The **Union** *Image*

CIVIL WAR AMERICA *Gary W. Gallagher, editor*

The **Union** *Image*

Popular Prints of the Civil War North

Mark E. Neely Jr. & *Harold Holzer*

The University of North Carolina Press Chapel Hill & London

© 2000

The University of North Carolina Press

All rights reserved

Designed by Richard Hendel and

Eric M. Brooks

Set in New Baskerville and Clarendon

by Eric M. Brooks

Printed in Hong Kong by C & C Offset

Printing Company Limited

The paper in this book meets the guidelines for

permanence and durability of the Committee on

Production Guidelines for Book Longevity of the

Council on Library Resources.

Library of Congress Cataloging-in-Publication Data

Neely, Mark E.

The Union image: popular prints of the Civil War North /

Mark E. Neely, Jr., and Harold Holzer.

   p.   cm.

Includes bibliographical references and index.

ISBN 0-8078-2510-7 (alk. paper)

1. United States—History—Civil War, 1861–1865—

Pictorial works.   2. United States—History—Civil War,

1861–1865—Art and the war.   3. Historical prints,

American.   I. Holzer, Harold.   II. Title.

E468.7.N44   2000

973.7—dc21   99-18486

          CIP

04 03 02 01 00   5 4 3 2 1

FRONTISPIECE

D[ominique]. C. Fabronius, after William Morris Hunt, *The Bugle Call.*
Copyrighted by Hunt, Boston, 1863. Lithograph, 17³⁄₁₆ × 13⁷⁄₁₆ inches;
chine collé size, 20⅞ × 16⅞ inches. (*The Metropolitan Museum of Art,
Harris Brisbane Dick Fund, 1932*)

To the memory of

DON E. FEHRENBACHER

1920–1997

CONTENTS

The **Union** *Image*

Introduction. Flag Mania

Our Heaven-Born Banner

The 4,000 shells that rained on Fort Sumter in Charleston, South Carolina, on April 12 and 13, 1861, claimed not a single human life. The only Union martyr to the attack that ignited the Civil War turned out to be the American flag—exposed to thirty-four hours of merciless bombardment, shot down by the enemy, rehoisted on a "jury mast extemporized on the parapet," and then finally hauled down in resignation, rather than disgrace, by the overpowered Federal forces.[1]

The tragic fate of the old Stars and Stripes ignited a patriotic firestorm in the Northern states, and those emotions in turn unleashed yet another bombardment, this one of patriotic prints: engravings and lithographs that would commemorate the great battles and leaders of the coming war, beginning with Fort Sumter, its defender Major Robert Anderson, and particularly its battered flag. "The Constitution, the Union, and the Flag," wrote Abraham Lincoln, had alike been "assailed by parricidal rebellion."[2]

Over the next four years of fighting, and many more years of remembering after Appomattox, affordable, mass-produced pictures illuminated stories of Civil War courage, victory, and defeat. These prints, often framed and proudly displayed in the parlors, dining rooms, and libraries of Northern homes, bore silent witness to their owners' immutable commitment to the federal Union and their readiness to make the unprecedented sacrifices necessary to preserve it. The Union presence in Charleston may have died when Fort Sumter surrendered, but with its death the Union image was born.[3]

The New York City lithography firm of Currier and Ives, which had earned its reputation and market preeminence in part by issuing timely prints of newsworthy events, many of them illustrating disasters, predictably became one of the first to respond pictorially to the nation-rending attack. The firm's *Bombardment of Fort Sumter, Charleston Harbor* (fig. 1) offered a news-hungry public a convincing depiction of the beleaguered fort—and its grand flag—engulfed in smoke.

Cannon fire was shown roaring back at the fort's attackers, though in truth An-

FT MOULTRIE.

CUMMINGS PT.

BOMBARDMENT OF FORT SUMTER, CHARLESTON HARBOR.
12th & 13th of April, 1861.

Figure 1. Currier and Ives, *Bombardment of Fort Sumter, Charleston Harbor. / 12th & 13th of April, 1861.* New York, 1861. Lithograph, 8¾ × 12¾ inches. This bravura battle scene was likely among the first popular prints to depict the shelling of Sumter. It showed the fort smoldering under a barrage of fire bright enough, the viewer was invited to believe, to light up the pre-dawn Charleston sky. Cummings Point, from which much of the damaging bombardment emanated, can be seen at right; Fort Moultrie, to the northeast of Sumter, is visible at left. The print bathed the fort's defiantly flying colors in a cloud of white smoke, portraying the flag still flying from a makeshift staff that had already been struck down around noon on April 13 and was quickly repaired and reerected as the bombardment continued. Even though its artists were not present to record the scene (they likely consulted the New York illustrated newspapers), the Currier and Ives firm had a long and successful record of depictions of disasters involving fire. Nathaniel Currier's first news print had portrayed a steamboat fire off Long Island (Albert K. Baragwanath, *One Hundred Currier and Ives Favorites* [New York: Crown Publishers, 1979], 7). (*Library of Congress*)

derson had not offered much resistance because the garrison, housing but seventy men, was too small. He returned fire only sporadically, mostly detailing his tiny command to put out the threatening fires that periodically ignited when incendiary shells struck the installation's wooden barracks. Although the commander of the besieged fort would soon emerge a Northern hero, he was not universally praised in the first published descriptions of the bombardment, many of which were riddled with what a contemporary called "bogus conjecture." One dispatch actually maintained that a treacherous Anderson, who hailed from the slave state of Kentucky, was "*gradually* blowing up" his own fort, "with the supposed intention of escaping seaward." Another advanced the libel that "Major Anderson had displayed his flag at half mast, as a 'signal of distress.'"[4]

Yet, while enduring what was, after all, the first Union defeat of the war, Major Anderson accomplished one symbolic victory: safeguarding the honor of the American flag. In his initial conference with Confederate emissary Louis Wigfall on the terms of surrender, he had insisted on the right to salute "the United States flag as it was lowered." The dramatic ceremony that ensued on April 14 was marred, and ultimately hallowed as well, by an accidental explosion inside the fort that killed two of Anderson's men, the only fatalities that week at Sumter. But it was not lost on Northerners that Anderson had defied his conquerors to ensure the dignity of his nation's emblem. Anderson would take justifiable pride in the way in which he had departed Sumter, "with colors flying and drums beating . . . and saluting my flag with fifty guns." In so doing, he handed patriots at home, and the image makers who served them, a great theme.[5]

Thus the first prints of Sumter were quickly supplanted by those depicting the American flag under attack. These constituted the earliest manifestations of the Union image, and the prints produced afterward, depicting myriad battlefields and generals, were almost all similarly patriotic in purpose. Many of them featured battle flags billowing over heroic troops; some were tinted in deep hues as if to echo the red of the bleeding wounded, the white of the cannon smoke, and the blue of the Federal uniforms. One the first portraits of Anderson himself, offered in May 1861, was advertised "for the benefit of the Families of those who may fall in defense of the Flag of the United States."[6]

During the war to come, publishers' lists of engravings and lithographs would demonstrate a greater quotient than ever of patriotism. Far more than news illustrations or domestic decorations designed principally for "beautiful effect," as one guardian of the American hearth expressed it, they came quickly to reflect strong beliefs and deep emotions. Civil War prints mirrored their owners' love of country, pride in its military achievements, reverence for its heroes, and in some instances, support for the destruction of slavery. At the outset, before news of a single battlefield victory reached the public, before a serious thought about emancipation entered the national dialogue, there was the symbolic flag of Fort Sumter and the riot of red, white, and blue (sometimes only suggested in engraved or lithographed black and white) that its fate at Charleston inspired throughout the North. Depictions of the symbolic flag of Fort Sumter rallied Northerners to the defense of the Union. These simple images came to serve as pictorial calls to arms.[7]

Major Anderson had no way of knowing that he would return to the North a hero. As the vessel transporting him and his men from Charleston docked in New York harbor, Anderson doubtless believed that they would be icily received. Instead, according to a reporter who arrived with them, they were greeted by a "fever of excitement" that "throbbed and billowed" through the city.[8] Many people were surprised that New York rallied so fervently to the defense of the Union. The city was a Democratic Party stronghold, and only weeks before, when the Republican president-elect had arrived in the metropolis en route to Washington for his inauguration, he had been greeted politely but without much warmth. More recently, some of the city's elected officials had been pondering their own declaration of secession. But Anderson's arrival erased notions of partisanship, unleashing "a popular outburst of loyalty to the Union . . . a thrilling and almost supernatural thing to those who participated in it." As one eyewitness recalled, it "was the period when the flag — *The Flag*—flew out to the wind from every housetop . . . and when . . . wildly excited crowds marched the streets demanding that the suspected or the lukewarm should show the symbol of nationality as a committal to the country's cause." Before long, flag fever spread to all the "great cities." When an awed observer worried that "the people have gone stark mad," a friend replied, "'I knew they would if a blow was struck against the flag.'" Echoed an elderly college professor in Massachusetts, "The heather is on fire. . . . The whole population, men, women, and children, seem to be in the streets with Union favors and flags."[9]

Major Anderson himself helped feed the flag frenzy by bringing to New York not only his fellow Sumter veterans but also the very flag that had withstood the bombardment (and could be seen in Currier and Ives's print, as "gallantly gleaming" as the original star-spangled banner that survived the rockets' red glare at Fort McHenry). "Show your colors," the press urged its readers, and retailers responded by offering three-by-four-foot flags for fifty cents each.[10]

On April 19, Anderson stepped out onto the pediment of an office building on flag-festooned Broadway in Lower Manhattan to help the city bid farewell to its Seventh Regiment as it marched off to war in response to Lincoln's April 15 call for volunteers. Thomas Nast made a sketch of the scene on the spot, which he later turned into a large painting. Dominating Nast's composition, waving from a pole on the building from which Anderson waved, was the most mammoth American flag of all: the tattered flag of Fort Sumter. A portion of its field of stars, along with a single red stripe, had been ripped from the whole, yet even torn, it flew majestically above the soldiers leaving for battle.[11]

From a slightly different, but no less inspiring, vantage point, New York lithographers Sarony, Major and Knapp issued their own view of the departure of the Seventh Regiment (fig. 2). While the Sumter flag was not so easily discernible in the scene, the red, white, and blue could be seen flying from flagpoles, windows, and rooftops. Soldiers marching in formation on the street carried flags, and onlookers gathered atop commercial buildings waved them. Flags seemed to be everywhere.[12]

The next day, between 50,000 and 100,000 New Yorkers jammed into Union Square to see Anderson once again at a pro-Union rally, described as "the most immense and astonishing demonstration ever seen in this, or . . . any other country." That day the square's equestrian statue of George Washington shared its pedestal with a new adornment: the same great banner of conquered Fort Sumter. In the presence of the sacred relic, an orator implored the crowd to "rally to the star-spangled banner so long as a single stripe can be discovered, or a single star shall shimmer from the surrounding darkness." In response, onlookers waved flags of their own; larger flags hung from the windows of the surrounding buildings, and even ships in the harbor hoisted their American flags. One observer estimated that 100,000 flags flew in New York that day, a veritable "feast of the American flag." Co-

DEPARTURE OF THE 7TH REGT N.Y. S M. FRIDAY APRIL 19TH 1861
VIEW OF BROADWAY, COR. COURTLAND ST

Figure 2. Sarony, Major and Knapp, *Departure of the 7th Regt. N.Y.S.M. Friday April 19th 1861. / View of Broadway, Cor. Courtland St.* Published for *D. T. Valentine's Manual for 1862*, New York, 1861. Lithograph, 6¾ × 9½ inches; also issued as a separate-sheet print, 14 × 20 inches in size. Onlookers crowd the streets of Broadway and wave American flags of every size from windows, rooftops, and streets, as volunteers of the Seventh Regiment march toward the ferry terminals on their way to the defense of the capital a few days after the fall of Fort Sumter. According to the *New York Times*, "The American colors were everywhere—on the house tops, on flagstaffs, on ropes stretched across the streets" (*New York Times*, April 20, 1861). In this print, even the street-level window awnings of the shops seem to boast an American flag stripe motif, and in hand-colored versions they were in fact tinted red. The overall result is a panorama of national colors, evoking the defiant spate of flag-waving with which the North responded to the attack on the flag on April 14, 1861. (*Macculloch Hall Museum, Morristown, New Jersey*)

lumbia College professor Francis Lieber dubbed it "the day of flags," recalling later that New York's response to the "reckless arrogance" and "treasonable cannon" at Sumter was "in the flag of our country—waving from every steeple and School-house, from City Hall and Court House, from every shop window and market stall, and on the head-gear of every horse in the busy street."[13]

A New York journalist aptly dubbed the patriotic frenzy "flagmania." Before long, one local firm would claim to have sold 10,000 flags. By May a publisher of en-velopes with small patriotic flag-motif vignettes printed in the upper left-hand cor-ners proudly advertised that he had sold a quarter of a million such envelopes, which reprinted the warning that General John Adams Dix had defiantly issued upon the news of Louisiana's secession: "If anyone attempts to haul down the Amer-ican flag, shoot him on the spot."[14]

Soon making their appearance as well were prints embodying similar sentiments, designed in large formats to serve as permanent decorations inside the homes of aroused, banner-waving patriots. Once again leading the nation's printmakers, Cur-rier and Ives turned its focus on the national symbol with *The Union Volunteer*, copy-righted five weeks after the fall of Fort Sumter, a prompt visual response by mid-nineteenth-century standards. The lithograph featured a young recruit, one hand raising his sword, the other clutching his beloved flag. Emphasizing the inspiration for the image was this resonant, timely verse:

> O'er Sumters walls OUR FLAG again we'll wave,
> And give to traitors all a bloody grave.
> OUR UNION and OUR LAWS maintain we must;
> And treason's banner trample in the dust.

At least two variations on the theme followed. One was *The Flag of Our Union* (fig. 3), published twenty-four days after *The Union Volunteer*, featuring a soldier who now bore a striking resemblance to the second hero of the war, Colonel Ephraim Elmer Ellsworth. Ellsworth had been shot to death by a Confederate sympathizer in Alexandria, Virginia, on May 24, 1861, after cutting down a Confederate flag visible from the White House across the Potomac River. Currier and Ives completed its flag-waving trilogy with *The Spirit of 61. / God, Our Country and Liberty!!*, copyrighted May 21, 1861, replacing the flag-waving soldier with a symbol of the nation itself, Columbia, still hoisting sword and flag. Here was a subtler, but still unmistakable, reference to the flag's unhappy fate at Charleston. At Sumter, the flag had been low-ered; now it must be raised again:

> Up with the Standard and bear it on,
> Let its folds to the wind expand.
> Remember the deeds of Washington,
> And the flag of our native land.[15]

PUBLISHED BY CURRIER & IVES

Entered according to Act of Congress in the year 1861, by Currier & Ives, in the Clerk's Office of the District Court of the United States, for the Southern District of New York.

152 NASSAU ST NEW YORK.

Nov. 15, 1861.

THE FLAG OF OUR UNION.

STRIKE— till the last armed foe expires,
STRIKE— for your altars and your fires!

STRIKE— for the green graves of your sires,
GOD— and your native land!

P. S. Duval and Son and its rival in Philadelphia, Thomas Sinclair, similarly capitalized on public sentiment with lithographs entitled, respectively, *Our Country's Flag* and *The Stars and Stripes Forever*, the latter accompanied by a verse confidently predicting that the "Sacred Flag" would again flutter "in the Breeze." E. B. and E. C. Kellogg of Hartford issued *The Flag of Our Union . . . Three Cheers for the Red, White and Blue*, and Philadelphia's Louis Rosenthal paired the powerful images of the threatened flag and its original defender, George Washington, in a stirring scene, *Raising the Flag May 1861* (plate 1). The print showed men, women, and children, military volunteers and civilians alike, marching past Clark Mills's famous equestrian statue of George Washington in the nation's capital; above the statue waves an American flag. Several onlookers can be seen raising both hands over their heads to hail the unfurled banner, in a fanciful scene that surely owed a debt to the outburst of patriotic passion that erupted at New York's Union Square when the Sumter flag was placed on the Washington statue there.[16]

Still the enduring symbol of the Union itself, and therefore the emblem of all those determined to preserve it in its peril, the flag now reflected, too, an aggressive desire by angry Northerners to repay the insult heaped upon the banner when it was fired upon at Charleston. The public fury was roused not only by the newspapers and Anderson's fortuitous appearances in the print publishing center of New York, but through another dependable route to the public heart: the church. On April 28, two weeks after the surrender of Fort Sumter, Henry Ward Beecher took to the pulpit of his Plymouth Church in Brooklyn to sanctify the colors that two departing companies of the local Twenty-fourth Regiment planned to carry off to war. Many of the soldiers were members of the church, which had contributed $3,000 to equip them.[17]

In a stirring performance, Beecher argued that the flag had not only been fired upon at Sumter, but had been desecrated as well. His impassioned report drove his listeners into such a frenzy that he had to plead for their silent attention. "That flag which Russia could not daunt, nor France intimidate, nor England conquer," Beecher cried, "has gone down beneath the treacherous States within our own Union." Then, re-creating an image that echoed the pathos of Christ's walk to the cross, he bemoaned the desecration of the flag in Charleston:

> Do you know that when it was fallen, in the streets of a Southern city, it was trailed, hooted at, pierced with swords? Men that have sat in the Senate of the United States ran out to trample upon it; it was fired on and slashed by the mob; it was dragged through the mud; it was hissed at and spit upon. . . . That this flag should, in our own nation, and by our own people, be spit upon, is more than the heart of man can bear.[18]

It was almost more than his audience could bear as well. "It is not a rag," the preacher shouted. "It is a whole national history. It is the Constitution. It is the government. It is the free people that stand in the government on the Constitution.

Forget not what it means; and for the sake of its ideas, rather than its mere emblazonery, be true to your country's flag." Beecher was, of course, calling for something more than revenge; his own brand of flag-waving embraced the tenets of the founding of the republic and the basic notion of "inalienable rights." To Beecher, a Union worth saving was a Union without slavery. Remember, he begged his listeners, "the American Flag has been fired upon by Americans and trodden down because it stood in the way of slavery. . . . Thank God Washington is dead, and has not lived to see the infamy and disgrace." Conveniently forgotten was the fact that Washington was a Southern slaveholder. Nothing would do now, Beecher concluded, but to carry the flag "into our national capital, until Washington shall seem to be a forest, in which every tree supports the American banner. And it must not stop there."[19]

Indeed, it did not stop. The acclaimed landscape painter Frederic Edwin Church, for example, responded to the Sumter crisis with an effort that soon inspired a notably successful popular print. In May 1861, while exhibiting one of his better-known works, *The Icebergs*, the proceeds from which Church earmarked for a war charity, he let it be known that he was working on a new painting. It would be, the *New York Times* reported, "a symbolical landscape embodying the stars and stripes. It is an evening scene, with long lines of red and gold typifying the stripes and a patch of blue sky with dimly twinkling stars in a corner for the Union." In its final form, the spectral image of the venerated flag seemed to unfurl from the leafless trunk of a dead tree. Church called his dreamlike work *Our Banner in the Sky*. One art historian has observed that its message was nothing less than that "Union victory was ordained by natural history."[20]

The patriotic frenzy notwithstanding, some art critics of the day were initially unmoved. Commenting in June 1861, the *New York Tribune* complained that the artist had taken too many "liberties" with nature in creating his celestial contrivance, and a few weeks later the *Hartford Courant* dryly observed that "'the spacious firmament on high' is not gifted in the manufacture of American flags." That spring, copublishers Goupil and Company and M. Knoedler (in whose gallery Church often exhibited) paid the artist $200 for the right to issue a chromolithographic reproduction (fig. 4). The appearance of the chromo moved the *Boston Transcript* to praise the Church picture as a "happy inspiration," and patriotic inspiration rather than the faithful rendering of nature was the realm of popular prints. By August even the *Tribune*'s recalcitrant critic referred to *Our Banner in the Sky* as a "most felicitous conception." The chromo's publication was accompanied by a pamphlet that described the work, delineated the "History of the Stars and Stripes" since the Revolution, and excerpted several poems about the flag, including the entire first stanza of "Key's Star-Spangled Banner," which the publishers boasted "will illustrate the subject and its treatment in the print of 'OUR BANNER IN THE SKY.'"[21]

Trumpeting the recent surge in patriotism, particularly among artists, the pamphlet touted the print as "one of the most characteristic and novel results of this patriotic enthusiasm . . . which electrified the North, West, and East," reminding po-

"Our Banner in the Sky."

THE sudden and simultaneous outburst of patriotism which electrified the entire North, West, and East of America, as well as many isolated points and baffled hearts in the South, when the Flag of the country was insulted and the Government defied and betrayed, found no more hearty or instant response among any class of our citizens than the Artists—several of whom immediately volunteered for the war in defense of the Union—and many of whom sent valuable works, the choice productions of their genius, to be sold in aid of the Patriotic Fund; while others exhibited elaborate and new pictures, in behalf of the same just and noble object. One of the most characteristic and novel results of this patriotic enthusiasm which inspired the artists was a felicitous "Study" of Morning Clouds, by FREDERICK E. CHURCH, wherein, by a perfectly natural but ingenious stroke of skill and fancy, he made the sun-lit vapors of the dawn and the lingering stars in the firmament wear the aspect of "OUR BANNER IN THE SKY." The publisher believing this spirited and significant, as well as beautiful sketch, will prove eminently acceptable to all patriots and lovers of art in the land, has caused it to be reproduced in the shape of an effective print, colored like the original, both in oil and water-tints. Poetry as well as painting recognizes "OUR BANNER IN THE SKY," both figuratively and actually, in some of the most popular lyrics of national poets, the following extracts from which, together with a brief history of the American Flag, will illustrate the subject and its treatment in the print of "OUR BANNER IN THE SKY:"

> Oh! say, can you see by the dawn's early light,
> What so proudly we hailed at the twilight's last gleaming,
> Whose broad stripes and bright stars through the perilous fight,
> O'er the ramparts we watched, were so gallantly streaming;
> And the rockets' red glare, the bombs bursting in air,
> Gave proof through the night that our flag was still there.
> Oh! say, does the Star-Spangled Banner still wave
> O'er the land of the free and the home of the brave?
>
> *Key's Star-Spangled Banner.*

> Flag of the seas! on ocean wave
> Thy stars shall glitter o'er the brave;
> When death, careering on the gale,
> Sweeps darkly round the bellied sail,
> And frighted waves rush wildly back,
> Before the broadside's reeling rack,
> *Each dying wanderer of the sea*
> *Shall look at once to heaven and thee,*
> And smile to see thy splendors fly
> In triumph o'er his closing eye.
>
> *Drake's American Flag.*

> Ay, tear the tattered ensign down!
> Long has it waved on high,
> *And many an eye has danced to see*
> *That banner in the sky;*
> Beneath it rang the battle-shout,
> And burst the cannon's roar;
> The meteor of the ocean air
> Shall sweep the clouds no more!
>
> *Holmes' Old Constitution.*

tential buyers that "when the Flag of the country was insulted" at Sumter, there had been "no more hearty or instant response among any class of our citizens" than from artists like Church. *Our Banner in the Sky*, the brochure claimed, ranked as "one of the most characteristic and novel results of this patriotic enthusiasm." Now, "the publisher believing this spirited and significant, as well as beautiful sketch"

Figure 4. Goupil and Company, after Frederic Edwin Church, *Our Banner in the Sky*. Published by M. Knoedler, New York, 1861. Chromolithograph, 7½ × 11¼ inches. An American flag appears in a dark, threatening sky in this patriotic allegory based on a painting by the great landscape artist. Writing in 1871, an early biographer of the artist remembered that the image was well received by a "generous and appreciative public" who regarded the work as "striking, bold, and imposing—very imposing." A leaflet issued to herald publication of the chromo described its flag-venerating design this way: "A felicitous 'Study' of Morning Clouds by Frederick [*sic*] E. Church, wherein, by a perfectly natural but ingenious stroke of skill and fancy, he made the sun-lit vapors of the dawn and the lingering stars in the firmament wear the aspect of 'OUR BANNER IN THE SKY'" (*"Our Banner in the Sky"* [New York: Goupil and Company, 1861], leaflet in New York Public Library; Gerald L. Carr, *Frederic Edwin Church: Catalogue Raisonné of Works of Art at Olana Historic Site*, 2 vols. [Cambridge: Cambridge University Press, 1994], 1:276, 498). (*New York State Office of Parks, Recreation, and Historic Preservation; Olana State Historic Site*)

would "prove eminently acceptable to all patriots and lovers of art in the land, has caused it to be reproduced in the shape of an effective print, colored like the original, both in oil and water colors." The marketing effort must have seemed almost irresistible.[22]

Goupil's chromo even inspired an original poem in tribute to its success. On July 29, 1861, one Champion Bissell published in the *New York Tribune* a poem, "Suggested by Seeing . . . OUR FLAG IN THE SKY [*sic*]." Wrote the admiring poet:

> To you reserved to show the eye
> The lustrous star, the reddening sky,
> The morning streaks of rosy hue
> The ample field of lurid blue,

The glittering white that points the way
Where leaps the sun to cloudless day. . . .

What is this banner? 'Tis the sense
The type of all our permanence,
Drawn from the glories of the sky,
Again we bid them wave on high,
Arranged by Art's immortal laws,
The symbol of a nation's cause. . . .

Such Flag may never trail to dust!
We can defend it, and we must. . . .[23]

Within weeks, Goupil reported $1,500 in sales; *Our Banner in the Sky* became a best-seller. Chastened, the *Tribune*'s art critic reevaluated the work as one of Church's "distinguished successes."[24]

Despite occasional inspiration by painters like Frederic Edwin Church, print-making was driven more by business considerations than artistic ones. The industry was guided by public demand and characterized by imitations and outright piracies that sometimes defied seldom-enforced copyright laws. On September 6, for example, Sarony, Major and Knapp of New York issued a lithograph entitled *Our Heaven Born Banner* (fig. 5). The image supposedly had been "created" by a local artist named William Bauly, who had exhibited at the National Academy of Design in 1859; in reality, it was little more than a martial version of Church's *Our Banner in the Sky*. Instead of a flag floating from a branchless tree, here was a flag that seemed to float from the upright bayonet of a Zouave sentry. Otherwise, as in Church's original, the Stars and Stripes appeared eerily and reassuringly within the national firmament.[25]

Sarony, Major and Knapp concurrently issued *Fate of the Rebel Flag* (fig. 6), in which a Confederate warship was shown burning and sinking in a sea strewn with the detritus of battle, the smoke and flame metamorphosing into an image of the enemy colors, as vivid as the Union flag that hovered above the Zouave in the companion print. Here, however, the flag was destined not to wave over the land of the free, but to perish in a watery grave reserved for traitors. It might well be thought of as the apogee of the flag-inspired printmaking that dominated the early image of the Union after Sumter.

In a matter of months, printmakers from New York, Boston, Philadelphia, Cincinnati, and other publishing centers in the North began to devote their attention to the emerging heroes of the Civil War and the bloody events that roiled the nation week after week over the next four long years. Depictions of imaginary flag-filled skies yielded to those of gallant charges on corpse-littered battlefields. But the flag showed its staying power as the armies marched under it and rallied to it in many a print of Civil War combat.

OUR HEAVEN BORN BANNER

Published by W. SCHAUS 749 Broadway New York.

Figure 5. Sarony, Major and Knapp, after William Bauly, *Our Heaven Born Banner*. Published by W. Schaus, New York, 1861. Chromolithograph, 10 × 12½ inches. Issued several months after the Goupil and Company chromo and obviously inspired by that original, this print suggested that the celestial phenomenon imagined by Church against the backdrop of a symbolic dark night sky had recurred in the promising dawn of Union resistance to secession. Here the spectral flag appears to fly from the upraised rifle of a sentry who stands on a cliff overlooking what appears to be Fort Sumter in the distance, in an improbable Hudson River landscape (the fort sits in the low tidewater of South Carolina, not a mountain lake). Rather than disguise its indebtedness to Church's original concept, Sarony, Major and Knapp issued this derivative update complete with lines from the same extract from poet Joseph Rodman Drake's "The American Flag" that Goupil and Company had reprinted in its advertising pamphlet for *Our Banner in the Sky*. The verse concluded: "She mingled with its gorgeous dyes / The milky baldric of the skies, / And striped its pure celestial white, / With streaking of the morning light." (*Library of Congress*)

The words of Joseph Rodman Drake's 1835 poem, "The American Flag," printed to accompany Sarony, Major and Knapp's *Our Heaven Born Banner*, reveal both the unrelenting national veneration for the flag and the powerful emotional response that allegorical images like Church's and Bauly's could exact:

> When Freedom from her mountain height
> Unfurled her standard to the air,

Figure 6. Sarony, Major and Knapp, after William Bauly, *Fate of the Rebel Flag*. New York, 1861. Chromolithograph, 10 × 12¼ inches. A companion chromo to *Our Heaven Born Banner*, this dramatic scene depicts a Confederate vessel plunging into the deep, stern first, as the consuming fires form the image of the similarly doomed rebel flag. The debris floating in the sea in the foreground, a pictorial convention of naval prints, nonetheless suggests here that the ship is one of many enemy vessels destroyed this day, although Union naval victories were all but unknown in September 1861, when this print was copyrighted. More important, perhaps, the bolt of lightning striking the ship from the upper left is meant to suggest that ship and flag have been destroyed not by man but by God—a vivid expression of the post-Sumter conviction in Northern states that theirs had become a holy cause. (*Library of Congress*)

> She tore the azure robe of night
> And set the stars of glory there.[26]

The American flag prints that virtually unleashed the Union image helped "set the stars of glory" on the American consciousness.

Four years to the day after Union soldiers had hauled down the flag of Fort Sumter, Major Robert Anderson returned to Charleston with the same tattered banner to hoist it high above the rubble that was now all that remained of the garrison he once commanded. The successful military and naval campaign to recapture Charleston and Fort Sumter would be referred to years later in the official records of the war as the campaign to restore the flag at Sumter. On hand in 1865 to deliver an oration on the occasion was the same Henry Ward Beecher who had so stirred his Brooklyn audience back in April of 1861. Gazing anew at the proudly waving battle flag, Beecher recalled: "Once it was shot down. . . . After a vain resistance, with trembling hand and sad heart, you withdrew it from its height, closed its wings, and bore it far away, sternly to sleep amid the tumults of rebellion and the thunder of battle. . . . Glory to the banner that has gone through four years, black with tempests of war, to pilot the nation back to peace without dismemberment."[27]

"Some future day a Napier will picture the final drama," Beecher predicted, referring to the late British historian. "[It] will form a picture of *War* and *Peace*."[28] But Americans did not have to wait for another Napier to form that picture. As early as 1862, at least one printmaker foresaw the restoration of federal authority, and with it the restoration of the supremacy of the American flag (prematurely, as it turned out, for the war would rage for another three years). M. H. Traubel's lithographed allegory, *The Triumph* (fig. 7), depicted the forces of liberty, humanity, and freedom, joined by heroes from the American past, gathered under a mammoth, billowing flag to herald the defeat of the evil forces that had kept slaves in chains and threatened democracy and Union.

Just as the firm had been among the first with its timely images of war, beginning with Sumter, Currier and Ives would be the first to portray the Sumter flag as a banner of peace. In *The Old Flag Again, Waves Over Sumter* (fig. 8), an exultant staff officer planted the standard into the debris-littered ground where the fort had once stood.

The Union image had come full circle.

In this book we propose to examine the popular prints of the Civil War that poured from the presses in Northern cities between the lowering of the flag at Fort Sumter in 1861 and its triumphant raising there in 1865. We will examine as well the prints that later recalled the conflict, especially those published during the great revival of interest in the war in the 1880s and early 1890s. As Oliver Wendell Holmes Jr. put it, there were "two Civil Wars": the "war in fact" and "the war in retrospect." This was true in iconography as well as history, and we strive to classify both kinds of pictures and subject them to rather different analysis.[29]

The number of Civil War images was too great to permit final judgments about the extent of their coverage, the frequency with which subjects appear, or their sources. Publishing records remain virtually nonexistent, making it all but impossible to answer the frequent question, "How many copies were printed?" We have examined major public archives of old prints from New York to California, and we have maintained contact with private collectors and dealers, resources that cannot be ignored in the study of popular prints. We have seen a wide variety of original images, as well as adaptations of period photographs and paintings, along with second and third variants of earlier prints. For us, the path from research to book has been one not only of discovery, but of careful distillation, an effort to find both unusual and representative prints to suggest this vigorous period of image making.[30]

Figure 7. M. H. Traubel, *The Triumph*. Philadelphia, 1861. Chromolithograph, 16 × 21 inches. King Cotton, a monstrous "Hydra of Human Discord," a serpent representing the treachery of secession, and the national shame of slavery all fall before the righteous advance of "Humanitas" in this symbol-rich allegory predicting ultimate Union victory. As figures representing Justice, Christianity, and Liberty emerge from the heavens on the wings of an American eagle to stamp out the fires of rebellion, a pantheon of American heroes—including Washington, Jefferson, and Franklin—joins them. Billowing above all is a colossal American flag, bathed in rays of sunlight, crowning the imminent victory over the forces of evil. Meanwhile, a pillar of state, burning at right, engulfs the enemy banner, an early Confederate flag, in its flames. This ambitious print bore little resemblance to the simpler, more homespun graphics typical of this period of flag mania in the Northern popular arts. (*Library of Congress*)

We have been interested in this subject for twenty-five years. Over that long period, we have lived in different parts of the country and worked for different museums and universities. We have been able to gather bits of information from a printmaker's brochure here or a newspaper advertisement there. But in the end what has proved notable is not the nature of the documentary evidence about the uses of popular prints but the sheer lack of it. Once the student of popular prints goes outside the borders of the images themselves, there is little to go on. We have not been able to find definitive evidence from newspapers, pamphlets, advertising ephemera, books, or manuscripts about the uses to which their original owners put popular prints of the Civil War.

Today these prints are principally used as illustrations for magazines, books, and other publications. Serious collectors remain rather few, connoisseurs are fewer still, and galleries and museums rarely offer exhibitions so closely focused in subject matter. A brief caption is about all such prints get, whether it be for the purpose of selling them to prospective buyers, explaining them to strolling museum patrons, or describing them to magazine readers. But captions do not do these images justice, and their conventional use as illustrations, in fact, essentially misleads readers. Many popular prints are valueless as illustrations of events and inferior to photographs as portraiture or landscape. What popular prints illustrate is not events or personalities but the popular culture of the times. A popular print depicting the Battle of Fredericksburg is more illustrative of popular patriotism in the parlor than of military maneuver at the scene. It tells us as much about the values of the makers and purchasers of the images at home as it does about the actual clash of arms at the front. Besides, there is more to be seen in popular prints than can usually be pointed out in the tightly restricted space offered by a caption, and much room for comment on what appears within the margins of the prints themselves. We want to show that they merit study and, in some cases at least, extended comment.

We will not always restrict our comments to what appears within the borders of the prints. There are clues, if not definitive proof, to be found elsewhere in regard to their uses and meaning. In fact, the absence of much conventional historical evidence is itself the greatest piece of evidence of their place in the nineteenth century. While oil paintings, even in the still artistically backward New World, enjoyed annual and special competitions and exhibitions, as well as regular coverage in urban newspapers and occasional analysis in magazines and books, popular prints did not. And while the new medium of photography still seemed novel and gained occasional extended commentary and exhibition, prints, by the time of the Civil War, seemed as old as the republic itself, and rather commonplace. They were rarely the focus of exhibitions, nor were they the subjects of reviews in magazines or newspapers.

They *were* common, and apparently they were sold mostly to common people by common people. An advertisement in an 1864 issue of *Harper's Weekly*, for example, sought "agents, dealers and country" stores to sell "splendid steel engravings" along

THE OLD FLAG AGAIN, WAVES OVER SUMTER.

RAISED by Capt. Bragg of Gen. Gillmore's Staff on the 18.th February 1865.

Lith. by Kimmel & Forster 254 & 256 Canal St. N.Y.

with "prize packets" and "novelty packets." Prospective salesmen were promised a "great chance to make money," with the assurance that "$10 *invested will yield nearly $50.*" A week earlier, the New York engraver H. H. Lloyd had placed a notice in *Harper's* seeking agents to sell their lines of "the best war maps . . . and portraits."[31]

An article in that same illustrated weekly toward the end of the war reminded readers that efforts at popular art from 1861 through 1865 had "enabled the poorest boy in the land to own a portrait of the bravest hero." Noting the importance that its own newspaper cuts and other, presumably separately published, sheets had attained for ordinary Americans, the paper attested: "All over the country, thousands and thousands of the faces and events which the war has made illustrious are tacked and placed and pasted upon the humblest walls. Whole regiments have had portraits of a beloved officer, whole corps of a commander." Pictures within the pictures in popular prints also occasionally attest to their use. If a lithograph is depicted hanging on the wall in the background of a domestic image, the viewer is to infer, often, that the household depicted is a humble one.[32]

Paintings were produced on commission from wealthy patrons, but engravings and lithographs were sold in shops or hawked by itinerant peddlers, sometimes selling from pushcarts. Customers outside the cities where they were published could answer newspaper advertisements and purchase them by mail. After the war, old veterans sold them—to other old veterans. At Christmastime, they were offered by booksellers as holiday gifts. They appealed to common people by arousing basic sentiments; during the war, naturally, patriotism was foremost among these, and it remained the driving force in later years as well. The flag never disappeared as a significant focus for battlefield scenes in popular prints: these offered the stuff of inspiration, admiration, even worship.

If this "hero worship" bore a complicated and anomalous relationship to the country's antimilitarist republican heritage, the purchasers of the prints, the artists who designed them, and the printers who produced them hardly noticed. Some images were products of new and sophisticated print publishing technologies. But the images themselves were seldom as sophisticated as the techniques of lithography, engraving, and printing. Nor were the images as self-consciously referential as some

opposite

Figure 8. Currier and Ives, *The Old Flag Again, Waves Over Sumter. / Raised by Capt. Bragg of Gen. Gillmore's Staff on the 18th February 1865.* New York, 1865. Lithograph, 12 × 9 inches. By the time Federal forces reoccupied Sumter, nearly four years after the bombardment that ignited the Civil War, the fort had been reduced to rubble by months of Union shelling. One observer remarked of the ruin at the time that it "was hardly possible to do the walls any further damage" (Harold Holzer and Mark E. Neely Jr., *Mine Eyes Have Seen the Glory: The Civil War in Art* [New York: Orion Books, 1993], 39). Nevertheless, the return of Old Glory to its original place there later inspired a major ceremony and oration (an event that is not well remembered because it occurred the same day as Lincoln's assassination). The hero of this lithograph, Henry M. Bragg, was the aide-de-camp of General Quincy Adams Gillmore, the Union commander who demanded the surrender of Fort Sumter back to the Union in August 1863 and then proceeded to shell the fort's walls when the Confederates refused. (*Library of Congress*)

of the traditions on which they drew. More can be said about these popular prints than the customary captions allow, but we must not say too much—or make claims for them that overreach their simple emotional and artistic appeals.

The prints reported contemporary events of the war and later reminded Americans of the salient historical landmarks of the conflict through a visual language of inspiration. People were, in a modest way, committed to these colorful and heroic pictures. Photographs might arouse curiosity, and woodcuts in the illustrated press could provoke shock or stimulate admiration, but people hung engravings and lithographs in their homes for all to see. They hung them there for themselves, to be looked at over and over again. Prints provided decorative beauty and inspiring sentiment, things that journalism and photography did not offer. People bought prints that reflected their values, commitments, and ideals and used them as modest domestic altarpieces in that most sacred room of the Victorian home, the family parlor. Prints were not sources of news alone; they were sources of inspiration.[33]

Though these pictures were meant to inspire and were therefore generally one-sided, the reader should beware of thinking of popular prints as "propaganda." The United States government did not produce a single one of these prints. The War Department apparently did not even order or print recruiting posters. Commerce and popular taste mixed together to produce popular prints, but official ideologies and party platforms had nothing directly to do with them.

Nor, generally, did the sophisticates who patronized other media. When Oliver Wendell Holmes Sr. in 1863 instructed his *Atlantic Monthly* readers who wondered "what war is" to "look at these"—the gruesome photographs of carnage from the Battle of Antietam by Alexander Gardner—he spoke as an elite New Englander through the pages of a consciously highbrow literary magazine. And when the young Henry James declared in 1866 that the "taste of the age is for realism," he, too, spoke for and to an American elite. The *Atlantic* did not comment on popular battle prints. They did not form part of the taste on which Henry James offered such perceptive observations.[34]

Prints existed alongside the world of James and Holmes. Engravings and lithographs were popular, but with "other" people, those who did not leave behind columns of criticism and analysis. They did not leave behind much of anything written by hand, in fact, let alone printed in type. But popular prints help us to understand the Civil War world as common people saw it. Connoisseurs, as far as we know, did not yet collect prints, and critics seldom reviewed them, yet they deserve comment and merit attention as something more than "Americana," that soft category of "collectibility" that in the twentieth century began to include the humble efforts of popular lithographers and engravers.

The persistent popularity of engravings and lithographs in an age of photography defied Henry James's vaunted movement toward "realism." Some postwar prints even approached the antiphotographic in style. In November 1861, about seven months after the first shots were fired at Fort Sumter, the editor of *Harper's Monthly* reflected on the surge of patriotic emotion that had gripped those who remained at home. "While the hum of war is heard far away," he wrote, "we see only the romantic aspect, and feel only the stirring excitement."

Popular prints may have shown only the romance and excitement of the Civil War, but they showed those things very well. To some degree, they helped create them, and their impact on collective American memory may have been substantial.[35] We seek in this book to recall and reveal the culture that nurtured popular prints of the Civil War—pictures that brought the war home to America and then helped the nation remember it for generations to come.

The Defenders of the Union

Heroic Tradition and the Popular Military Portrait

"Won't you buy a splendid portrait of Gen. Grant?" asked a most intelligent peddler, six months from England, of a country friend at one of our hotels a few days since. "No, Sir; I do not want it." "Ah! then you will take this of Gen. McClellan?" "No, no; I wouldn't have that *any how." "Ah, Sir," resumed the peddler, waxing confidential, "I sell more of McClellan now than I do of Grant; but if I only had* Gen. Lee, *I could sell ten times as many of him as I can of McClellan—and to the same men."[1]*

Like most items that appeared in the partisan press of the Civil War era, the above story had a political point to make. But leaving aside the anti-McClellan animus of the pro-Republican *New York Tribune*, in which it appeared, one can see in the anecdote, unconsciously revealed, one of the ways popular prints were distributed to the people. The itinerant salesman of the story, a recent immigrant lacking knowledge about American politics, offered his customers portraits of the heroes of the summer of 1864. Ulysses S. Grant's stock was down in August, as his Virginia campaign stalled in the face of ferocious Confederate resistance. McClellan's stock was up, for though he had not yet been nominated for president, he was everywhere being touted as the most likely Democratic challenger to President Lincoln.

The idea that such portraits were tailored for an unsophisticated "country" audience shopping in the metropolis helps explain the often crude craftsmanship of the popular print—especially in the form of lithographs, which were generally less expensive and more quickly made than their more carefully wrought cousins, steel engravings. It explains as well the surprising absence of comment on them in the genteel magazines or the newspapers of the era. Even the illustrated weeklies largely ignored them, and, after all, papers like *Harper's Weekly* trafficked in the same kind of art, though for browsing rather than displaying. The *New York Tribune* reviewed books weekly and covered exhibitions of art conscientiously, but finding mention of popular prints in the *Tribune*, or any other nineteenth-century printed or manuscript sources, is nearly impossible. Photography earned more attention, for it offered something the time-tested engravings and lithographs did not: novelty.

The anecdote also reminds us of the outpouring of McClellan images before 1865. To examine the print bins of America's great repositories of old engravings and lithographs without precise knowledge of the events of the American Civil War would invite the conclusion that McClellan was its great hero. In fact, he became the war's goat, more so than the Confederate generals who eventually went down to defeat, and to this day he is the subject of belittling biographies and scathing historical criticism. But it was not always so. McClellan was a frequent subject of Union military portrait prints, and it is easy to understand why he was, for a time, so popular: he was young, handsome, and colorful, and he commanded vast armies in great battles. He was also genuinely charismatic. When Secretary of the Navy Gideon Welles ruefully complained in his diary that McClellan "likes show, parade, and power," he was listing the attributes that also defined the general's public appeal. The mere sight of him could inspire spontaneous cheers among his troops. "The soldiers," one of his staff officers explained, "fairly loved to look upon him." For a time, so did the patrons of popular prints.[2]

As always, printmakers searched for heroes who would stir their customers. One typical 1861 patriotic lithograph, *Loyal Americans*, portrayed General Winfield Scott, General Robert Anderson, Colonel Ephraim Elmer Ellsworth, and General Benjamin F. Butler. Another, *The National Political Chart*, also issued in 1861, presented portraits of Scott, Anderson, and Lieutenant Adam Slemmer, commander of the distant Union outpost of Fort Pickens in Pensacola, Florida, for a time a possible flash point of war like Fort Sumter. Such were the first military heroes of the Civil War North.

Within a matter of months, others would supplant them. The pages of *Harper's Weekly*, though never stooping to acknowledge war prints in their editorial copy, did feature advertisements that suggest the ebb and flow of both early wartime military reputation and the commercial appeal of print portraits of these heroes. In October 1861, for example, J. C. Buttre of New York offered by mail, at fifteen cents apiece, "finely engraved" 10-by-12-inch portraits of "Gens. Scott, M'Lellan, Wool, Banks, Fremont, Sigel, Anderson, Dix, Butler, Sprague, Lyon, Com. Stringham, Col. Ellsworth, &c." In November Buttre was promoting a nine-figure group portrait, *Generals of Our Army, 1861*, featuring most of these same officers, along with *Officers of Our Navy, 1861*, depicting Samuel F. Du Pont, Henry Hall Foote, and seven other men. Not until 1862, interestingly, did Buttre add a group portrait of political celebrities (Lincoln and his cabinet), by which time the old individual portraits, like that of Ambrose E. Burnside, had been discounted in price 33 percent to only ten cents.

Firms like Buttre's sent their mail-order catalogs to individuals on receipt of a postage stamp to cover mailing costs but also continuously sought agents to sell prints in the field. An indication of the ongoing effort in the industry to secure agents to sell in distant markets was evident in L. W. Lucas's advertised offer to send, at two dollars per dozen and twelve dollars per hundred, the firm's latest "fine steel engravings, exquisitely accurate, with fac-simile autographs, of the prominent officers of the Army, Navy, or State . . . by mail to any part of the country."[3]

General Winfield Scott was one of the figures frequently featured in these early prints. He was an authentic military hero to be sure, but of the war with Mexico some thirteen years earlier. Now old and enfeebled, he would soon relinquish his command. Currier and Ives's 1861 cartoon, *The Old General Ready for a "Movement"* (fig. 9), showed him trapping Confederate generals P. G. T. Beauregard and Gideon Pillow at Manassas and Memphis, respectively, but the scatological double entendre in the caption was surely not lost on print buyers and revealed something of the price of fame: occasional tasteless references, even in the restrained nineteenth century. Such images were not destined for the home, where Scott's fame rested secure, for a time, in print portraits.[4]

The group portrait *Loyal Americans* depicted three newer, younger heroes with Scott, but they had earned their fame for reasons other than battlefield triumphs. General Butler had successfully occupied Baltimore after riots there threatened to cut off Washington from the flow of Union troops. Colonel Ellsworth had been shot to death by a pro-Confederate innkeeper in Alexandria, Virginia, after hauling down a Confederate flag from the top of the building. And General Anderson, "hero" of Sumter, was lionized in the North after surrendering his fort. Such, one might conclude, was the state of Union iconography early in the first year of the Civil War: put bluntly, it seems to have been focused, with few exceptions, on elderly heroes, losers, and martyrs.

Northern printmakers wasted little, if any, time on Confederate portraits, with the exception of New York lithographer Jones and Clark's early, and apparently unique, portrait of Robert E. Lee.[5] As the *Tribune* anecdote revealed, the universal assumption was that anyone who purchased a portrait print of a Confederate hero was a traitor as well, and, significantly, the peddler in the *Tribune* story had no Lee portraits to sell.

Genuine patriotic sentiment was attached to these print images, though it is difficult to recapture that emotion now, when we tend to view them as quaint "Americana." The rapid development of printmaking earlier in the century had made it possible for many ordinary Americans to patronize an artistic tradition once reserved exclusively for royal courts. The taste for equestrian portraits of warriors in armor and death scenes on sanctified fields of battle dated to medieval England; it became so widespread when these were made available to the masses as display engravings that the eighteenth-century philosopher David Hume warned against the adulation that such images stimulated. He called it what, in effect, it was: "hero-worship."[6]

The tradition quickly moved to the New World, notwithstanding America's deep-seated aversion to military authority and standing armies. As early as 1811 a Russian

THE OLD GENERAL READY FOR A "MOVEMENT".

Figure 9. Currier and Ives, *The Old General Ready for a "Movement."* New York, ca. 1861. Lithograph, 10¾ × 13¾ inches. General Winfield Scott, portrayed as far younger than his seventy-five years, sits atop a mound, labeled "Richmond," covering a foxhole and waits for the creature labeled "Jeff" to emerge into the noose he patiently dangles to entrap him. (Prints showing Davis being hanged as a traitor would soon become common.) Meanwhile, the old general firmly uses his boots to hold by their tails foxes named "Beauregard" and "Pillow." In its haste to produce a topical cartoon, Currier and Ives mistakenly used John C. Breckinridge's portrait for Gideon Pillow's and Pillow's likeness for Davis's. The print suggested that Scott's patience was a strategic virtue, but it may also have mocked "Old Fuss and Feathers" by depicting him squatting, implying in the caption that he was more constipated than aggressive. Certainly the pose was undignified and inglorious, to say the least. The scatological scheme of making the capital of the Confederacy into Scott's toilet bowl was somewhat obscured by depicting it as a foxhole. (*Library of Congress*)

visitor to the United States noted the proliferation of portraits of America's first and greatest military hero: "Every American considers it his sacred duty to have a likeness of Washington in his home, just as we have images of God's saints. Washington's portrait is the finest and sometimes the sole decoration of American homes." Twenty years later, Gustave de Beaumont, who accompanied Alexis de Tocqueville to America, reported that "prints of Washington dark with smoke" were still "firmly pasted over the hearths of . . . many American homes." In the realm of fiction, Mark Twain's Huckleberry Finn encountered in one "mighty nice house . . . pictures hung on the walls . . . mainly Washingtons and Lafayettes, and battles." For years, though he turned from the military life in true Cincinnatus style to become the country's first president, Washington would remain most often portrayed not in the civilian garb of the presidency, but in the uniform of the Continental army.[7]

The heroic connotations that could be suggested by military portraiture were evident in political campaigns throughout the nineteenth century, whenever old heroes sought civilian office. Andrew Jackson, for example, might be portrayed in derisive caricatures as a skeletal old man in a black suit, but in many of the prints designed to extol his virtues, he remained the uniformed hero of the Battle of New Orleans. William Henry Harrison was similarly portrayed in the campaign of 1840, and "Old Rough and Ready," Zachary Taylor, was so often depicted in uniform in campaign prints of 1848 that his opposition countered with banners showing its candidate for vice president, William O. Butler, wearing *his* old military uniform, complete with epaulets, though he had earned less distinction as a warrior.[8]

In the early months of the Civil War, it would have been difficult to discover hanging above any northern hearth a separate-sheet portrait of a truly triumphant Union military hero. The period was clouded with military failures, especially in the East. General Irvin McDowell, who led Union forces to defeat at Bull Run in July 1861, was not even portrayed by Currier and Ives, which depicted dozens of war celebrities. Had McDowell sacrificed his life on the field, he might have inspired pictures, for Edward D. Baker achieved status as a martyr when he fell at the equally disastrous engagement at Ball's Bluff. The difference between dead and defeated generals was great—a point not lost on Philip H. Sheridan, who once justified his battlefield fearlessness by saying, "I have never in my life taken a command into battle, and had the slightest desire to come out alive unless I won."[9]

One of the most popular of the early Union heroes in prints proved to be Colonel Ellsworth, the first Union officer killed, who seemed in death not only to represent the best of young American manhood, but to symbolize to each of the nation's parents and wives the harrowing possibility that war could strike at every family in the North. "In size, in years, and in youthful appearance, a boy only, his power to command men, was surpassingly great," a deeply saddened Lincoln wrote to Ellsworth's mother and father. The president seemed to speak for an entire nation of admirers when he added: "So much of promised usefulness to one's country, and of bright hopes for one's self and friends, have rarely been so suddenly dashed, as in his fall." What was more, Ellsworth had died hauling down a Confederate flag, a detail that was surely not lost on patriotic Northerners still in a flag-waving frenzy following the assault on the American standard at Fort Sumter.[10]

Ellsworth was famous before his martyrdom. He had formed a peacetime volunteer unit called the U.S. Zouave Cadets and accoutred them in the trim jackets, billowing, gaudily colored pantaloons, and white puttees that Zouaves had adapted from North African uniforms. Ellsworth's Chicago company earned added distinction by winning a national drill team championship and then traveling throughout the North, accompanied by a brass band, to demonstrate their acrobatic routines.

When war broke out, the indefatigable drillmaster formed a company of New York Fire Department Zouaves and led them across the Potomac River to Alexandria on May 24, 1861.

The only Confederate troops guarding the city fled before Ellsworth arrived, but when he reached the Marshall House on King Street, he decided to storm up its stairs and cut down the huge enemy flag that had been vexingly visible as far away as the White House on the other side of the river. As he headed downstairs clutching his trophy, James W. Jackson, the infuriated proprietor, blasted at Ellsworth with a double-barreled shotgun, killing him instantly. Ellsworth was but twenty-four years old.

It was a shot heard around the North, in part because one of the men accompanying Ellsworth up those stairs was Edward H. House of the *New York Tribune*, who reported on the colonel's martyrdom immediately. House's presence suggests that the action had been what in later years might be called a publicity stunt; if so, it backfired tragically. Within minutes after Ellsworth's death, other correspondents converged on the scene, several of whom, understanding immediately the symbolic importance of the event, were moved to cut souvenir pieces from the Marshall House flag, even as it lay on Ellsworth's body to cover him. Over the next few days, they, too, celebrated Ellsworth in reports published throughout the North. Ellsworth, a friend of the Lincolns before the war, was given a funeral fit for a commanding general in the East Room of the White House, and a nation joined in the mourning through reports in the press.[11]

The printmakers quickly followed suit. James L. Magee of Philadelphia reacted quickest of all, producing a depiction of the shooting and a memorial portrait on May 29 and June 1, respectively. On July 10 in New York, D. Appleton and Company published a depiction of the Marshall House, "rendered memorable," its caption reminded potential buyers, "by the death of Col. Ellsworth at the hands of Jackson the proprietor after the capture of the secession flag." Earlier, on June 6, an Ohio publisher had issued a facsimile of Ellsworth's final letter to his parents, in which he had termed his imminent march into Alexandria "the performance of a sacred duty."[12]

For weeks, publishers registered their latest Ellsworth pictures at copyright offices in New York and Philadelphia. More than eighty pictures appeared in all—dignified portraits based on photographs, action scenes re-creating his death, and lithographed covers for funeral dirges and requiem marches. Explicit in at least one of these prints was the point that Ellsworth was heir to an American tradition of military heroism: J. C. Upham entitled his dual portrait *The First Officer Killed in the Revolution, Warren—The First Officer Killed in the Present Rebellion—Ellsworth*. In truth, the Marshall House was no Bunker Hill, the hallowed site where Joseph Warren had given his life in 1775. But Ellsworth's youth, precocity, spruce good looks, dashing style, and cruel death surely combined to make him a popular martyr. Many Ellsworth prints bristled with warlike or pugnacious titles like "Remember Ellsworth" and "Avenge Ellsworth! War to the knife, the knife to the hilt."[13]

The myriad Ellsworth death scenes varied in accuracy and detail. A typically earnest effort was the lithograph produced by Currier and Ives of New York (fig. 10). It realistically showed Ellsworth's gaping (and bleeding) wound but erroneously positioned it near the colonel's stomach rather than over his heart, the area that the shot actually pierced (as an examination of the surviving uniform reveals). Moreover, Currier and Ives depicted innkeeper Jackson simply raising his rifle and firing at Ellsworth. In truth, one of Ellsworth's men had first batted away Jackson's rifle with his own, a diversion that, tragically, might have helped send the deadly shot directly into the young colonel.[14]

The printmakers differed in presenting the details, but they all seemed to sense immediately Ellsworth's symbolic importance to the Union. In the words to a "Song on the Death of Colonel Ellsworth the Gallant Zouave," published to accompany a print of his death, an unidentified poet summed up the national feeling for the colonel with a tribute to his courage that suggested that Ellsworth's bold action had been tantamount to preserving the Union itself. With no deaths recorded on the larger field of Fort Sumter, Ellsworth's sacrifice in a way sealed the vow of revenge in innocent blood:

> When he saw Treason's proud banner waving,
>   No danger his valor could quell,
> And when his hands tore it asunder,
>   By a coward assassin he fell.
> T'was Ellsworth, the gallant Zouave,
> T'was Ellsworth, the gallant Zouave,
> Who tore down the banner of treason,
> And perished our Union to save.[15]

As New York diarist George Templeton Strong noted of the martyred officer, "He could hardly have done such service as his assassin has rendered the country. . . . His murder will stir the fire in every northern state." Indeed, lithographer Edward Mendel issued a richly illustrated cover for an 1861 Ellsworth requiem march featuring the late colonel's portrait all but enveloped by American flags.[16]

Ellsworth was the first, but not the last, Union martyr to attract interest from Northern printmakers. General Nathaniel Lyon's heroic death in August 1861 at the Battle of Wilson's Creek in Missouri inspired tributes from the ever timely printmaker J. L. Magee (Currier and Ives had copyrighted a Lyon portrait on June 24, before his death, at a time when many in the North were crediting the general with saving the border state of Missouri for the Union). Other famous casualties earning pictorial tributes included Colonel Baker, portrayed on a funeral march cover by Lee and Walker in November 1861, a month after his death at Ball's Bluff, and General Philip Kearny, killed at the Battle of Chantilly in September 1862 and portrayed in *Last Reconnoissance*, by an unknown printmaker, soon thereafter.[17]

A century after the triumph of victors like Grant and Sherman, it challenges his-

Brownell. Entered according to act of Congress in the year 1861, by Currier & Ives, in the Clerk's Office of the district Court of the United States, for the Southern District of New York. Jackson.

DEATH OF COL. ELLSWORTH,

after hauling down the rebel flag, at the taking of Alexandria, Va.__ May 24th 1861.

torical imagination to find in today's print archives so many portraits of heroes whose fame did not last—men like Franz Sigel, the German-born commander who became a major general in early 1862. The number of prints devoted to this figure far outweighed his contributions to the war effort. Sigel performed with reasonable success at the Battle of Pea Ridge in March 1862 but otherwise earned little distinction in service of the Union. But for German Americans, one of the largest and fastest growing ethnic groups in the North, Sigel was an authentic hero; he became a touchstone for immigrant enthusiasm for the Union cause.

Currier and Ives's *Genl. Franz Sigel. / At the Battle of Pea-Ridge, Ark.* (fig. 11), copyrighted on August 27, 1862, typified the popular printmakers' resort to traditional cavalier imagery in the absence of reliable firsthand accounts from the front. It depicted Sigel on horseback as he resolutely led his troops in a picturesque charge that helped turn the tide at that battle. Sigel admitted that at the Battle of Wilson's Creek a year earlier, he wore "a blue woolen blanket over my uniform and a yellowish slouch hat, giving me the appearance of a Texas Ranger." The garb was designed to ensure, Sigel stated frankly, that he "was not taken" by the enemy. The ruse worked, but it would hardly do for printmakers like Currier and Ives to portray a battlefield hero in disguise. Their portrait of Sigel leading his charge at Pea Ridge depicted him in standard Union regalia, waving a plumed cavalier's hat in the bargain. When lithographer Louis Kurz, also German-born, and then working in the heavily German city of Milwaukee, produced his own portrait of Sigel at Pea Ridge for a sheet music cover, he gave the general the blanket he wore that day, but instead of portraying a ranger's hat, he dressed Sigel in what appeared to be a brimless fur cap, giving him the appearance almost of a Cossack. This at least was the kind of hat in which he had been photographed at the beginning of the campaign. The result was still inspirational.[18]

Sigel was not the commander of Union forces at Pea Ridge; General Samuel R. Curtis was. But it would be difficult to ascertain that fact from the prints and other popular representations of the fight. Sigel fought well that day, perhaps better than he would ever fight again, but he was Curtis's subordinate, and the victory be-

---

opposite

Figure 10. Currier and Ives, *Death of Col. Ellsworth, / After Hauling Down the Rebel Flag, at the Taking of Alexandria, Va. May 24th, 1861.* New York, 1861. Lithograph, 12¾ × 8¾ inches. Ellsworth's death was widely reported in the press, and the detailed published descriptions probably helped Currier and Ives construct this scene. Ellsworth had cut down the Confederate flag flying atop the Marshall House and was on his way downstairs when the innkeeper, James Jackson, shot him at point-blank range. Corporal Francis E. Brownell, who had accompanied the young colonel, then shot Jackson in the face, killing him instantly. (Ellsworth's "Avenger" would himself inspire prints by both T. W. Strong and J. H. Bufford.) Ellsworth was a small man in life, but in death he assumed outsized proportions, as in this print. Currier and Ives did not copyright the lithograph until November 15, 1861, suggesting perhaps that the printmakers took some time to research and prepare their lithograph, a luxury they would seldom employ in competition to market Civil War news prints in years to come. More likely, after the Union debacle at Bull Run, the firm was desperate for heroes whose portraits Northern audiences would be eager to purchase. (*Library of Congress*)

Figure 11.
Currier and Ives, *Genl. Franz Sigel. / At the Battle of Pea-Ridge, Ark. March 8th 1862.* New York, 1862. Lithograph, 13¾ × 9½ inches. All the elements of classic military portraiture—the hat-waving commander, the rearing horse, the inspired troops, the nearby loyal lieutenants, fallen soldiers, and overturned cannon—are employed here to invest Franz Sigel's performance at Pea Ridge with the trappings of full military glory. Little concession is made to the cold weather that Sigel and his men confronted that winter in Arkansas; Sigel is depicted as a summer warrior, doffing his plumed hat to urge on his soldiers. He had undeniable appeal for German American print buyers, of whom there were many in Currier and Ives's headquarters city of New York. At the same time, he was the subject of anti-German prints like *Valiant Men Dat Fight Mit Sigel,* etched, ironically, by a fellow German, the pro-Confederate Maryland artist Adalbert J. Volck. (*Library of Congress*)

PUBLISHED BY CURRIER & IVES,   Entered according to act of Congress, in the year 1862, by Currier & Ives, in the Clerk's Office of the District Court of the United States, for the Southern Dist. of New York.   152 NASSAU ST NEW YORK.

GENL FRANZ SIGEL.
At the Battle of Pea-Ridge. Ark. March, 8th 1862.

longed to the commander. After the engagement, however, numerous soldiers from Sigel's division, disproportionately German in origin, spread stories in their hometown newspapers and to their congressional representatives that Sigel was the true hero of the battle, that he dissuaded Curtis from retreating after setbacks on the first day of fighting, and that he led the decisive attacks the next day. That view prevailed in the press, and Curtis stoically resigned himself to letting it stand without objecting.[19]

An accurate portrayal of Sigel's contributions at Pea Ridge would have celebrated not his hat-waving leadership, but rather his professional direction of the artillery. A graduate of a European military academy, Sigel knew the technical aspects of warfare, and on the morning of March 8, 1862, he performed his best work, overseeing the artillery batteries, well placed on a rise, that shattered Confederate infantry and rendered them vulnerable to attack by Union infantry. He personally sighted some of the guns, but he surely accomplished the work on foot, not on horseback, though prints always showed him mounted. Suggesting individual acts of courage and dash on horseback, rather than depicting the triumph of the ugly machines of destruction wielded by the Union artillery, was a constant error of the pictorial chroniclers of the Civil War. In truth, the formulaic dismounted artillery piece being rushed over by charging infantrymen, found in the Sigel lithograph and in many others, ironically reinforced the idea of the insignificance of artillery.[20]

Enthusiasm for Sigel continued to run high. The Philadelphia printmaker Feodor Fuchs's 1862 lithograph, *Major General Franz Sigel, United States Army, / As Colonel on the Battlefield of Carthage* (fig. 12), portrayed the action of July 5, 1861, when Sigel's troops were chased from that Missouri city by a Confederate flanking action led by a politician-general who could boast none of Sigel's military training or experience. Clearly, Sigel's status as a German American hero made the matter of his military record secondary.[21]

Fuchs's handsome print, which owed much to the European traditions of military uniform prints, is redeemed from the criticism it deserves as a depiction of war by excellent portraiture and careful draftsmanship. Only a circus rider could sit so calmly and erectly athwart a horse running at full tilt. And General Sigel was not so much wasp-waisted as slight of build; such exaggerated figures were characteristic of European uniform and costume illustrations of the day.[22]

Sigel had succeeded to command when the impetuous General Nathaniel Lyon fell at Wilson's Creek, but the two generals had in common an asset that would make the images of both attractive in the early months of the war: they were heroes of the West, the only theater of the conflict then witnessing Union victories. In response, E. B. and E. C. Kellogg, the Hartford lithographers whose close coverage of the battles and leaders of the war paralleled that of Currier and Ives, published *Brig. Generals Nathaniel Lyon and Franz Sigel* in 1861, and Louis Prang of Boston followed the same year with *Genl. F. Siegel and Late Genl. N. Lyon* (fig. 13). The latter image looked very much like the former, except that in Prang's version, Lyon hovers in the clouds, acting as divine inspiration for Sigel.

Galloping on the battlefield or flying through the clouds alongside a dead comrade, Sigel was an inspiration to Northern printmakers—an appeal probably enhanced for reasons of ethnicity. Sigel enjoyed exalted status in lithography, a medium dominated by fellow Germans; publishers like Kurz, Prang, and Fuchs, all

Figure 12. F[eodor]. Fuchs, *Major General Franz Sigel, United States Army, / As Colonel on the Battlefield of Carthage, July 5th, 1861*. Philadelphia, 1862. Lithograph, 14½ × 19 inches. Rendered with impeccable draftsmanship, this highly flattering portrait suggested even more strongly than Currier and Ives's Pea Ridge print that Sigel's appearance on the field of battle was capable of rallying his troops. Image notwithstanding, Sigel and his army retreated from the Carthage battlefield. (*Library of Congress*)

German-born, portrayed Sigel early. Printmaking helped temper the prejudices of the greater culture. The heyday of the anti-immigration Know-Nothing Party was five years past at most, and prejudice against the "Dutch" remained strong. Confederates denounced the Union invaders as "Hessians" or labeled them the immigrant dregs of the Northern cities, while within the Union army itself, some soldiers blamed fellow soldiers of German stock for any incidents of rape or pillage. The heroic prints of Franz Sigel, however brief their vogue, showed that German-born soldiers could be well worth honoring.[23]

Many of the eastern generals celebrated in prints early in the war faded even more quickly than did Sigel in the West. Toward the end of the first year of the war, a significantly changing Union military order could be glimpsed in group military

GEN^L. F. SIEGEL AND LATE GEN^L. N. LYON.

THE HEROES OF MISSOURI

Published by L. PRANG & Co. 34 Merchants Row Boston.

Designed & drawn with Pen on Stone by E. ACKERMANN.   Printed by L. PRANG & Co Boston.

Figure 13.
E[mil]. Ackermann, *Genl. F. Siegel and Late Genl. N. Lyon. / The Heroes of Missouri.* Published by L. Prang and Company, Boston, 1861. Lithograph with tintstone, 11 × 10 inches. Sigel had served under Lyon at Wilson's Creek, and this print suggested that even in death, Lyon continued to watch over his German-born lieutenant. Their appearance together, the martyr inspiring the hero, suggests how strong was the appeal of these veterans of the western theater in the first year of the Civil War. (*Anne S. K. Brown Military Collection, Brown University*)

portraits like *Union Generals*, *The Champions of the Union*, and *Lloyd's New Political Chart.* The last named featured portraits of President Lincoln, Generals Scott and John Wool, Major Anderson, and Lieutenant Adam Slemmer, commander of the Union garrison at Fort Pickens, Florida. The three-foot by two-foot posters sold for twenty-five cents, promoted by publisher H. H. Lloyd of New York with advertisements that cited "large, new, colored portraits . . . finely colored on excellent paper." As early as June 1861, Lloyd had advertised among its "Charts and Portraits, designed expressly for the times," a "new and Elegant" print, priced at twenty-five cents, around whose central scene showing Zouaves trampling on the rebel flag, could be found "correct portraits of Generals Scott, McClellan, Butler, Fremont, Banks, and Prentiss; Colonels Ellsworth, [Michael] Corcoran, and several others . . . size 27 × 37 inches."[24]

In a similar vein, *A Council of War in '61* offered portraits of President Lincoln, Secretary of State William H. Seward, and Secretary of War Simon Cameron listening intently as General Scott discusses military strategy at what appears to be a White House meeting with several Union generals. Among the officers who join the imaginary council there stands another figure, thrust so awkwardly between Cameron and Butler that it almost looks as if the artist inserted him into the scene at the last minute. Even as his colleagues glance improbably at each other in unnatural poses dictated by the separate, rigid photographic portraits that the printmaker copied, this general gazes almost fiercely at Scott. He is George B. McClellan, Scott's eventual successor.

By the time Sarony, Major and Knapp produced a similar scene, *The Defenders of the Union* (plate 2), a print later reproduced as a *carte-de-visite* for the newly popular photograph albums designed to display them, McClellan had become more prominent. Here the early heroes were all seated behind a table dominated by Scott. The only officer who shares the foreground with the venerable Mexican War hero is McClellan. Perhaps unintentionally, but tellingly all the same, the two officers stare at each other across the table. And it is McClellan who gestures; Scott is now reduced to listening.

With great promise, McClellan took command of the Army of the Potomac on July 27, 1861. Although a brilliant organizer, he was given to delay and would not move his army until Lincoln directly ordered him to do so the following January. Unfortunately, McClellan's ingenious plan to capture Richmond bogged down after an elaborate campaign along the Virginia Peninsula and ended in retreat that summer. In September 1862 he did lead the Union to success at Antietam, although his was less complete a triumph than President Lincoln had hoped for. Nonetheless, it proved sufficient to enable Lincoln to issue the Emancipation Proclamation—and more than enough to convince McClellan that he deserved historical vindication. "My military reputation is cleared," the general insisted after the victory. "I have shown that I can fight battles & *win* them." He felt confident that "one of these days history will . . . do me justice in deciding that it was not my fault that the campaign of the Peninsula was not successful." McClellan's prediction proved wrong, except where the printmakers were concerned. They never ignored George B. McClellan— quite the contrary. In light of his collapsed reputation in modern times, however, the large number of print tributes from the war era seems anomalous.[25]

Like other generals, McClellan entered the war with notions of leadership that were soon to become outdated. Undeniably, he looked impressive on horseback, even when printmakers stressed his elaborate uniforms and the supposed foreign dominance of his staff, as in Sarony, Major and Knapp's dashing *The Commander of the Union Army / And His Staff* (fig. 14), which pointed out that several of McClellan's chief staff officers were European. The print was copublished by Goupil in Paris.[26]

The gap between image and accomplishment widened. J. H. Bufford's portrait (fig. 15), depicting McClellan in a resplendent uniform, complete with epaulets, placed him on the battlefield, his hand resting on an artillery piece aimed at the enemy. McClellan would admit, "The duties of my position were such as often to make it necessary for me to remain in the rear," adding, "It is an awful thing." That confession signaled a watershed moment in the responsibilities of command. The modern general was no longer needed on the field of action, personally inspiring his soldiers with upthrust saber or brilliant horsemanship. He was required at the rear, surveying vast fields with telescope or binocular, directing lieutenants from afar. It was an unheroic style of command, as historian John Keegan has pointed out, and while it fit the needs of modern war, it challenged image makers to conceive of new ways to pay tribute to successful generals. Where McClellan was concerned, printmakers stubbornly preferred the old forms, even if they no longer reflected reality.[27]

Before long, McClellan had become not only the most frequently portrayed of all Union heroes, but a representative heroic figure so familiar to print audiences that he did not have to be identified in captions. Currier and Ives's sentimental home-front scene, *The Brave Wife* (fig. 16), for example, showed an officer with a remarkable resemblance to McClellan about to take leave of his family to join the war. For a time, he surely seemed to most print buyers to be the quintessential military hero, the ideal of noble military portraiture. Even the commander in chief was not immune to the McClellan image fever. In March 1862 the Boston representative of the London Printing and Publishing Company sent Lincoln three engravings of the general, and the president retained one for himself. "The Engraving is very beautifully executed," he acknowledged in a letter, "and the likeness is perfect." McClellan signed print portraits of himself for other admirers (fig. 17) and, judging by the absence of other examples, appears to have been one of the few Civil War celebrities who did so.[28]

Dismissed by Lincoln in 1862, the general temporarily faded from view. But McClellan's image would take a distinctive and not always flattering new turn in 1864, when he reemerged as the Democratic candidate for the presidency, inspiring a new wave of print portraiture as well as vicious cartoons that harked back pointedly to the military setbacks for which he had been more often than not excused by the printmakers of 1861 and 1862. (That election-year image is considered in a separate chapter.)

Less famous men than McClellan also enjoyed their brief brush with pictorial

THE COMMANDER OF THE UNION ARMY

fame, and an adaptable printmaker might accommodate the uncertainty of rises and falls in reputation with an ingenious use, and reuse, of lithographic stones. To save the time required for artists to compose new designs whenever a new military celebrity emerged, printmakers could quickly insert new portraits onto existing designs and reissue the results as "new." Such recycled adaptations also obviated the need for thorough research—and saved artists' time in the bargain. No wartime printmaker made more frequent or more ingenious use of this system than Ehrgott, Forbriger and Company of Cincinnati.

The firm issued a series of military portraits around 1862 that offered stock equestrian poses, into which were inserted, in almost amusement park, head-through-the-hole fashion, a succession of portraits of the latest military heroes. The result might be called an assembly-line gallery of subjects, most of whom later suffered diminished reputation, though their onetime, if fleeting, fame is borne out by their appearance in these lithographs. To produce the prints, Ehrgott, Forbriger created the design on a lithographic stone, printed as many copies as it thought would sell to admirers of the subject, and then erased the face, inserted a new one, and printed yet another set of portraits.

General John A. McClernand, an early hero in the West who was later removed from important posts by General Grant, thus shared the same pose as the martyred Nathaniel Lyon, for example. Their portrayals differed only in the prop each holds in his right arm: Lyon waves his hat, McClernand a saber. In another pairing, General Jefferson C. Davis (fig. 18), who won early acclaim at Pea Ridge and Corinth but later fell into disrepute when he murdered a fellow general in Louisville, and General Joseph Hooker (fig. 19), who was later defeated at the Battle of Chancellorsville, ride over identical landscapes. Ehrgott, Forbriger went on to adapt the design yet again for a portrait of General William Rosecrans, who scored a triumph at the Battle of Stones River on December 31, 1862, but faltered at Chickamauga the following September. The printmakers also used the Hooker-Davis equestrian

opposite
Figure 14. Sarony, Major and Knapp, *The Commander of the Union Army / And His Staff.*
Copyrighted by M. Knoedler, published by Goupil and Company, New York and Paris, 1861.
Lithograph with tintstone, 21 × 17½ inches. Prints depicting General George B. McClellan charging across battlefields on handsome steeds were common during the Civil War. This print showed McClellan in epaulets, a richly plumed bicorne hat, and a flowing cloak—garb that made him appear more European than American. To emphasize the general's Continental look—this picture was, after all, published for French as well as American audiences—the lithograph noted that several of McClellan's key lieutenants were French. From left to right, the staff officers in the background are "Col. [Henry F.] Clarke, Le Duc de Chartres, Le Compte de Paris, and Genl. [Stewart] Van Vliet." Chartres, "the little duke," as McClellan referred to him, was a member of France's royal but exiled House of Orleans, and the Comte de Paris was the pretender to the French throne. Both the duke and the count were nephews of another McClellan intimate, the Prince de Joinville, whom McClellan once called "a noble character . . . true as steel" (Stephen W. Sears, ed., *The Civil War Papers of George B. McClellan: Selected Correspondence, 1860–1865* [New York: Ticknor and Fields, 1989], 76, 114, 135–36). (*Anne S. K. Brown Military Collection, Brown University*)

Entered according to Act of Congress in the year 1861 by J.H.Bufford in the Clerk's Office of the District Court of Mass.

MAJOR GENERAL GEORGE B. M'CLELLAN.

Lithographed & Published by **J.H.BUFFORD**, 313. Washington St. Boston.

portrait as a model for a sheet music cover entitled "Rosecrans' Victory March" (fig. 20).

Ehrgott, Forbriger performed this pictorial sleight-of-hand with many military celebrities, including those from the naval side of the war. One such set included Commodore Andrew Hull Foote (fig. 21), one of the heroes of the assault on Fort Donelson in February 1862, Commander John A. Dahlgren (fig. 22), who presided over both the Washington Navy Yard and the Bureau of Ordnance and later commanded the Union blockading squadron in Charleston, South Carolina, and Commander David Dixon Porter, who won early fame leading the naval expedition to relieve Fort Pickens in Florida.

In all, Ehrgott, Forbriger issued at least forty-five separate military portraits, employing no more than twelve different lithographic stones, repeatedly inserting different heads on previously designed bodies in order to save money and time in rushing out prints of the latest promising military heroes. A survey of known works reveals that the firm produced the following groups of pictures:

Group 1 (seven portraits; equestrian, right arm outstretched): Generals George G. Meade, Ulysses S. Grant, George B. McClellan, Ambrose E. Burnside, Robert C. Schenck, Lovell H. Rousseau, and Lewis Wallace.

Group 2 (five portraits; seated at table): President Abraham Lincoln, Secretary of the Treasury Salmon P. Chase, Governor of Indiana Oliver P. Morton, Military Governor of Tennessee Andrew Johnson, and Governor of Ohio David Tod.

Group 3 (four portraits; equestrian, arm outstretched, horse rearing): Generals Daniel E. Sickles, George H. Thomas, Quincy A. Gillmore, and George Stoneman.

Group 4 (three portraits; equestrian, hat in hand with arm outstretched): Generals Alexander McDowell McCook, Robert L. McCook, and Ebenezer Dumont.

opposite
Figure 15. J[ohn]. H. Bufford, *Major General George B. McClellan*. Boston, 1861. Lithograph, 12 × 9 inches. Around the time this heroic print was published, McClellan sent some photographs home to his mother, which the photographer "insisted on taking," he wrote, "by main force & violence." In truth, McClellan proudly sat before the cameras as often as any other celebrity of the Civil War era, and the abundance of resulting images produced a healthy flow of models for engravers and lithographers. But only printmakers could add the atmosphere of war—in this case an artillery piece, the smoke of battle, and a soldier on horseback. The print may have exaggerated McClellan's proximity to such action, but not his dress. "I appeared today for the first time in full tog," he wrote his wife in August 1861, "chapeau, epaulettes, etc—& flattered myself 'we' did it well—at least [Brig. Gen. William F.] Barry [McClellan's chief of artillery] and [Captain] Charles P. Kingsbury [chief of ordnance] told me they were quite jealous about what their wives said" (Sears, *The Civil War Papers of George B. McClellan*, 85, 88–89). (*The Lincoln Museum*)

PUBLISHED BY CURRIER & IVES,   152 NASSAU St. NEW YORK.

THE BRAVE WIFE.

The wife who girds her husband's sword,
  'Mid little ones who weep or wonder,
And bravely speaks the cheering word,
  What tho' her heart he rent asunder,—

Doomed nightly in her dreams to hear,
  The bolts of war around him rattle,
Hath shed as sacred blood as e'er,
  Was poured upon the plain of battle!

opposite
Figure 16. Currier and Ives, *The Brave Wife.* New York, ca. 1861. Lithograph, 12¾ × 8¾ inches. Although he was not identified by name as the central figure in this sentimental "farewell" print, the departing officer of this lithograph, his belt being buckled by his adoring wife, was probably meant to portray George B. McClellan. The viewer is thus encouraged to believe that he experienced the same kind of tearful departure from his family as officers and common soldiers alike were then experiencing throughout the North. Certainly the soldier's appearance in this print strongly suggests that McClellan quickly came to symbolize the Union army itself—and the sacrifice each soldier made by leaving home to serve the country. Currier and Ives made one error in presenting McClellan here as the military's Everyman: although the printmakers portrayed a little boy crying at left, the McClellans' son, George Jr., was not born until 1865. The printmakers managed to insert a little advertisement for themselves by including a framed heroic military print on the wall of the "Brave Wife's" home. (*The Harry T. Peters Collection, Museum of the City of New York*)

JEFFERSON C. DAVIS

BRIG - GEN - U.S.A

JOE. HOOKER.

MAJ GEN⊥ U.S.A.

Figure 19.
Ehrgott, Forbriger
and Company,
*Joe. Hooker /
Maj. Genl. U.S.A.*
Cincinnati, ca. 1863.
Lithograph, 10¾ ×
9¾ inches. One of
this Ohio publisher's
array of stock prints
with interchangeable
heads, this portrait
of General Joseph
Hooker presented
him, appropriately,
as a dashing officer,
yet the likeness failed
to do full justice
to his appearance:
Hooker was one
of the handsomest
generals in the
Union army.
Immensely popular
with his troops, he
led the Army of
the Potomac to
disastrous defeat
at the Battle of
Chancellorsville.
This print was
undoubtedly
published before
that loss took place.
(Abner Doubleday,
*Chancellorsville
and Gettysburg*
[1882; reprint,
New York: Da Capo
Press, 1994].)
(*Library of Congress*)

opposite
Figure 18. Ehrgott, Forbriger and Company, *Jefferson C. Davis / Brig. Genl. U.S.A.* Cincinnati,
ca. 1863–64. Lithograph, 10¾ × 9¾ inches. There is no discernible difference between this version
of Ehrgott, Forbriger's standard equestrian portrait and the alternative version featuring General
Hooker. Popular demand for portraits of this officer was surely brief. Davis was burdened not only
with the same given and family names as the president of the Confederacy, but with a spotty record
that included a feud with his commanding general, William Nelson, at Louisville that ended
tragically when Davis shot Nelson to death in a hotel. Although he was never tried for the murder,
Davis was never promoted to the rank of full major general, despite subsequent successes at Stones
River and Chickamauga. (Ezra J. Warner, *Generals in Blue: Lives of the Union Commanders* [Baton
Rouge: Louisiana State University Press, 1964], 115–16.) (*Library of Congress*)

Figure 20.
Ehrgott, Forbriger and Company, "Rosecrans' Victory March." Published by J. Church Jr., Cincinnati, 1863. Lithographed sheet music cover, 10¾ by 9¾ inches. A tribute likely inspired by Rosecrans's successful Chattanooga campaign in 1863, this third variant of the standard Ehrgott, Forbriger equestrian portrait placed it within an authentic-looking battle scene, with artillery firing at left and soldiers charging at right. Rosecrans holds a telescope, the appropriate "weapon" for a commanding general on a large field, and as a shell explodes in front of him, the horse's head tilts upward—a subtle but clever adjustment from the Hooker and Davis versions of the image. (*Library of Congress*)

opposite

Figure 21. Ehrgott, Forbriger and Company, *Commodore Foote / U.S.N.* Cincinnati, ca. 1863. Lithograph, 9¹⁵⁄₁₆ × 9⁵⁄₁₆ inches. With other ironclad gunboats—known as "Pook's Turtles"—steaming in the foreground and background alike, Commodore Andrew Hull Foote poses almost nonchalantly on the armored deck of one such vessel, clutching the kind of dress sword that would surely have proven useless in a naval battle. In truth, Foote had been injured by a shell while on the deck of an older vessel, the USS *St. Louis*, during the attack on Fort Donelson in February 1862. He was on crutches when he next commanded, at Island No. 10 in April, and thereafter was restricted to desk duty in Washington. He died in 1863. (Patricia L. Faust, ed., *Historical Times Illustrated Encyclopedia of the Civil War* [New York: Harper and Row, 1986], 265–66.) (*Library of Congress*)

COMMODORE FOOTE,

U S N

Lith. &published by Ehrgott,Forbriger &C° Cin.

COM. DAHLGREEN.

U.S.N.

Group 5 (three portraits; equestrian, with horse standing still): Generals William H. L. Wallace, John E. Wool, and Ormsby M. Mitchel.

Group 6 (three portraits; standing): Admirals David G. Farragut and Samuel F. Du Pont and Captain John L. Worden.

Group 7 (three portraits; standing on deck): Naval Commanders John A. Dahlgren and David Dixon Porter and Commodore Andrew Hull Foote.

Group 8 (five portraits; equestrian, facing right): Generals Henry W. Halleck, John C. Frémont, William B. Franklin, and Samuel R. Curtis and Colonel Ephraim Elmer Ellsworth.

Group 9 (three portraits; equestrian, gloved right arm outstretched): Generals Jefferson C. Davis, Joseph Hooker, and William S. Rosecrans.

Group 10 (five portraits; standing beside horse): Generals John Adams Dix (see fig. 94), William T. Sherman (see fig. 95), Louis Goldsborough, Benjamin F. Butler, and David Hunter.

Group 11 (two portraits; equestrian): Generals Henry W. Halleck and Benjamin F. Butler.

Group 12 (two portraits; equestrian, arm outstretched waving, respectively, hat and saber): Generals Nathaniel Lyon and John A. McClernand.

Such tricks of the trade were hardly new. They had frequently been employed by British engravers. As a historian of those early engraved images has pointed out: "The demand for a topical plate would sometimes last only a few weeks. Between them, the engraver and the publisher evolved the expedient of altering and adapting plates to their immediate need. Obviously, it took much less time to burnish out the head . . . than to engrave an entirely new plate." It was even easier with lithographs, whose process did not alter the surface of the stone as engravings did their steel and copper plates.[29]

The range of subjects depicted in this series suggests that Americans continued to yearn for heroes—and their portraits. In 1862 a publisher named Evert A. Duyckinck launched his *History of the War for the Union, Civil Military and Naval,* perhaps the first ambitious history of the conflict. Issued to subscribers in thirty-two softcover volumes, the series featured not only "national" and "impartial" reportage, as readers were reminded, but also fully realized print art: a series of five-by-seven-inch frontispiece engravings, one per issue, based on specially commissioned paintings by the respected artist Alonzo Chappel.[30]

An advertisement for the series noted: "Every pains [*sic*] has been taken, both in its artistic and literary developments, to present a work worthy of a permanent place in the American library and by the American fireside, in the homes of the American people." The notice invited special attention by suggesting a dearth of

opposite
Figure 22.
Ehrgott, Forbriger and Company, *Com. Dahlgreen. / U.S.N.* Cincinnati, 1863. Lithograph, $9^{15}/_{16} \times 9^{5}/_{16}$ inches. No records of copyright exist to indicate which of these man-on-tinclad prints was published first, but the setting was certainly inappropriate for a portrait of John A. Dahlgren, his name here misspelled in the caption, who commanded the Union blockading squadron in Charleston in 1863, a fleet comprised of monitors and ocean-going screw vessels. The only concession the printmaker made to the differences between the two naval heroes was the distinctive head-gear worn by each. Otherwise, the poses and background designs were left precisely the same. (*Library of Congress*)

comparable portraiture available elsewhere: "The Pictorial Department will exhibit a novel feature, never before, we believe, carried out in any similar undertaking—in a series of FULL LENGTH PORTRAITS, presenting the most vivid representation of the characters, with suitable accessories. . . . These portraits have been drawn from the best authorities, expressly for the work, by ALONZO CHAPPEL, and engraved on steel in the highest style of art."[31]

Such pictures were of so much better quality than the printing that publisher Johnson and Fry provided for the history itself that it was inevitable that many subscribers would remove the prints from the flimsy paper volumes and frame them for their homes. That temptation may explain why surviving runs of the Duyckinck history are scarce, and complete sets, with illustrations intact, even scarcer. But the engravings themselves, long ago torn from their bindings, are plentiful, known to almost anyone who visits used and rare book shops in search of Civil War materials.

Books were not the only medium to focus on the personalities of the war. In 1863 New York publisher I. W. Lucas advertised for twenty-five cents each, or two dollars per dozen, "fine etched engravings[,] exquisitely accurate," depicting "the prominent officers" of the army and navy.[32] The growing vogue for family photograph albums convinced other printmakers to issue work in the still smaller *carte-de-visite* format. In 1861 Elias Dexter of New York, for example, issued *carte*-sized engraved portraits of Robert Anderson and a beardless, still largely unknown general named William T. Sherman. Louis Prang of Boston published a series of flag-and-eagle-festooned lithographic *cartes*, each tinted with blue or red, for a series entitled *Officers of Our Union Army, Navy: Their Lives, Their Portraits*, issued in 1862 both individually and in large sheets, featuring dozens of portraits at a time, suitable for wall display. The vogue for these miniaturized images was brief, however. Although publishers continued to issue photographs of prints for years, no series was published after Prang's. When it came to photography, patrons seemed to prefer the real thing rather than reproductions of prints made in other media.

During the early years of the Civil War, portraits of generals vastly outnumbered those of admirals. In one sense, it is difficult to explain this phenomenon. Admiral David Glasgow Farragut, for example, triumphed at New Orleans early in 1862 but stimulated only a few known print portraits (fig. 23). One factor inhibiting such production may have been the remote kind of war the navy fought. Battles were conducted on oceans and inland waterways far from the Northern cities where new photographs could be taken that might be used as models for prints. As Admiral David Dixon Porter so keenly observed after the war:

> Our Army was full of writers who could delineate in the most happy manner all the events that were transpiring around them—they were also ready with the pencil; the photographer, while he traveled with the army, would spend his days in photographing every noted scene, reprints of which were spread broadcast over the Union, bringing the movements of our armies as clearly before the millions

of people in the North as if the battles had been reflected in a mirror . . . but there were no such means of bringing the Navy before the public. Naval ships did not travel with reporters, photographers or sketchers, there was no room for these on board ships, and if perchance some stray reporter should get on board, the discomfort of a man of war, the exacting discipline, and the freer life in camp sent him back to shore.[33]

The problem of the absence of photographic models of naval heroes can be seen in a rare group portrait of Union naval officers by an unknown printmaker (fig. 24). Tellingly, it exists only in unfinished form; two of the faces on the carefully drawn, uniformed bodies remain blank, as if the artist waited in vain for models that would help him render the portraits he was never able to complete. The result may have been a proof copy pulled from the press so the artist could insert additional newsworthy portraits into a stock scene that had previously featured notables from another era. The sole known surviving example of the print exists in this incomplete form.

Among the early land heroes, many were honored not only in print but in song as well, and the two arts met in the medium of illustrated sheet music covers. Kept on the piano in the family parlor, such pictures could take on a role akin to prints hung above the hearth. Lee and Walker of Philadelphia quickly emerged as one of the most prolific publishers of such material; a wartime list of the firm's "songs, waltzes, polkas, marches &c. embellished with handsome lithographs" included a number of military themes. Among them were a "Buell Quickstep," celebrating General Don Carlos Buell, for thirty cents, an "Ellsworth (Colonel) Funeral March," billed as "the only correct likeness published on music," for sale at fifty cents, and "Lyon's Funeral March," boasting a "superb likeness of the great patriot and soldier," at twenty-five cents, as well as marches dedicated to John Pope, William Sprague, Halleck, John F. Hartranft, McClellan, and Sigel. Of course, to keep the Civil War theme in perspective, the overwhelming majority of Lee and Walker's titles were of decidedly nonmilitary interest—"Beautiful Venice," "Gentle Maiden," "How Sweet Are the Roses," and "The St. Lawrence Tubular Bridge Polka Mazurka," to name a few.[34]

In the end, prominence in prints proved fleeting without battlefield success. General Ambrose E. Burnside, for example, was a natural subject for early prints, with his distinctive muttonchop side-whiskers (a style so identified with him that it eventually bore the elements of his name—"sideburns"). He was appealing enough to inspire Edward Sachse, a Baltimore lithographer, to produce *The Burnside Landing at Roanoke* in 1862. That same military success also resulted in a lithographed sheet music cover by Boston printmakers Benjamin B. Russell and Henry Tolman, "General Burnside's Grand Triumphal March" (fig. 25). But their popularity proved short-lived. Once the general led the ill-fated attack across the Rappahannock River at Fredericksburg in December 1862, precipitating one of the worst Union slaughters of the war, Burnside's portraits were destined for iconographical oblivion.[35]

REAR ADMIRAL D. C. FARRAGUT.

Figure 24. [Printmaker unknown], [*Union Naval Officers*], ca. 1862. Lithograph, 11¾ × 26¹⁵⁄₁₆ inches. The dearth of photographic models for the Union's early naval heroes may have hindered completion of this print by an unknown lithographer, who has left blank the faces of two of the standing figures at left. Evidently the artist was waiting for reliable models that never arrived, and the print project was abandoned. Group portraits as finely executed as this one necessarily used costly artistic talent. The publisher has attempted to save his investment in careful artwork by removing heads and replacing them with more timely portraits, thus updating his lithographic stone. Note the odd angles at which heads are perched on the bodies of the seated figure second from left, as well as the officer standing next to him. Portrayed in the work are, left to right, John L. Worden, Andrew A. Harwood, David G. Farragut, Theodorus Bailey, Samuel F. Du Pont, Charles H. Davis, Andrew H. Foote, Silas H. Stringham, Louis M. Goldsborough, Charles Wilkes, and David D. Porter. (*National Portrait Gallery*)

opposite
Figure 23. J. H. Bufford, *Rear Admiral D. G. Farragut.* Boston, ca. 1864. Hand-colored lithograph, 11⁷⁄₁₆ × 8⅜ inches. The steely gaze and characteristic faint smile of America's first rear admiral are aimed directly at the viewer in this handsome portrait probably inspired by Farragut's great victory at Mobile Bay on August 5, 1864. The hulking fortress in the background is Fort Morgan, past which Farragut's fleet stormed under the admiral's memorable order, "Damn the torpedoes! Full speed ahead!" But the printmaker missed a major opportunity by failing to show the admiral as he really appeared that day: tied to the rigging of his flagship, the *Hartford*, so he would still be able to command in case he was wounded. (*National Portrait Gallery*)

GENERAL BURNSIDE'S GRAND TRIUMPHAL MARCH.

BOSTON
Published by HENRY TOLMAN & Co 291 Washington St.

CHICAGO
ROOT & CADY.

NEW YORK
S.T. GORDON.

ALBANY
EDWIN PARKHURST.

Figure 25. [Printmaker unknown], "General Burnside's Grand Triumphal March." Published by Henry Tolman, Boston, 1862. Lithographed sheet music cover, 10 × 13 inches. Dedicated "To Brigadier General A. E. Burnside, Commanding 3d Naval & Military Expedition to the South," this illustration for a musical tribute celebrates Burnside's early successes along the North Carolina coast. Enjoying success on both sea and land, Burnside's forces overpowered a Confederate fleet at the Albemarle Canal and captured Roanoke Island, New Bern, Beaufort, and Fort Macon. By the end of 1862, however, Burnside lost the Battle of Fredericksburg, and his appeal as a Union icon abruptly ended. (*Library of Congress*)

George G. Meade was another commander who rose quickly to pictorial prominence, only to fall nearly as swiftly. Less than two weeks after Meade triumphed at one of the most important battles of the war, Currier and Ives rushed out an equestrian portrait of *Maj. Genl. George G. Meade at the Battle of Gettysburg.* The last guns had been fired in that Pennsylvania town on July 3; the print was copyrighted on July 13, a lightning response. Meade surely deserved the honor, but his heroics had been displayed mainly at headquarters, planning the three-day battle, and not on the field itself. Although the German American general Carl Schurz commented that "there was nothing in his appearance or his bearing . . . that might have made the hearts of the soldiers warm up to him," Meade appeared in the Currier and Ives

MAJOR GEN^L JOHN C. FREMONT.
U.S. ARMY.

print on horseback, sword upraised, charging against unseen enemies and inspiring his soldiers forward. Within two years Meade, subordinated to Ulysses S. Grant's command, would disappear from Civil War iconography, except as a supporting character in scenes showing Grant and his staff.[36]

The only other early officer besides McClellan to enjoy sustained exposure in popular prints was John C. Frémont. But he came to the Civil War with a national reputation that had already been celebrated in popular prints. More than a decade earlier, Frémont's expeditions across the treacherous mountains of the West had earned him the title of "Pathfinder" and made him a celebrity; by 1850 his lithograph by Francis D'Avignon was included in Mathew Brady's *Gallery of Illustrious Americans*. The Frémont image underwent a metamorphosis in 1856, when he was nominated by the new Republican Party as its first candidate for president, inspiring a number of campaign prints.[37]

Once the war began, Frémont was featured in the uniform of the Union army. It was his third persona in American iconography—that of general. Assigned to the western theater by President Lincoln himself, Frémont quickly ran afoul of his commander in chief by ordering, on August 30, 1861, the emancipation of slaves owned by pro-Confederate citizens of Missouri. Lincoln, worried that the action could trigger the secession of neighboring Kentucky, revoked the order and ultimately relieved Frémont of his command.[38]

Whether right or wrong, self-aggrandizing or humane, Frémont created for himself an enthusiastic constituency, and printmakers were prompt to feed the new interest in him. Louis Prang included him in the *Officers of Our Union Army and Navy* series of *cartes-de-visite*; Currier and Ives responded with a handsome three-quarter-length vignette portrait (fig. 26) that showed the general looking altogether unconcerned over the controversy swirling about his command, and wearing the type of beard he had last affected during his days as Pathfinder of the West.

Frémont returned briefly to command in mid-1862 in the newly formed Mountain Department of Western Virginia, but after failing to distinguish himself in battle, he was dismissed and replaced by General John Pope. This time Frémont asked to be relieved and left military service for good. But his image would resurface a fourth and final time two years later, when he emerged, briefly, as a third-party candidate for the presidency (see fig. 66).[39]

By then, George B. McClellan had joined Frémont in this new tier of Civil War military iconography, not as a politician-turned-general, a description that fit many of the early failures in the Union military pantheon, but as a general-turned-politician. The Civil War produced many changes in the popular culture, and one of the most telling was the fact that two of its early generals, McClellan and Frémont, men who squandered early fame or failed to win major battlefield successes, turned to politics. Until then, generals who sought the White House—Jackson, Harrison, Taylor, Scott, and, of course, Washington—were unblemished war heroes. The early years of the Civil War produced defenders and pretenders, but no Washington.

In Camp and on Campaign

Eyewitness Portfolios of Soldier Life

Although popular prints of the Civil War most often depicted soldiers, military events, and naval actions, at the time they were not so much aimed at soldiers and military history enthusiasts as at the people at home who had opportunity to purchase them, frame them, and display them. The motive of reassurance therefore ranked close to patriotism in animating the images. Certainly Thomas Nast's 1863 sketch of a snug campfire scene with soldiers roasting a pig (fig. 27), adapted into a print that year by Currier and Ives (fig. 28), held little in it to worry a mother or sister or father of a soldier.

Artists who were eyewitnesses might occasionally make drawings suggesting deprivation on the march or theft of civilian property in the field, but the buyers of prints for the home were probably not interested in such depictions. These images had their place in journalism, in sobering photography, or in comic commentary on the passing scene, but print customers at home seem to have wanted pictures that reassured them that their loved ones and heroes were thriving, not suffering, as they marched into battle to save the Union.

One printmaker, Charles Magnus of New York, who began his career lithographing commercial letterhead designs, produced numerous small, hand-colored scenes showing Union regiments in clean-looking camps. The Magnus prints were in a way precursors of the picture postcard from scenic vacation destinations. With a branch office located in Washington, D.C., Magnus could create individualized pictures as soon as a new regiment arrived to encamp in nearby Virginia or Maryland and then sell them to soldiers eager to send reassuring pictures back home to worried families. Similarly, Louis Rosenthal of Philadelphia issued a series of 7-by-10⅝-inch prints in 1862 showing New York, Rhode Island, New Jersey, and Pennsylvania units drilling, camping, working with mules, piling wood outside their tents, braving winter, and playing games in camp, all the pictures ringed with gilt borders as if to crown the subjects' activities.[1]

So powerful was the motive of reassurance that what was destined to become one of the most famous prints of the Civil War era, Sarony, Major and Knapp's *Union Prisoners at Salisbury, N.C.* (fig. 29), based on an eyewitness sketch by Otto Boetticher, showed its subjects not cowering behind barricades or wallowing in filth but gathered in a bucolic setting to play a game of baseball. As perhaps the first image of what was to become the national sport, the print gained fame even beyond its considerable merits as a depiction of Civil War soldiers' life, and many who know it as an early illustration of baseball have no idea it actually depicts a prisoner-of-war camp. Printmaker J. H. Bufford of Boston developed such reassuring scenes as *Commissary Department*, in which soldiers line up for hearty meals while a butcher hacks away at a huge joint of meat, and *Field Hospital*, showing a Virginia hospital that exudes order and efficiency.[2]

Scenes of soldiers recuperating in military hospitals were designed to honor those who tended the sick and wounded but no doubt also heartened the parents and wives of the victims. Even a mourning scene like Hugh Young's *Graves of the Highlanders / Soldiers Cemetery, Knoxville, Tenn.*, published by Charles Hart in 1864, could offer the consoling caption in verse: "Their country's soldiers, living their simpler story, / But dead, her best defence and her undying glory." As the later

Figure 27. Thomas Nast, untitled sketch, December 1861. Pencil and wash on paper, 4 × 6 inches. The artist may have set too difficult a task for the printmaker when he submitted this sketch for adaptation. The scene is lighted only by a crescent moon and a campfire. The sketch was preserved by the artist in his sketchbook. (*John Hay Library, Brown University*)

fame of *The Burial of Latane*, a Lost Cause icon for the South, would reveal, people were concerned that the soldiers who died on campaign would receive decent burial.[3]

Generally, the efforts of soldier-artists and artist-correspondents to depict the Civil War soldier's life were not transformed into separate-sheet prints until after the war. To say in the title of a print published during the Civil War that it was based on an eyewitness observation of the event obviously added cachet to the image, and such statements were made whenever possible, but ultimately, popular prints offered reassurance, patriotism, and decoration. Journalism and photography were more the realms of sensationalism, criticism, and eyewitness accuracy. However, a

Figure 28. Currier and Ives, after Thomas Nast, *Life in the Camp. / Preparing for Supper*. New York, 1863. Hand-colored lithograph, 15¾ × 21⅓ inches. Popular lithography was not quite equal to the severe contrasts of light and shadow in artist Nast's original conception of this scene. Currier and Ives sentimentalized it by adding more figures, a depiction of camp, details of landscape, and more light. (*Anne S. K. Brown Military Collection, Brown University*)

UNION PRISONERS AT SALISBURY, N.C.

DRAWN FROM NATURE BY ... R. OTTO BOETTICHER.

New York, Published by ...   ...Broadway.

Figure 29. Sarony, Major and Knapp, after Otto Boetticher, *Union Prisoners at Salisbury, N.C.* New York, 1863. Lithograph, 20¾ × 37¼ inches. Artist Boetticher seemed to have in mind producing a memento for "graduates" of the Confederate military prison at Salisbury, North Carolina. He created portrait likenesses of Union officers and men playing baseball. The artist could hardly have aimed wider of the mark of national feeling than in this image, which created an almost collegiate ambience at a time when Northern patriots were denouncing the undernourishment of Union prisoners of war and their suffering in vile conditions. Over the years, the importance of this print was transformed entirely when it became known, and frequently reproduced, as perhaps the earliest image of the "national pastime." (*Library of Congress*)

handful of artists saw their eyewitness sketches transformed into popular prints, and some of them issued their pictures in portfolios containing several images.

J. Nep Roesler, an artist serving in the Forty-seventh Ohio Volunteer Infantry, hit upon the idea as early as anyone. Yet his work, despite eyewitness derivation, unsophisticated charm in depiction of rumpled and bored soldiers, and pioneering insight into packaging the visual image of the Civil War, is now all but forgotten. The reason had little to do with the quality of the prints; rather, the lithographs based on his work were doomed to obscurity because this infantryman-artist participated in a campaign small in scale and early in the war, which, despite lasting and important results, was forgotten in the later preoccupation with "decisive" battles.

The western Virginia campaign of 1861, as historian Richard Curry aptly observed, led to the permanent severance of West Virginia from the Old Dominion, thus affecting Civil War strategy and forever altering the map of the United States.

Ohio troops were in the forefront of this action.[4] Roesler, who served as a corporal of the color guard of his regiment, made his mark early: his portfolio depicting the campaign in West Virginia was published by Cincinnati lithographers Middleton, Strobridge in 1862. However, the great battles of 1863 like Gettysburg and Vicksburg, the declining reputations of George B. McClellan and William Rosecrans (the Union generals who led the earlier campaigns in West Virginia), and enormous casualties later in the war all dimmed the national memory of this earlier struggle.

Moreover, Roesler depicted a campaign in which terrain dominated technology, and by the twentieth century the myth of the American Civil War would run quite the other way, portraying a conflict in which Northern industrial technology triumphed over Southern agrarianism. Such an interpretation diminished chances for a recovery of appreciation of Roesler's essentially pastoral works. They are not often used as illustrations today, let alone studied and collected, and they deserve a better fate.

The campaign in western Virginia began for Roesler's newly recruited Ohio regiment in August 1861. It did not require an artist's eye to notice the scenery on the march into western Virginia in high summer. The regimental historian, Joseph A. Saunier, recalled vividly the train ride into Virginia from Ohio: "The surface of the country is very broken and rugged, forming pretty valleys and rough and frowning mountains. One moment we run along the side of a deep and dark chasm, then across a deep fill, with rough and rocky valleys on each side. . . . The scenery is weird and wild, yet beautiful, and only a few villages greet our sight. No level ground, nothing but hills and mountains."[5] Little wonder that an artistically inclined soldier, his head brimming with the landscape conventions of American romantic art, responded viscerally to the countryside and produced a series of prints that in many instances emphasized the landscape a good deal more than the soldiers on campaign. (Indeed, one of the prints depicts no soldiers, other human figures, or signs of human habitation at all.)

Corporal Roesler, about whose artistic training nothing is known, may never have read a word of art criticism, but he worked within the visual assumptions of the age. Those were well stated by a critic of the day, who noted:

> In historic painting or in high ideal art Americans have as yet achieved few triumphs. We attribute this largely to the total lack in this country of great galleries and museums, where the young artist can find grand inspiring suggestions in these higher departments of work. On the other hand, landscape . . . is just what our artists find most within the reach of their attainment. Nowhere can be found more suggestive, instructive, and inspiring surroundings than amid our own American scenery.[6]

As an artist, Roesler is as remarkable for his landscape skills as for his clumsiness in rendering human figures. This was a common failing in American artists of the period, most of whom had opted for training in landscape depiction before the war, when it seemed that nothing of historical significance would ever happen in the young republic. With the onset of war, Roesler, like many artists, proved ill-equipped to deal properly with historic events. It is a shame that his professionally rendered Virginia landscape did not ultimately contain pickets and scouts as convincingly drawn as the terrain.

Roesler found the landscape inspiring. Even when depicting masses of troops, he tended to see them conforming to the contours of the landscape, not overcoming or overwhelming it. He saw an army that climbed over and around rocks and waded through streams. Engineering was often depicted as incomplete or, in the case of domestic architecture, tumbledown. To Roesler, the rough nature of western Virginia shaped the war more than war shaped the landscape.

In *Camp, Gauley Bridge* (fig. 30), Roesler did provide an unusual image in which telegraph wires strung from poles figured prominently, along with a jury-rigged device for pulling boats across an unbridged river. But customarily his artistic eye was not much attracted to feats of modern engineering. Those are best documented in the works of the war's photographers, some of whose efforts were commissioned by the engineering branches of the armed services.[7]

Roesler opted for an intimate soldier's-eye view of picket posts and campfires. He created skilled images capturing the rough grandeur of the Appalachian countryside, but he proved less well equipped to depict the dazzling sweep of a modern mass army on campaign. That challenge attracted the regimental historian, who, unlike the visual artist, could invoke sound as well as sight:

This was Gen. Rosecrans' supply depot or base, and was crowded with officers, soldiers, stragglers and settlers. It seemed to our unaccustomed eyes and ears a babble, verily. There was a confusion of tongues, a profusion of oaths, the shouting of trainmasters, the braying of mules, the swearing of teamsters, the din of brass bands, the whistle of locomotives, the frenzied screams of the babies and frightened children of the refugees, and the hoarse voices of the officers giving commands, but the long line of white-topped wagons with its guards, lengthening always, and continually moving out of "park" to a particular point, and winding thence away over and around the hills until it was lost to view in the beautiful foliage of the deciduous forests fringing the road, showed that order and system held sway even here.

For Roesler, soldiering was a more nature-bound enterprise: his stoic pickets and lounging soldiers might almost be hunters or shepherds, except for their uniforms. "Order and system," as invoked by the official regimental historian, are less in evidence in the artist's portfolio of soldiers in nature, and a train whistle would seem almost a sacrilege in his world.[8]

Among the prints that featured nature was *Thunder-storm. / (Big Sewell Mountain) / (Reconnoissance)* (fig. 31), which employed rocky precipice, wind, rain, sinuously threatening trees, and low storm clouds to highlight the predicament of the scouting soldiers (the vigilant sentinel in the foreground is almost a fixture in Roesler's work). The commonplace details of a picket post and the casual poses of the soldiers seen in *Pickets in the Woods* (fig. 32) are among Roesler's most winning depictions. Particularly noteworthy is the veteran soldier's touch: though Roesler sketched dozing, smoking, and generally relaxed men, he inserted the vigilant guard on duty, watching in the other direction, as well. As experienced soldiers knew, they never pitched camp without posting guards or putting out pickets.

The real subject of Corporal Roesler's portfolio was not war but nature. In fact, the viewer can improve several of the lithographs by covering the human figures. In

Sketched fr. nature & drawn on stone by J. Nep Roesler Corpl of Color Guard Comp. G. 47ᵗʰ Regᵗ OV·USA

Printed by Ehrgott, Forbriger & Cᵒ, Cincinnati.

CAMP, GAULEY BRIDGE.

Figure 30. Ehrgott, Forbriger and Company, after J. Nep Roesler, *Camp, Gauley Bridge*. Cincinnati, 1862. Lithograph, 12 × 16 inches. Old and new technologies cross paths in this view of a Union camp in the western Virginia campaign of 1861. The telegraph lines in the foreground are the work of the Federals, while in the distance the local commerce continues by flatboat, a mode of transportation last widely used in the first three decades of the nineteenth century. The destruction of the bridge necessitates pulling Union soldiers across the river in a flatboat—which must be the way the pickets traveled across the river from camp. (*Chicago Historical Society*)

Entered according to act of Congress in the year 1862 by J. Nep. Roesler in the Clerks office of the District Court of the Southern District of Ohio.

Sketched fr. nature & drawn on stone by J. Nep. Roesler Corpl. of Color Guard Comp. G 47th Regt OV·USA

Printed by Ehrgott, Forbriger & Cº, Cincinnati.

THUNDER~STORM.
(Big Sewell Mountain)
(Reconnoissance.)

Figure 31. Ehrgott, Forbriger and Company, after J. Nep Roesler, *Thunder-storm. / (Big Sewell Mountain) / (Reconnoissance)*. Cincinnati, 1862. Lithograph, 12 × 16 inches. A young picket in a poncho clutches his hat against the rain and wind in Roesler's romantic evocation of a storm atop Big Sewell Mountain. The soldier stands guard while mounted scouts observe a Confederate camp through a telescope. Absent the picket in the foreground, the image of wild and sublime landscape paid homage to the romantic vision of nature familiarly embodied in the paintings of the Hudson River School. The distressed picket is likely based on Corporal Roesler's firsthand experience. (*Chicago Historical Society*)

Thunder-storm, for example, if the sentinel in the foreground is removed from view, the image of nature stands very well alone. Roesler knew best how to depict romantic nature's tangled trees, rough rocks, and enveloping foliage. For a juxtaposition of sublime nature with the casual charm of his images of pickets on guard, see *Picket on Lover's Leap. / (Road to the Log House) Camp Anderson* (fig. 33).

By September 10, 1861, Roesler's Ohioans had not only marched and picketed and scouted but also met the Confederates at the Battle of Carnifax Ferry. Though

Entered according to act of Congress in the year 1862 by J. Nep Roesler in the Clerk's office of the District Court of the Southern District of Ohio.

Sketched it nature & drawn on stone by J Nep Roesler Corp! of Color Guard Comp. G 47ᵗʰ Reg! OV-USA

Printed by Ehrgott, Forbriger & Cᵒ, Cincinnati.

PICKETS IN THE WOODS
after the Engagement, near the Drill Ground, C Andrsn

Figure 32. Ehrgott, Forbriger and Company, after J. Nep Roesler, *Pickets in the Woods / After the Engagement near the Drill Ground, C[amp] Andrsn.* Cincinnati, 1862. Lithograph, 12 × 16 inches. In this unusual subordination of nature drawing to human figures, Roesler offered a study of solitude as six pickets, who do not interact in the image, patiently occupy their lonely post. The lumpy human figures offer a contrast in skill of delineation with the nicely rendered foliage in the right foreground. Yet the figures are not without interest, from the sentinel jarringly facing away from the viewer toward the enemy to the central picket preoccupied with sewing a button on his tunic. (*Chicago Historical Society*)

the Forty-seventh stood in reserve throughout the battle, the unit suffered some casualties. Roesler's attempt to depict the battle did not make a convincing print. By October 9 the Ohioans had gone into Camp Anderson near Hawk's Nest, which afforded them breathtaking new views of spectacular scenery, cataracts, waterfalls, gorges, and forests—irresistible subject matter for an artist interested in landscape. Roesler duly recorded Hawk's Nest—without a single soldier in the view—and Lover's Leap, a 700-foot-high perpendicular cliff, the alleged point of departure from life of two ill-fated rustic lovers. The regimental historian, who perhaps saw too much war to retain a sanitized and romantic view of death, related the legendary suicide by saying, "So they went to the cliff, and locked arms, and threw themselves down the cliff. Of course they went down and were mashed to a jelly."[9] By late November the army had moved to Gauley Mountain or Tompkins Farm. Snow began to fall and they went into winter quarters, leveling great circles on hillsides to place circular Sibley tents, in the center of which a sheet-iron stove was

PICKET ON LOVER'S LEAP
(Road to the Log House) Camp Anderson

Figure 33. Ehrgott, Forbriger and Company, after J. Nep Roesler, *Picket on Lover's Leap. / (Road to the Log House) Camp Anderson.* Cincinnati, 1862. Lithograph, 12 × 16 inches. Union pickets huddle around a fire while the ever-watchful sentinel gazes away from them. The figures are dwarfed by the perilously tossed-up rocks and the skillfully drawn trees. Note, at right, the exposed leg of a picket sleeping in the lean-to shelter of tree branches. Such images went beyond the work of printmakers from the East, among them L. N. Rosenthal of Philadelphia and E. Sachse of Baltimore, who issued stock scenes of camp life during the early years of the war, probably for soldiers to send home the way tourists today send relatives postcards. Rosenthal alone published at least thirty-two such prints, showing such aspects of camp life as working with mules, piling wood, and pitching tents. (*Chicago Historical Society*)

placed, and around which the twelve or fifteen occupants warmed themselves throughout the cold winter months.[10]

In the idleness of winter quarters, Corporal Roesler had time to perfect the sketches that he sent to Cincinnati to be published by Ehrgott, Forbriger and Company. The resulting portfolio of twenty prints, called *The Civil War in West Virginia, as Sketched by J. Nep Roesler*, appeared in 1862, with the claim that the artist sketched from nature and made the drawings on stone, a feat he could have accomplished only by obtaining leave to return to Ohio for a season, as lithographic stones were far too heavy and cumbersome to tote on campaign.[11]

Roesler was not tethered to the conventions of battle art or battle narrative. Unlike the regimental historian of the Forty-seventh Ohio (who possessed above-average talent for his task), he was not infatuated with the generals and leaders of the regiment. None of Roesler's print titles—unlike many that followed from other artists and printmaking firms during the war—featured the names of the commanding general for the campaign or the colonel of the regiment. While other artists often featured portrait likenesses of the officers and placed them in commanding positions, Corporal Roesler fixed his artistic gaze on the common soldiers of the regiment. That outlook was forward-looking.

He was also remarkably forward-looking in his devotion to images of soldiers on picket. The Union soldiers, huddled in big tunics, greatcoats, and cloaks, peering under their broad-brimmed and tall-crowned hats, almost disappear in their loose clothing. They generally appear cold and jam their bare hands into pockets or stick them under their blanket rolls. These are military images but not militaristic ones. The soldiers by no means dominate—nature does. There are real soldiers in these images, though the superficial observer may fail to realize it because they wear the stiff Hardee hats and full equipment of the 1861 quartermaster's regulation issue, which would be much altered by seasoned soldiers later in the war.

Roesler ignored many of the parlor-room conventions of small popular patriotic prints. Only in *Crossing to Fayetteville* (fig. 34), perhaps his best combination of soldier and landscape in one image, can an American flag be seen (at left). The portfolio of twenty prints thus contains but a single image with a flag in the foreground and no image in which the flag is the focus—despite the fact that Corporal Roesler served in his regiment's color guard and must have been duly imbued with the importance of the colors! Roesler's ability to escape patriotic convention, as well as his real skills as a landscape artist, gave his portfolio a special place among popular prints of the Civil War. The democratization of the war's depiction in popular prints—featuring rumpled pickets on guard like Roesler's—would come long after the war was over.[12]

Among the few wartime depictions of army life in popular prints, another portfolio came from Winslow Homer, an artist who, unlike Corporal Roesler, was destined for great fame. Homer began his professional career as an apprentice to Boston lithographer John H. Bufford. The artist later recalled this first printmaking

Entered according to act of Congress in the year 1862 by J. Nep Roesler in the Clerks office of the District Court of the Southern District of Ohio

Sketched ft. nature & drawn on stone by J. Nep Roesler Corp¹ of Color Guard Comp. G 47ᵗʰ Reg¹ OV-USA

Printed by Ehrgott, Forbriger & Cᵒ. Cincinnati

CROSSING TO FAYETTEVILLE.

Figure 34. Ehrgott, Forbriger and Company, after J. Nep Roesler, *Crossing to Fayetteville.* Cincinnati, 1862. Chromolithograph, 12 × 16 inches. In Roesler's best military image, a river crossing, an obvious hazard of the western Virginia campaign, halts a Union column while it waits for flatboats. The drummers adjusting their instruments and the infantrymen checking their equipment or waiting for instructions from their mounted officers are all well integrated into the challenging terrain. (*Chicago Historical Society*)

experience as a period of "bondage" and "slavery." He relocated to New York in 1859 to learn to paint, joined *Harper's Weekly* as an artist-correspondent, and went off in October 1861 to follow the Union army on campaign in Virginia. "I am instructed to go with the skirmisher's in the next battle," he wrote expectantly to his father. "I get $30. per week RR fare paid."[13] Homer left to cover the army a second time in April 1862, sending back a number of drawings to *Harper's.*

By 1863 the artist was painting seriously and beginning to exhibit his canvases at the National Academy of Design, but his work in the field of popular prints was not

Figure 35. Cover to Winslow Homer, *Campaign Sketches, Part 1, Containing 6 Plates.* Published by L. Prang and Company, Boston, 1863. Lithograph, 14 × 10⅞ inches. The illustrated cover of Homer's portfolio offered the best of the images in the set, this backlit, mysterious, and contemplative soldier standing and reflecting, rather than marching off to heroic duty. When the portfolio was first published, Homer told Prang, "The cover is very neat and the pictures look better than they would in color" (Lloyd Goodrich, *The Graphic Art of Winslow Homer* [New York: Museum of Graphic Art, 1968], 10). Prang was still offering the portfolio in 1868. (*Prang's Chromo*, January 1868, photocopy in the Print Collection, New York Public Library). (*Gift of Charles G. Loring; courtesy Museum of Fine Arts, Boston*)

yet behind him.[14] In the summer of 1863 Homer contracted with another Boston lithographer, Louis Prang, to produce *Campaign Sketches*, a portfolio of six prints. By December Homer wrote to his publisher, "The stone was received all right. I shall commence it very soon, probably send it to you a week from Wednesday." The portfolio of lithographs—*The Letter for Home, Foraging, Our Jolly Cook, The Coffee Call, A Pastime,* and *The Baggage Train*—appeared in 11-by-14-inch format, priced at $1.50 for the set.[15] In 1864 they were advertised as "Campaign Sketches.—Designed and drawn on stone by Winslow Homer. A series of spirited Camp scenes sketched on the spot by Mr. Homer and executed in high artistic style in crayon. These sketches are sold in sets of 6 copies put up in a neat cover."[16]

The cover was "neat" indeed, and Homer offered the best of the *Sketches* there, a backlit image of a common soldier (fig. 35). Such an image announced that the portfolio would be the work of a master figure artist and that artistic characterization would be more important than military verisimilitude. Homer's choice of backlighting the figure cast a dark and somewhat mysterious shadow over most of the infantryman's face. Mystery, philosophy, introspection, and melancholy were qualities rarely demonstrated in the brash figures of popular lithography representing the

Figure 36.
Winslow Homer,
The Coffee Call.
Published by
L. Prang and
Company, Boston,
1863. Lithograph,
14 × 10⅞ inches.
By obscuring the
eyes of some figures
with the bills of their
kepis, or soft hats,
Homer lent them
an air of mystery
or melancholy that
redeemed them from
the comedy with
which other figures
were endowed. Note,
for example, the
soldier with his
hands in his pockets
at right. Homer's
initials, reversed,
appear on the
barrel at right. Years
later, when Prang
defended the art
of lithography to
Homer, the artist
insisted, "What you
say about the lith tint
being the best means
of expression for an
artist I cannot agree
with you" (Homer to
Prang, November 22,
1895, original in the
Archives of American
Art, Washington,
D.C.). (*Gift of Charles
G. Loring; courtesy
Museum of Fine Arts,
Boston*)

American Civil War. They were qualities that Roesler could aspire to only in rendering landscape: he did not have the command of figure to make more philosophical exploration possible. But they were qualities of Homer's later searching works, and one sees forerunners of such figures even in *Campaign Sketches*.[17] Not a soldier like Roesler, Homer necessarily had the outlook of the behind-the-lines observer rather than the participant. His figures have a studied quality about them, and one could not imagine the presence in his works of one of Roesler's sentries, facing away from the artistically arranged group that provides the focus of the print.

Homer had difficulty taking the medium of lithography seriously; he considered it the realm of humor and burlesque but not, perhaps, of serious art. Thus in *The Coffee Call* (fig. 36) a greatcoated soldier with eyes hidden by his cap bill shared the foreground with a near-comic figure with his hands thrust in his pockets, standing before a background that featured a man dancing a jig in front of a tent. The unfortunate sense that lithography cannot contain serious subject matter emerges from that print into the foreground of *Our Jolly Cook*, a depiction of a caricatured African American camp cook dancing wildly to a fifer's tune before assembled white soldiers.

Where humor did not dictate the contents of popular prints, sentimentalism often did, and Homer succumbed to a sentimental theme in *The Letter Home* (fig. 37), a conventional hospital scene in which a genteel female visitor writes a letter for a wounded hero. Although he began concentrating on painting, Homer returned to the print medium in 1864 with the first of two series of essentially comic, *carte-de-visite*-size chromolithographs called *Life in Camp* (fig. 38; see also plate 3).

Such series of prints, not tied to any particular newsworthy event of the war, were evidently conceived of by their creator, Louis Prang, as holiday gifts. Both *Campaign Sketches* (at $1.50) and *Life in Camp*, series 1 and 2 (at fifty cents for each set of twelve cards), were advertised in the *New York Tribune* around Christmas and New Year's, along with a great number of other Prang series of birds and other flora and fauna.[18] (The *Sketches*, in light of Homer's later reputation, would have made a good purchase, but not as good as another portfolio offered the same Christmas: 150 of John James Audubon's immortal elephant-folio *Birds of America* at less than $400.)

Oil painting would ultimately unleash Homer's talents, and he would leave behind the theme of war and, with rare exception, the medium of popular prints. A little of that future can be glimpsed in the lithographed cover of *Campaign Sketches*, and careful examination of *Life in Camp* reveals in rough form the subject matter of two of Homer's wartime canvases. But the artist realized the limiting conventions of the popular medium. *Campaign Sketches*, after all, was called *Part 1*, but *Part 2* never appeared.

Another artist who, like Homer, gained later fame also produced a little-known group of Civil War images. Although the work of Alfred E. Matthews is well known to collectors of prints of the American West, his name is not as familiar among students of the Civil War.[19] Yet many know the early work of Matthews in the Civil War

Figure 37. Winslow Homer, *The Letter for Home.* Published by L. Prang and Company, Boston, 1863. Lithograph, 14 × 10⅞ inches. Sentimentalism and the conventions of illustration took charge of this Homer lithograph for the *Campaign Sketches* portfolio. Note the extreme elongation of the woman's forearm, the long thin shoe protruding from her skirt, and the almost dainty gesture by the wounded soldier. Homer did not picture the spittoons that likely sat near the beds of the myriad tobacco chewers. The artist's initial "H" appears in the floorboards at lower left. (*Bequest of W. G. Russell Allen; courtesy Museum of Fine Arts, Boston*)

without realizing that they do. His lithographs depicting western campaigns of the war are distinguished by their bleak wintry landscapes and by the antlike swarming of the armies. In later years, *Century* magazine, commissioning illustrations for its famous Battles and Leaders series, could find no better depictions of the Battle of Stones River, fought in Tennessee December 31, 1862–January 2, 1863, than Matthews's prints. *Century*'s editors copied Matthews's work, crediting the source only as "From a Lithograph." *Century* also used four of his Vicksburg prints.

Each magazine engraving, which later illustrated the Century Company's four-volume work *Battles and Leaders of the Civil War*, carried a signature near its margin, but that belonged to the artist who adapted Matthews's work for Century. Adaptation was necessary, for the prints, originally published by Middleton, Strobridge and Company of Cincinnati on pieces of paper roughly 11 by 14 inches in size, were reproduced as 2⅝-by-4⅞-inch part-page cuts in the books. Adapted by E. J. Meeker and a fine illustrator named Walton Tabor, the tiny illustrations necessarily simplified the images.

Matthews's lithographs deserved the compliment *Century* paid them. Among the better ones from the series on Stones River was *Charge of the First Brigade, Com-*

Figure 38. L[ouis]. Prang and Company, after Winslow Homer, *Life in Camp, Second Series* (twelve stiff cards mounted in an album). Boston, 1864. Chromolithographs, each 4 × 2⅜ inches on album page 13¾ × 12½ inches. Sentimentalism and humor vie with eyewitness observation in this series of *carte-de-visite*-size chromos for display in parlor albums. The depiction of "Extra Ration" (top right) may have been inspired by Currier and Ives's *Life in the Camp*. The portrayal of "Our Special" artist at lower right is a self-portrait of artist Homer. For a detail from the first series of chromo cards, see plate 3. (*The Metropolitan Museum of Art, Harris Brisbane Dick Fund, 1947*)

manded by Col. M. B. Walker, on the Friday Evening of the Battle of Stone River (fig. 39), lithographed as usual by Middleton, Strobridge. Perhaps its ability to capture the nature of Civil War combat stemmed from Matthews's experience of the battle, for his regiment, the Thirty-first Ohio Volunteer Infantry, was fully engaged in the action. He was probably aided by the unusual winter backdrop, allowing the depiction of a greater sweep of combat without the visual interference of forests in full foliage (except for the evergreens present). Most Virginia battles were difficult to render visually because of the dense forests that covered parts of the famous battlefields. Since Civil War armies, until the final winter of the war, customarily went into winter quarters rather than engage in combat in the cold season, most battles were fought when forests were in full foliage and visibility was the most difficult.[20] Whatever the reasons, the lithograph appears not only true to the action as described in words by participants after the battle, but also suggestive of a common sort of confrontation on Civil War battlefields.

Much of the war, in both eastern and western theaters, was fought in the great woodland of the United States. The observations of military engineers articulated what artists must have seen when they studied the landscape of the war. In 1863 General Gouveneur Warren, chief engineer of the Army of the Potomac, described the famed theater of war in northern Virginia in these words:

> All our known topography in the entire region from the Potomac to the James River, and from the Blue Ridge to the Chesapeake . . . is a dense forest of oak or pine, with occasional clearings, rarely extensive enough to prevent the riflemen concealed in one border from shooting across to the other side; a forest which, with but few exceptions, required the axmen to precede the artillery from the slashings in front of the fortifications of Washington to those of Richmond. . . . It will aid those seeking to understand why the numerous bloody battles fought between the armies of the Union and of the Secessionists should have been so indecisive. A proper understanding of the country, too, will help to relieve the Americans from the charge so frequently made at home and abroad of want of generalship in handling troops in battle—battles that had to be fought out hand to hand in forests, where artillery and cavalry could play no part; where the troops could not be seen by those controlling their movements; where the echoes and reverberations of sound from tree to tree were enough to pall the strongest hearts engaged, and yet the noise would often scarcely be heard beyond the immediate scene of strife.[21]

Terrain in northern Virginia and elsewhere east of the Mississippi typically featured wooded areas more or less interspersed with areas cleared for farms. Often infantry combat consisted of concentrating forces behind or within wooded areas and perching them near the perimeter to peer out at and threaten enemy troops similarly gathered at the woodline on the other side of the cleared areas. When the action elsewhere on the battlefield demanded it, or when one side or the other thought it had the advantage of numbers or firepower, one side might venture forth into the clearing to attack the other side. The problems that such settings afforded an artist intent upon representing the sweep of action in a Civil War battle were formidable.

Stones River was fought in Tennessee, and artillery played a larger role than Warren's observations prepare us for, but the action developed as the terrain described by Warren dictated. Moses B. Walker's brigade, consisting of three Ohio infantry regiments (one of them Matthews's), one Indiana infantry regiment, and a battery of Michigan artillery, took a key part in the action. According to Walker's lucid after-battle report, his brigade occupied "a somewhat dense cedar forest" across from

CHARGE OF THE FIRST BRIGADE, COMMANDED BY COL. M. B. WALKER, on the FRIDAY EVENING OF THE BATTLE OF STONE RIVER,
January 2nd, 1863; in which the Rebels were repulsed with heavy loss, and driven behind their breastworks.
SKETCHED BY A. E. MATTHEWS, 31st REG. O. V. I.

Figure 39. Middleton, Strobridge and Company, after Alfred E. Matthews, *Charge of the First Brigade, Commanded by Col. M. B. Walker, on the Friday Evening of the Battle of Stone River* . . . . Cincinnati, 1863. Lithograph, 11 × 14 inches. Union troops, wearing their winter overcoats, approach the perimeter of trees in line of battle in this almost panoramic view of the fighting at the final day of the Battle of Murfreesboro (Stones River), Tennessee. The front two lines fire a volley on the enemy skirmishers visible in the open field at left. The Confederate line of battle appears to be drawn at the edge of the barren trees on the other side of the field. (*Library of Congress*)

Confederate forces that had shown themselves "in strong force upon the margin of the woodland immediately on my front." After a day—New Year's Day 1863—spent skirmishing and dueling with artillery at long range to feel each other out, the Confederate lines fell silent; the Union major general thought the enemy had probably withdrawn. He instructed Walker to test the theory by advancing. The eager soldiers leaped over their breastworks constructed of rocks and tree limbs in the woods, formed long straight lines of battle, and advanced. As Walker described the ensuing action:

> We had not advanced more than 300 yards beyond our breastworks when the rebel infantry opened a rapid fire on our right from the cornfield adjacent, and from the pickets in front of our center. My lines advanced under this fire, with the utmost steadiness and good order, a distance of 75 or 80 yards before a shot was returned. I then gave the order to commence firing. The front line, composed of the Seventeenth and Thirty-first Regiments, delivered a steady and well-directed fire. Then, as previously instructed, falling upon the ground to load, the Thirty-eighth Ohio and Eighty-second Indiana immediately advanced and delivered their fire, lying down to load. I then gave the order to fix bayonets, intending to finish the job with that weapon. The enemy, however, had fled precipitately before our volleys behind their breastworks in the woods. There being no corresponding movement on my right, and the battery on our left keeping up a most pertinacious fire, which put my lines in great peril should I advance, I withdrew the brigade again behind the breastworks.[22]

Matthews's print depicts the brigade's advance in two firing lines out of one perimeter of woods toward another. The first line fires a massed volley, as the second, the Indiana troops and the Thirty-eighth Ohio, comes forward. The artist apparently chose not to depict Colonel Walker's tactics, with one line lying on the ground to reload while the other fired over it. It might not have been readily apparent to print buyers what the ground activity was, and such prone positions for the soldiery did not fit the heroic conventions of battle art. The second line already bristles with bayonets, perhaps a liberty taken by the artist. The four infantry regiments, rather understrength for Northern Civil War units, embraced some 1,200 men, and the extent of the lines of battle in the print accurately suggests such scale.

All in all, Matthews had crafted a fine print. Although, like Colonel Walker, many commanders ordered bayonets fixed from time to time, they were seldom used; bayonet charges were unusual, and wounds from edged weapons caused few casualties in the war. Actions were decided by musketry or artillery before becoming the furious assaults on the enemy's lines that printmakers so often used to depict Civil War battles.[23] Walker suffered only two officers and twenty men wounded in the action, but casualties could be much higher if the enemy proved to be in strength in the other perimeter of trees or put up a more determined resistance. Colonel Walker fought a rather commonplace action here, and Matthews captured its essence well.

Matthews was equally capable of depicting the elevating possibilities of life in service to one's country. His sketch of *Rev. L. F. Drake, Chaplain 31st Ohio Volunteers, Preaching at Camp Dick Robinson, Ky., November 10th 1861* (fig. 40), was adapted by Middleton, Strobridge into a depiction of serene harmony among men, nature, and God. Remarkably, considering their audience and its pervading evangelical piety, popular prints underestimated the role of religion in the lives of Civil War soldiers, and few prints addressed the theme.

A. E. Matthews's series of Civil War prints anticipated not the camp life portfolios of Edwin Forbes, but the gaudier battle series later concocted by the lithographers of the postwar era. Matthews did not offer images of the soldier's life that he knew from close personal experience. He opted instead for sweeping images of combat, of which he as a common soldier could have seen but a tiny and likely confusing fragment. But his works proved rather different from the patriotic lithographs of the popular sort offered by Currier and Ives and other printmakers, and they were more accurate.

Matthews's contemporary Edwin Forbes had to postpone translating his eyewitness depictions of army life into fine prints until the war was over and he himself had learned the technique that might consecrate them as art. Forbes worked as an artist-correspondent for *Frank Leslie's Illustrated Newspaper* during the war, but none of his images appeared as separate-sheet prints at that time. Instead, his eyewitness sketches from the Virginia battlefields were copied on woodblocks by anonymous engravers in New York for reproduction as wood engravings in the illustrated newspaper. Naturally, most "special" artists hated the process of adaptation—seeing their original works altered by the haste-making hands of the staff engravers. Eventually Forbes was able to combine the freshness of his eyewitness vision with the popular reach of art engraving by teaching himself how to etch. In 1876 he produced a portfolio of forty etchings called *Life Studies of the Great Army.*

Although Forbes lacked Winslow Homer's artistic genius, he nevertheless solved the problem that dogged Homer's Civil War lithographs: the matter of medium. Artists associated lithography with popular art; it suggested patriotism, sentimentalism, and humor, but not serious artistic purpose. By mastering the finer art of etching, Forbes was able to lend to his sketches an artistic dignity usually reserved only for painting.

Forbes had labored on the portfolio long and hard. If we can believe his own testimony, he worked up the wartime sketches into drawing models for his portfolio in the period 1865–68. He then etched the copper plates from 1870 through 1875.[24] The etchings went on view at the Centennial Exhibition in Philadelphia in 1876, where they won a medal. They won prominent admirers as well. General William T. Sherman had his aide-de-camp buy the first set of proofs to decorate his new office under construction in the War Department in Washington. General Philip H. Sheridan had a set of the prints framed and hung around the rooms of his headquarters at the Military Division of the Missouri in Chicago. In the words of Horace

Figure 40. Middleton, Strobridge and Company, after Alfred E. Matthews, *Rev. L. F. Drake, Chaplain 31st Ohio Volunteers, Preaching at Camp Dick Robinson, Ky., November 10th 1861.* Cincinnati, 1863. Lithograph, 11 × 14 inches. Though many common soldiers scoffed at and ridiculed chaplains, many others attended services and evangelical revivals during the Civil War. The number of prints depicting religious services by no means matched the importance of religion in the lives of the wartime armies. (*Library of Congress*)

Binney Sargent, commander of the Department of Massachusetts in the powerful veterans' organization, the Grand Army of the Republic, the prints made "delightful decorations" for Grand Army posts in the North. Forbes went on to show them at the Union League Club in New York City. Newspaper critics, delighted by the fact that the prints were the skilled products of a native artist, took note of the medium and the technique, recognizing that the works were not "fancy sketches" but eyewitness representations, and commented as well on the everyday nature of the subjects.[25]

The medium also guaranteed Forbes's immunity to the influence of photography. He had seen what he depicted in person and had often sketched on the spot; he did not need photographs to know what the war really looked like. His images serve to remind us today of the pretensions of photography. For all its vaunted realism, photography generally demanded posed subjects, and the results failed to capture the homeliest details of camp life. Readers will search Miller's *Photographic His-*

Figure 41. Edwin Forbes, *Necessary Routine* [also known as *Washing Day*], part of Plate 8 from *Life Studies of the Great Army*. New York, 1876. Etching, 11 × 15⅞ inches. Though this soldier was drawn with what might have turned into comic elements in a popular lithograph—his kepi sideways on his head and his laundry drying on the muzzle of his rifle—Forbes endowed the marching Federal with both dignity and determination. On campaign, "time for drying was not to be thought of," the artist remembered after observing a scene such as this, "and shirts and socks and bandanna handkerchiefs were often attached to the muskets and fluttered and dried in the breeze as the soldiers marched along. The ever-rising clouds of dust did not improve the color of the washed garments" (Edwin Forbes, *Thirty Years After: An Artist's Story of the Great War* [New York: Fords, Howard and Hulbert, 1890], 169). (*The Metropolitan Museum of Art, Harris Brisbane Dick Fund, 1940*)

tory of the Civil War in vain, for example, for photographs of soldiers drying their laundry on the march, as Forbes depicts in *Necessary Routine* (fig. 41).[26]

The subtitle of Forbes's major Civil War portfolio is important: *A Historical Art Work in Copper Plate Etching Containing Forty Plates.* Forbes thus called specific attention to the plates as "art work" and spelled out the medium in lengthy detail. The few critical works on the artist fail to point out that the plates offered studies in black and white, or light and shadow; they often were meant to show what etching could do, or what Forbes could do as an etcher. And etching could do what photography could not: scenes at dusk or dawn, or lighted by fire, were beyond the reach of field photography during the 1860s. Even in his daylight scenes Forbes often preferred backlit subjects—also beyond the reach of photography at the time.

Figure 42. Edwin Forbes, *Through the Wilderness*, Plate 3 from *Life Studies of the Great Army*. New York, 1876. Etching, 11 × 15⅞ inches. Forbes recorded this scene after a torrential morning rainstorm turned passable roads into "quagmires." Heavy loads became "more than the animals could draw through the churned mass of mud," and as the artillery "toiled through the swamp-like roads" they lost "horses by the dozen in the mire." The artist watched as "horses and drivers assumed the same color, and the guns almost lost distinctness of form" (Forbes, *Thirty Years After*, 209–10). In sketching what he saw, and later etching the result, Forbes created what was destined to rank among the most frequently reproduced black-and-white images of the Civil War. (*The Metropolitan Museum of Art, Harris Brisbane Dick Fund, 1940*)

Among the plates that constituted studies of light and dark were *The Picket Line, Officers' Winter Quarters, Going into Camp at Night, Coffee Coolers, Tattoo and Reveille*, and *A Night March*.

The masterpiece of Forbes's portfolio was *Through the Wilderness* (fig. 42), a study in light and dark, though not a night scene or one lit by firelight. Here the dense shadows of the treacherously wooded Wilderness of northern Virginia caused the light and shadows. No other artwork depicting the Civil War in any medium offered a more vivid portrayal of mud, as the wheels of Forbes's cannon and limber appear almost fused with the earth. Forbes, famed as an animal painter before the war, appreciated the toiling horses and offered them sympathy in the sadly deflated image of the exhausted creature lying in the shadow of death at the lower left.[27]

Life Studies of the Great Army was a forward-looking portfolio that can claim important twentieth-century descendants. The recognizable heirs of Forbes's disheveled soldiers with their stooping posture, their baggy uniforms, and their humdrum chores were cartoonist Bill Mauldin's Willie and Joe, the World War II GIs. But Forbes proved too precocious artistically for his own good. The heyday of art etching in the United States lay in the twentieth century, and only the disillusionment with war engendered by World War I caused artists and cartoonists to let the posture of the soldier in art sag. More typical of Forbes's era were Ernest Crehen's lithographs of the official *Uniform and Dress of the Army and Navy of the Confederate States of America*, published in Richmond in 1861.[28] From their waxed mustaches and goatees to their tiny feet in neat black shoes, these French-inspired, stiff-backed dandies suffered few wrinkles in their jackets and pants, and it seems nearly certain that the slouching infantrymen in wrinkled uniforms depicted by Forbes constituted an artistic rebellion against the fanciful soldier of the traditional uniform print.

Although Forbes's 1876 portfolio earned both a medal at that year's centennial exposition and not insubstantial critical acclaim, it had little immediate influence. The 1880s were dominated by brightly colored portfolios of battles and leaders, packaged and promoted by large chromolithography firms. Depictions of the humdrum realities of camp life were as yet confined to a few oil painters and mostly awaited the next century.

The Domestic Blockade

3

The Home Front in Prints

> *We are about to meet once more, in the shock of battle, the invaders of our soil, the despoilers of our homes, the disturbers of our family ties. Face to face, hand to hand, we are to decide whether we are to be freemen, or the vile slaves of those who are free only in name. [General P. G. T. Beauregard, May 2, 1862][1]*

When Confederate generals harangued their armies before a battle, they did not remind the soldiers that they were defending the great planters and their slave property. Instead, they urged the men to defend home and hearth from the Yankee invader. Northern leaders could not avail themselves as easily of this effective message, for Southern armies rarely invaded the North and, on those rare occasions when they did, the Confederates did not penetrate very far. No enemy army ever marched through Massachusetts to make New England "howl." Northern civilians were rarely subjected to the horrors that beset, say, the citizens of Vicksburg, who were forced to live underground in rat-infested caves to escape the siege of 1863, or the residents of Atlanta, Columbia, and Richmond, who were engulfed in conflagrations that laid waste to entire cities. Yet Northern printmakers did not concede the image of the home to the enemy.

For many Northerners, the rebellion began as nothing more threatening than a picnic war. Hundreds of spectators from Washington had optimistically packed champagne and lunches and journeyed across Potomac River bridges in carriages to Manassas, Virginia, to enjoy the first—and, they mistakenly presumed, the last—battle of the war. When the Union army was defeated, the experience proved anything but enjoyable for the startled spectators. "There was a regular chariot race when the rout began," an aide to Confederate General J. E. B. Stuart boasted. "We found, occasionally, along the road, parasols and dainty shawls lost in their flight by the frail, fair ones who had seats in most of the carriages of this excursion."[2]

Modern interpretations of the impact of the Bull Run defeat on the North vary sharply. Most historians used to see it as a galvanizing and sobering event for the

North, echoing the contemporary sermon by the great Hartford Congregationalist Horace Bushnell entitled "Reverses Needed: A Discourse Delivered on the Sunday after the Disaster at Bull Run." "Peace," he said, "will do for angels, but war is God's ordinance for sinners, and they want the schooling of it often. In a time of war, what a sense of discipline is forced." But historian Michael C. C. Adams has offered an alternative view, noting the psychologically debilitating effect of losing the first battle of the war for the North, which already trembled at the idea of fighting the youths from the region of the country identified with tough rural virtues of riding, shooting, and woodcraft.[3]

Perhaps popular prints did not operate at quite such intellectual levels, but they did register in a way the profound effects of the battle on American opinion, for this battle alone led to ridicule in lithographs. In at least two, one European and one American, the humiliating flight from Virginia was sharply caricatured. Members of Congress who fled, including Senator Henry Wilson of Massachusetts and the famous antislavery congressman from Illinois, Owen Lovejoy, were specifically referred to in the American print, which offered in the background an image of Northern ladies and gentlemen as spectators fleeing the field in carriages. Northern printmakers would rarely again heap ridicule on the Northern army, and this little deviation from the path of steady patriotism on the part of American Civil War printmakers strongly suggests the trauma of the Bull Run defeat.[4]

But the Civil War did inspire domestic and sentimental prints. Stoic women and fatherless children became staples of Civil War iconography, along with scenes of home and hearthstone. The war proved well suited to such image making, for it was interpreted from the start as a domestic conflict. It has been described, then as now, as a brother-against-brother war, a family war. Abraham Lincoln had warned in 1858 of a "house divided," and at his inauguration as president in 1861 he had invoked the "mystic chords of memory" that he declared resonated not only from patriot graves and living hearts, but also from "hearthstones," the symbolic centerpiece of the American family. Now American families were under siege as surely as was the nation itself. To Harriet Beecher Stowe, maintaining the domestic family became no less essential than preserving the national family. Writing in 1864, she urged unity in words that left little doubt that she regarded family as the national metaphor: "Our country is now in the situation of a private family whose means are absorbed by an expensive sickness, involving the life of its head; just now it is all we can do to keep the family together; all our means are swallowed up by our own domestic wants; we have nothing to give for the encouragement of other families; we must exist ourselves; we must get through the crisis and hold our own."[5]

Not surprisingly, when printmaker Joseph E. Baker devised an anti-Lincoln lithograph, probably for the 1864 presidential campaign, he chose as his visual metaphor the maternal figure of Columbia demanding, "Mr. Lincoln, give me back my 500,000 sons." The title of the print is *Columbia Demands Her Children!* The grotesque Lincoln is unrepentant—Columbia's demands merely remind him of a joke—but it could not have been lost on audiences of the day that so much sacrifice had been rendered by the "children" of this divided national family. It is no wonder, as historian Reid Mitchell has observed, that many Northerners understandably "saw joining the army to fight for the Union as an extension of a man's duty to protect his family." Another historian, Gerald Linderman, has asserted that "the cement of armies" is courage; Mitchell countered that the cement of Civil War armies was "love of home."[6]

A culture so devoted to home and family would naturally seek inspiration from fathers, sons, and husbands sent into battle to protect the national house, as surely as such soldiers would find inspiration from those they left behind. As a Pennsylvania corporal named Frederick Pettit expressed it, "Those home influences will save many of our brave soldiers from a fate worse than death on the battlefield." Printmakers provided numerous depictions of "home influences," mostly pictures designed to reassure the families of Union soldiers, along with their widows and orphans, that their men were armed with inspiring thoughts about their homes. The printmakers offered icons testifying to what artist Lilly Martin Spencer had called, in the title to her best-known wartime domestic group, "war spirit at home." But they sometimes depicted a "home spirit at war" as well. One volunteer, Charles Harvey Brewster of Massachusetts, put it this way: "Everything that savors of home relishes with us." To such soldiers, moreover, the grimmer aspects of war service surely helped to glorify further the memory of home.[7]

In 1861 Currier and Ives nicely illustrated this heightened sense of the sanctity of home with *Off for the War, / The Soldier's Adieu* (fig. 43), in which a Union volunteer takes leave of his wife and son to join his regiment. The flowers that bloom behind the picket fence seem to suggest the bright hopes of the Federal cause, and the home itself, a two-story affair set amid what appear to be acres of lush property, is unmistakably worth fighting for. One can almost imagine wives throughout the reach of Currier and Ives's wide net of distribution eager to hang such lithographs in their parlors to testify to their loyalty to the Union cause and their pride in their husbands' bravery. The firm concurrently issued *Home from the War, / The Soldier's Return* (fig. 44), depicting the same volunteer returning from his brief tour of duty. He has grown a beard, evidence of his hard living on campaign, while his wife wears the same black dress with white lace collar that she wore when he departed, attesting perhaps to the sacrifices she made to maintain their home while he was away. The flowers in their yard are still in bloom; apparently one spring campaign has sufficed to quell the rebellion. Surely here was a pictorial tribute to the brief cycle of service required of the first ninety-day volunteers. Unfortunately, the war would last longer than Northerners first hoped and believed, and images of the home left behind grew more meaningful as terms of service lengthened from months to years.[8]

The vogue for depictions of life behind the lines was only beginning, and no printmakers proved more suited, either by sentiment or marketing acumen, to

Figure 43. Currier and Ives, *Off for the War, / The Soldier's Adieu.* New York, 1861. Lithograph, 9 × 7 inches. As he rests his rifle against the rocks outside his gate, a Union volunteer, newly uniformed, bids farewell to his wife and son, leaving behind a substantial-looking home to fight for his country. In a variant of this print, perhaps designed for members of the officer class, not the families of common soldiers, Currier and Ives showed the volunteer fully bearded, gave him emblems of rank on his uniform, inserted a saber and gaudy sash, and removed his knapsack, canteen, and rifle. The child was given a lace collar, as if to emphasize the family's wealth, and, to indicate that the volunteer was an important person, the print added a small knot of soldiers in the background waiting for their comrade to take his leave. (*Anne S. K. Brown Military Collection, Brown University*)

OFF FOR THE WAR,
THE SOLDIER'S ADIEU.

touch the national nerve on this issue than Currier and Ives. At the same time, it is important to understand that war pictures of all sorts never accounted for more than a part of the firm's business, and that home-front prints, in turn, never made up more than a fraction of the firm's wartime output. If Currier and Ives may be regarded as the country's leading lithography firm—and certainly it could claim the largest list of titles, based on surviving catalogs of the period—then the diversity of that list suggests that for many customers the walls of the family parlor remained off limits to war depictions. Domestic and sentimental images seemed best suited to the home. Harriet Beecher Stowe and Catharine Beecher, for example, would in 1869 recommend in their famed manual, *The American Woman's Home*, that women decorate their homes with "admirable" prints. But they specifically suggested only chromos of paintings like Eastman Johnson's *Barefoot Boy* and Albert Bierstadt's *Sun-*

Figure 44. Currier and Ives, *Home from the War, / The Soldier's Return.* New York, 1861. Lithograph, 9 × 7 inches. Now sporting a beard, but otherwise looking none the worse for his service in the military, the prototypical volunteer returns to the embrace of the wife he left behind. Evidently his service has been brief, for it still appears to be summer in the blooming garden behind the white picket fence. (*Anne S. K. Brown Military Collection, Brown University*)

set in the Yo Semite Valley. In the realm of painting, where history held prestige, sentimentalism and domesticity exerted appeal, too. By war's end, even as audiences South as well as North grew interested in depictions of battles and heroes, Mark Twain would visit the National Academy of Design's annual art exhibition in New York and ruefully note that "more than half of the paintings" were still "devoted to the usual harmless subjects," including "the same old pile of cats asleep in the corner."[9]

The range of subjects provided by printmakers during the war is apparent in the surviving copyright registry books in which Currier and Ives, along with local competitors, occasionally (but not always—the laws were, at best, loosely enforced) recorded its newest compositions to protect them from piracy. On January 14, 1863, for example, the same day Currier and Ives copyrighted its lithograph of the Battle of Fredericksburg, it also registered *Fruit and Flower Piece*, a Fanny Palmer print of a vase filled with flowers, strawberries, and cherries, and *Strawberries*, showing two baskets of berries next to a dish of morning glories. On May 18 of that year, the same day the firm registered its dramatic scene of Admiral David D. Porter's fleet running the Confederate blockade of the Mississippi at Vicksburg, Currier and Ives copyrighted two domestic prints, *Two Little "Fraid" Cats* and *An Increase of Family*. Mark Twain was perhaps closer to the truth about nineteenth-century art than he knew with his amusing observation about cats in the paintings at the National Academy. According to the *Currier and Ives Catalogue Raisonné*, the company produced 163 different Civil War prints. While producing those, Currier and Ives published about the same number of new titles on nonwar subjects. In 1862, of eighty-seven new titles, only thirty-five were nonwar; in 1863, of fifty-three new titles, twenty-nine were nonwar; and by 1864, of forty-nine new titles, thirty were nonwar. Apparently, the firm's interest in war subjects declined. The war was never Currier and Ives's only business, just as it was not by any means the total business of American society from 1861 to 1865.[10]

A fourth print was registered by the firm on May 18, 1863: *The Little Recruit*, in which a mother and daughter prepare a young boy for a game of war as other children frolic outside. This represented business as usual for Currier and Ives, which had long ago mastered the art of capitalizing on sentimental images of children. The firm had always gravitated toward prints of "little" subjects, sentimental, precious, and probably aimed at "feminine" taste. Evidence is hardly conclusive, but it seems likely that in the rigid separation of gender spheres in the era of the Civil War, the acquisition of popular prints for the home fell in women's realm. The famous Conningham checklist of Currier and Ives titles recorded an astounding 180 "little" portraits—from *The Little Alms Giver* to *The Little Zouave*, the latter being one of several such prints created during the war years showing youngsters, whose fathers were off at the real war, dressing up in imitation of their family heroes.[11]

One of these prints was inspired by a rough, but wonderfully evocative, 1862 sketch by Thomas Nast (plate 4), which he later pasted into his scrapbook of wartime art. It showed a domestic servant, comical brogans adorning her feet, raising her broom in mock defensiveness as she confronts the children of the house (including a little Zouave), who block the entrance to one of the rooms with chairs, pots, and a bottle aimed outward like a shoreline battery. It was refined and published as a large-folio lithograph by Currier and Ives (plate 5), entitled, appropriately enough, *The Domestic Blockade*. Patriotism and humor were the message to Americans in the 1860s, but rigidity of social class lines is readily apparent to modern viewers as well.

A companion piece after yet another Nast drawing, *The Attack on the "Home Guard"* (fig. 45) from 1864, presents a rather confused scene in which the family dog appears to be biting the cuff of a uniformed child as if to prevent him from cavorting with a little girl. The scene may be a parody of "Soldier's Return" scenes;

here the "return" is from a fight with the "home guard," in this case the family watchdog. The little girl is catching the boy and attempting to turn him back to face the "enemy." In either case, the subject is war-inspired play, but here one might infer a loss of innocence among a generation of children growing up in the crucible of war. These children do not live in caves as their Confederate counterparts are com-

THE ATTACK ON THE "HOME GUARD".

Figure 45. Currier and Ives, *The Attack on the "Home Guard."* Signed, lower right, "Th. Nast 9/63." New York, 1864. Hand-colored lithograph, 18 × 24 inches. A youngster dressed in an impeccable replica of a Union uniform attempts to mimic a tearful farewell with an adorable playmate, or perhaps tries only to flee the scene, but is thwarted by another "home guard"—the family dog who nips at the youngster's trouser cuff as if to remind viewers that, even playing at war, these children remained firmly attached to the safe sphere of home. The little onlooker who grasps an American flag while he laughs at the action reminds viewers that children, too, were expected to maintain patriotic fervor about the war. The assortment of domestic and mock-military props—the hoop and watering can stored on the wall at right and the miniature caisson in the bushes at left—suggests that traditional occupations, even among the young, have been supplanted by those that relate to war. (*The Harry T. Peters Collection, Museum of the City of New York*)

pelled to do, for example, in the besieged city of Vicksburg, but they are deprived of their fathers, which appears to be enough of a transformation to have inspired these prints. Perhaps the firm's ultimate statement on this theme was *The Little Hero*, whose subject was no soldier but, presumably, the child of one. What was surprising was that this time the child was a daughter, not a son. The girl is in her family parlor, standing at mock-attention, toting a large rifle. Unlikely gold braids decorate the shoulders of her dress. Staring down in benign approval is the portrait of a real soldier—the girl's father, we are meant to assume. The message of these prints was unambiguous: citizen morale and enthusiasm for the war effort, they suggested, remained high on the Union home front.

Yet such prints may have exaggerated the "war spirit at home" proposed by artist Lilly Martin Spencer. Readers of the classic novel on the Civil War at home, *Little Women*, for instance, will recall no similar scenes. On the contrary, even in antislavery New England, the March children did not parade around the dining room table in honor of their father, away because of the war, and the girls' suitors plan their futures with little or no thought to military service. When they dressed up in costumes, like the children in *The Domestic Blockade*, the March girls did not don uniforms and tote mock muskets; they performed classic melodrama. Even when Laurie, the boy next door, joined the troupe, Jo, Amy, Beth, and Meg gave no thought to staging something more military.

Still, the sacrifices that previously secure Northerners made to the Union cause took their inevitable toll. A real-life Union officer from Massachusetts pointed to the universality of such sacrifice when he commented: "At this time there was a good deal of despondency at home." As Louisa May Alcott understood after the local Concord, Massachusetts, company was sent off to the front, "In a little town like this we all seem like one family in times like these."[12] In such families, children inevitably began experiencing not play war, but real war. In 1862 a young people's magazine, *The Student and Schoolmate*, pointed out that "only a few years ago," Northerners "looked with a feeling bordering on contempt on military matters. . . . A military company was senseless pageant to be enjoyed by little boys and stupid men." But when Fort Sumter was attacked, the magazine contended, "the military spirit rose to a tremendous pitch of enthusiasm." By 1864 the magazine would exhort its young readers, in language not unlike the patriotic verse written at the time to stir adults:

> Should coming days he dark and cold,
> We will not sigh or murmur,
> For Grant has said, with courage bold,
> "We'll fight them here all summer."[13]

Currier and Ives would poignantly illustrate this transformation with *The Soldier Boy, / "On Duty"* (fig. 46) and its companion picture, *The Soldier Boy, / "Off Duty."* The former depicted a youthful recruit on guard duty, and the latter portrayed him leaning against a tree near the campfire. But these were not portraits of children imitating adults in homemade uniforms; these showed children brought too early to maturity, serving in the ranks as camp musicians, or perhaps even as fully armed soldiers. They were not exactly home-front prints, but they were not war prints, either: they vivified the tragic existence of a wartime purgatory somewhere in between, populated by children who in a peaceful world would have remained home. Instead, they were compelled by "war spirit" and other exigencies into premature adulthood, not to mention grave danger. The culture seemed willing to put its youth at risk at very early ages, as was the case with drummer boys, but the average Civil War soldier was rather old, the median age almost twenty-four.[14]

What is perhaps more revealing than how the printmakers treated the subject of children in war is how they chose not to treat it. Nowhere in the archives of Civil War popular prints are there realistic, disturbing portraits of teen-aged soldiers playing cards or serving as stretcher bearers—the kind of characters who later populate the canvases of camp musician-turned-artist Julian Scott. Perhaps the crucial difference was that Scott's paintings were created long after the war ended. Parents whose young sons were still at war probably wanted no reminders of the camp vices or bloodshed to which their children were being routinely exposed. In other words, the wartime print images were sentimental, without a hint of the drilling, gambling, and whoring also traditionally associated with a soldier's life. Children, however, confronted what many parents could not. They might read, in an 1862 issue of *The Student and Schoolmate*, a harrowing poem about the death of a fifteen-year-old drummer boy killed at Fort Donelson:

> And there let him rest, on the battle-field fearful,
> Where heroes, in thousands, repose at his side;
> And we'll think on his doom with a feeling less tearful,
> To know that for justice and freedom he died.[15]

Such children might yet be compelled themselves to die for justice and freedom. The war lasted long enough to allow tens of thousands of young boys to grow up and join the ranks. But for a time, the only acceptable role society granted their mothers was that of patient guardian of the hearthstone. Currier and Ives celebrated this prototypically passive heroine in *The Brave Wife* (see fig. 16), a lithograph notable at least in part for its poignant celebration of women. The print proved appealing enough to a twenty-two-year-old Union volunteer named Lester Frank Ward (later a noted sociologist) to inspire him to purchase a copy—along with *The Soldier's Dream*, *The Young Cavalier*, and a portrait of Lincoln—to send to friends and family.[16]

The Brave Wife may have been particularly appealing to the family of such a soldier, for it also provided beneath its caption a poem that celebrated not the bravery of volunteers, but the nobility of their spouses—and the unspoken understanding that each farewell might well be the last. In the words of the poem:

THE SOLDIER BOY,

"ON DUTY".

The wife who girds her husband's sword,
　　Mid little ones who weep or wonder,
And bravely speaks the cheering word,
　　What tho' her heart be rent asunder . . .

Doomed nightly in her dreams to hear,
　　The bolts of war around him rattle,
Hath shed as sacred blood as e'er,
　　Was poured upon the plain of battle.[17]

Wives might be comforted by the prints that suggested that in shedding their real blood "upon the plain of battle," their husbands' final thoughts had been directed toward home and family. *The Dying Soldier* (fig. 47), published by Thomas Kelly in 1864, presented precisely this scene. Here a handsome soldier lies dying on a battlefield, a rather lush one whose unscathed tree branches and wildflowers offer scant evidence that fighting had occurred there. He glances one last time at a locket that hangs from his neck. In a variation on the theme of the soldier's dream of home, the viewer is transported into the eye and mind of the dying soldier via a spectral image that rises above the clouds at the top of the scene, revealing the vision brought to mind by the locket. We see his wife, son, and daughter, the children playing, oblivious to their father's suffering on the faraway battlefield, the wife bent over in worry, but not yet mourning. Such touching scenes may well have served to comfort untold widows in the months of their bereavement.

Those who had not lost their husbands, but who worried nonetheless about not only their safety but, perhaps, their moral strength in camps filled with temptation, could take comfort from *The American Patriot's Dream, / The Night before the Battle* (fig. 48), whose side-whiskered soldier dreams of his triumphant return home and the welcome he anticipates from wife, child, and parents. As the verses below the caption explained:

Stretched on the ground the toil worn soldier sleeps,
　　Beside the lurid watch fire's fitful glare;

---

opposite

Figure 46. Currier and Ives, *The Soldier Boy, / "On Duty."* New York, 1864. Lithograph, 12½ × 8½ inches. Three years after the war began, as the copyright date of this print suggests, children barely old enough to understand secession and war in 1861 were suddenly thrust into service themselves. Available statistics, which if anything overestimated the age of Northern soldiers, the youngest and most zealous of whom understandably lied about their birth dates in order to enlist, show that large numbers of teenagers served in the ranks: 90,215 nineteen-year-old soldiers joined the Union army between 1861 and 1865, along with 133,475 eighteen-year-olds, 6,425 seventeen-year-olds, 2,758 sixteen-year-olds, 773 fifteen-year-olds, 330 fourteen-year-olds, and 127 who were only thirteen years old (*Ages of U.S. Volunteer Soldiers* [New York: U.S. Sanitary Commission, 1866], 5–6). The artist who drew this image likely copied the uniform from a soldier's photograph but had probably never seen a cannon, for the barrel of a Civil War cannon rested on the parallel wooden trails, not between them, as in this print. (*Library of Congress*)

The Dying Soldier

And dreams that on the field of fame he reaps,

Renown and honors, which he haste's to share,

With those beloved ones who gathering come,

To bid their hero, husband, father "welcome home,"

Fond dreamer may thy blissful vision be;

A true fore shadowing of the fates to thee.

Not all women remained at home wringing their hands helplessly over the dining room table, as their husbands in popular prints imagined them. The Civil War often transformed the roles of women. As historians Catherine Clinton and Nina Silber have argued, "wartime necessity" brought about "the breakdown of rigid gender categories and sexual barriers." Historian George Fredrickson has suggested that wartime home-front organizations staffed by women volunteers, like the United States Sanitary Commission, achieved a shift in the ideology of welfare and charity. Women's wartime gains would prove mostly temporary, but while the war raged, many oversaw households, maintained family farms as resolutely as their more fabled Confederate counterparts sustained their plantations, saw to the care and comfort of their families without help, and in some cases, aided the war effort directly by volunteering to nurse the wounded or raise funds for their care.[18]

Acknowledgment of these new roles for women came in a caption for a Frank Bellew cartoon in a wartime edition of *Frank Leslie's Illustrated Newspaper*, noting the "profound interest and deep sympathy of our wives and daughters for everything which concerns the honor and glory of the republic." Such women were quite unlike the helpless, angry Confederate Mary Boykin Chesnut, who saw her own privileged world shattered by wartime privation. "I think *these* times make all women feel their humiliation in the affairs of the world," she confided to her diary in the summer of 1861. "With *men* it is on to the field—'glory, honour, praise &c, power.' Women can only stay at home—& every paper reminds us that women are to be *violated*—ravished & all manner of humiliation. How are the daughters of Eve punished." In the North, largely unthreatened by enemy invasion, the daughters of Eve left their domestic Edens not in shame, but with valuable work to do. Printmakers occasionally recorded their transfiguration.[19]

Prints depicting female nurses in the war, for example, documented the opening of nursing as an important new profession for women. At the war's beginning, America's medical care was home-based, not hospital-based (except for charity cases), and the expectation was that military nurses would be males. It is no surprise, then, that Currier and Ives's 1865 lithograph, *The Angels of the Battle-field* (fig. 49), likened these pioneering hospital nurses to celestial guardians, for there are, literally, two angels in this battlefield scene tending to a wounded soldier: a winged angel from heaven, shining the light from a heavenly crown on the victim, and a devoted nurse, doing the useful earthly work of trying to stop the bleeding.

opposite
Figure 47.
A. Turrell, after a painting by H. B. Simmons, *The Dying Soldier*. Published by Thomas Kelly, New York, 1864. Mezzotint engraving, 24 × 18 inches. A wounded Union soldier spends his last living moments staring sadly at a locket hanging from his neck, containing a picture of his family, while imagining that his worried wife and small children wait anxiously at home, unaware that he has become a casualty of America's family war. This print may well have been designed for widows, to provide constant visual reassurance that their late husbands had breathed their last with thoughts of home and family uppermost. In 1870 Turrell issued a companion print, *The Orphans*, showing the same family visiting the dead soldier's grave. (*Library of Congress*)

Figure 48. Currier and Ives, *The American Patriot's Dream, / The Night before the Battle*. New York, 1861. Hand-colored lithograph, 8⅞ × 11⅞ inches. As his worried comrades huddle sleeplessly around a campfire in the background, no doubt nervously awaiting a confrontation with enemy forces at daybreak, the handsome Union soldier in the foreground dreams about returning home to his wife, child, and aging parents. Such scenes were meant to reassure families that their men in arms remained inspired, perhaps even protected and blessed, by thoughts of home and hearth. When the painter James Henry Beard dealt with the same subject in his 1865 canvas, *The Night before the Battle*, he preferred to depict soldiers' prebattle nightmares: the sleeping men in the Beard painting dream only of death, and skeletons walk the camp (Beard canvas in the Memorial Art Gallery, University of Rochester). (*Library of Congress*)

Today's viewers might not easily appreciate the progressive nature of this print, for no matter how tirelessly they worked, nurses did not win universal approbation; some Northerners clung to the belief that the battlefield was no place for women, and that those who defied tradition to nurse male soldiers were somehow indecent. Clara Barton recalled with bitterness hearing the "groans of suffering men" in one ear and "the appalling fact that I was a woman, whispering" in the other. She was

THE ANGELS OF THE BATTLE-FIELD.

Figure 49. Currier and Ives, *The Angels of the Battle-field*. New York, 1865. Hand-colored lithograph, oval, 13 × 18 inches. As a battle rages in the near background on a smoke-drenched field littered with corpses, a fearless Civil War nurse tends to the chest wound of a gravely injured soldier. An angel appears on the scene to bless his chances for recovery, holding her halo over the soldier's head and bathing him with its healing rays. The stars-and-stripes shields decorating the four corners of this composition add a patriotic imprimatur as well on the nursing enterprise, which still faced some criticism at home from those who believed women should not engage in such indelicate work. "The sight of . . . legless, armless, or desperately wounded" soldiers served to remind Louisa May Alcott, as she wrote in *Hospital Sketches*, that she was present at such scenes "to work, not to wonder or weep" (Louis P. Masur, ed., *"The Real War Will Never Get in the Books": Selections from Writers during the Civil War* [New York: Oxford University Press, 1993], 26). (*Library of Congress*)

eternally mortified that she had ever given the whispers any thought. Most nurses were "the objects of continual evil speaking among coarse subordinates," agreed the official history of the United States Sanitary Commission: they were "looked at with a doubtful eye by all but the most enlightened surgeons, and have a very uncertain semi-legal position, with poor wages and little sympathy." Even Frederick Law Olmsted, the founder of the Sanitary Commission, was reported as "impenetrably silent" when it came to women volunteers. Such unspoken disdain was "worse," one nurse confessed, "because we can't rebel at it."[20]

Relief efforts could also be professionally organized. From the outset of the war, the founders of the United States Sanitary Commission, organized in June 1861 to care for the wounded and the sick, concerned themselves with nutrition. "The difference between well-cooked digestible food and ill-cooked indigestible food consumed by a regiment during three months of actual service in the field is equivalent to a difference of at least forty percent in its available strength at the end of that period," a proponent of the Sanitary Commission declared in 1864. In a parallel effort, the Volunteer Refreshment Saloon created by the citizens of Philadelphia to provide lodging and meals to Union soldiers was said to have fed more than 800,000 troops during its existence.

A colorful lithograph designed to celebrate that noble experiment came from James Queen of that city (plate 6), one of several prints issued there to commemorate the patriotic generosity of the citizens. But the print also commemorated the women who, as the earliest official histories of the Sanitary Commission acknowledged, had helped sustain it. "The women were clearer and more united than the men," Henry Bellows recalled in 1867, if only "because their moral feelings and political instincts were not so much affected by selfishness and business, or party considerations." To Bellows, "the women of America had at least half of its patriotism in their keeping." Such women not only purchased and displayed prints, they inspired them.[21]

The Sanitary Commission offered women the opportunity to join the war effort, to find a useful outlet for what the organization's *Bulletin* called "the motherly love which kept swelling up night and day in millions of hearts, and flowed out toward the tented fields in such a stream as threatened to overrun all boundaries." Posing the question "What can women do to help save the Nation?," a Sanitary Commission volunteer from Chester County, Pennsylvania, insisted: "The mere fact of this question being asked is . . . a most encouraging sign. It shows that we are becoming awake to the great interests and duties of the hour." Now the "power of right," exemplified by virtue, love, and religion, could become as potent as the "power of arms." She concluded by warning women throughout the North: "These are strong, earnest days, and woe to the woman . . . who stands idly gazing by the highway, while the chariot wheels of destiny roll on to their grand fulfillment." By 1864 a St. Louis army inspector would praise the commission as "the best medium through which to send material comforts to the sick of the army."[22]

In 1863 the women of the Sanitary Commission began organizing fairs, staging mammoth charity bazaars in Boston, Cincinnati, Chicago, New York, and a number of smaller cities as well, which featured such attractions as captured Confederate battle flags, livestock, musical instruments, books, homemade food, and the latest farm implements, along with autographed letters, paintings, and prints. Such events were as impressive and wide-ranging as annual state fairs; the only difference was that the money they raised went to a charity that benefited the soldiers. To printmakers Ensign and Bridgman of New York, these volunteers "on the battle field," "in the parlor," "in the hospital," and "at the fair" were nothing less than—in the words of the caption to the firm's celebratory engraving, *United States Sanitary Commission*—"Heroines of the War."[23]

To stock New York's Great Metropolitan Fair, organizers exhorted farmers to "bring gifts from their barns, their stalls, their dairies, and their poultry yards," while the "creators" and "dealers" in fine arts were urged to "send their contributions for exhibition and for sale." But these gatherings were to offer more than merchandise. They were expected to reflect "moral power" as well, in the words of the organizers of Chicago's Great Northwestern Fair, "to convince the South of the folly of persisting in its madness against a United North." At the Great Northwestern Fair, this "moral power" was evidenced at an art gallery displaying some 500 pictures, which attracted 20,000 visitors.[24]

At least one of these extravaganzas, the Brooklyn and Long Island Sanitary Fair, which opened at the Academy of Music on February 22, 1864, not only displayed and sold images of the war, it inspired them. Like all fair-goers, those in Civil War Brooklyn expected to be amused, to spend money, and to eat. Here they could sample "chicken pie, roast beef and veal, pork and beans, white and brown bread, potatoes in various styles, pickles, tea, coffee, cider, puddings, and mince and pumpkin pies." The full bill of fare cost fifty cents, and all of it was set up in one of the fair's major attractions, a "New England Kitchen," where waitresses served in costume and quilting bees and a New England wedding were staged as special attractions. The exhibit inspired the following description in the *Daily Morning Drum-Beat*, the fair's official newspaper:

> The kitchen contains four large tables all set out in a delightfully primitive style and most refreshingly free from the effeminate luxuries of this degenerate age: for instance napkins and butter knives. The viands are set forth on the most uncompromising of earthen ware—blue plates, eight brown bowls and big saucers. A pitcher of molasses takes the place of refined "syrup," and there is nothing on the table to remind the visitor that he is in a fashionable and wealthy city.[25]

Sanitary fairs like Brooklyn's, however, displayed more than quaint and vanishing domestic arts. They were important showcases for other arts as well. The Brooklyn fair exhibited paintings by Frederick Kensett, Albert Bierstadt, Asher B. Durand, and Arthur F. Tait. Henry Ward Beecher lent his collection of engravings of works by Italian artists, and a "curious picture of a Berdan sharpshooter" was offered by one "W. Homer" (Winslow Homer also produced a firsthand drawing of the fair's special post office booth, which was engraved for *Harper's Weekly*).[26]

Art of a more popular order also found its way into the fair's New England Kitchen. There one could find "a very remarkable copy, by Mr. Paine, of the President's Emancipation Proclamation . . . [with] a good portrait of Mr. Lincoln, and a fancy border, at the foot of which is a spirited picture of the Union Soldier on picket guard." Mass-produced photographic editions of this 1864 print, copyrighted by Joseph E. Paine and published in New York by Stadtfeld, would bear the inscription: "Original given to the Brooklyn Sanitary Fair, Feb. 22, 1864, and by a subscription of $500, bought of the fair, and presented to Abraham Lincoln, President of the U.S." Altogether, the Brooklyn Sanitary Fair raised $402,000 for the Union wounded.[27]

The Brooklyn fair inspired a series of commemorative prints as well. (The Great Central Fair in Philadelphia later that year would also generate a lithographic depiction, but from a distant, bird's-eye perspective, lacking the close-up detail provided for Brooklyn.) Arthur Brown, a lithographer from across the East River in Manhattan, issued five prints of the Brooklyn Sanitary Fair, showing Knickerbocker Hall; views from the dress circle and a view of the Brooklyn Academy of Music, site of the fair; two views of the academy stage, where volunteers sold thousands of dollars worth of books, flowers, and fancy goods; and, of course, the New England Kitchen (fig. 50).[28]

In truth, not all of the war's impact on domestic culture offered acceptable subject matter for parlor prints. Some women had gone beyond volunteerism to seek work as government clerks. But females who labored to sustain themselves, rather than the males serving in arms, were not deemed suitable subjects of engravings and lithographs, all of which, after all, were published by male-run establishments. There are no known separate-sheet prints depicting Civil War women on the job—except for nurses. But one even more socially unacceptable home-front phenomenon did inspire a print cartoon, clearly to discourage other citizens from following the same path. In *Candidates for the Exempt Brigade* (fig. 51), lithographer William Trowbridge touched on the roles of shirkers, croakers (doomsayers), and their female coconspirators. His 1862 print depicted a hatchet-faced woman who has just used a knife and hammer to slice the finger off a coward seeking a medical exemption from service. But here the cringing male is clearly the object of greatest scorn. The woman is portrayed as red-nosed, suggesting that she was drunk when she mutilated the shirker. In a culture in which women were still idealized, it would not do to suggest that a female could knowingly participate in such an unpatriotic, hideous deception. More typical was A. B. Walter's 1865 print, *Woman's Mission*, whose caption contained a dedication "to the Patriotic and Benevolent Ladies of the Union who By their Devoted Services Aided their Country in Its Trying Hour and Comforted Its Brave Defenders."[29]

Even the tireless female volunteers of the Sanitary Commission and other charity organizations sometimes longed for a return to their prewar spheres. This yearning for domestic tranquility was suggested by the appearance of "home from the war" prints that churned off the presses even as the war itself continued, but its first volunteers completed their service. It is perhaps instructive that the number of surviving "return" subjects outnumber the "leaving for war" prints devoted to the encouragement of recruitment. The notion of the house divided and reunited—one of the reigning metaphors of the Civil War—could even inspire one imaginative lithographer to conjure up a postwar meeting in hell among Satan, Benedict Arnold, and Jefferson Davis. This particular print was perhaps appropriately entitled *A Proper Family Reunion.*[30] Currier and Ives's *The Union Volunteer. / Home from the War*

BROOKLYN SANITARY FAIR, 1864.

NEW ENGLAND KITCHEN.

Figure 50. A[rthur]. Brown, *Brooklyn Sanitary Fair, 1864. / New England Kitchen*. New York, ca. 1864. Hand-colored lithograph, 16 × 20¼ inches. One of four prints issued to commemorate the successful charity fair that opened in Brooklyn in February 1864, this lithograph depicted one of its most popular exhibits, a New England–style kitchen that offered authentically costumed waitresses serving hearty food. The fair's official newspaper described the scene immortalized in the print this way: "The great monster fireplace has, with a kind consideration its early freaks had given us little right to expect, benignly consented to stop smoking, and acts its part with the quiet gravity of its puritanical progenitors. Before it stands an old-fashioned spinning-wheel, whereat an industrious dame of the olden time may be seen faithfully and patiently at work." One of the chairs in the scene was a 150-year-old-relic that its owner had buried for safekeeping when he joined the Union army. When he was killed, "it was exhumed" and installed in the kitchen, where it became "one of the most interesting objects in the Sanitary Fair of 1864" (*Lincoln Lore*, no. 1749 [November 1983]: 3–4). (*The Lincoln Museum*)

Figure 51. W[illia]m. E. S. Trowbridge, *Candidates for the Exempt Brigade.* New York, 1862. Lithograph, 13½ × 16 inches. "Oh Lord! Oh Lord! how it hurts," the shirker, "Adam Cowherd" (note the pun on his last name), yells after the grim-looking woman at left has wielded her knife to sever his index (trigger) finger from his now profusely bleeding hand. The doctor of dubious repute at right comforts him with the knowledge that "'twont hurt but a minute and then you can get one of those": a certificate of medical exemption from Union service. "He affirms," according to the perjured medical certificate the doctor clutches, "that it was cut off while digging post holes." Meanwhile, the severed finger itself lies hideously on a tree stump, blood still trickling toward the ground, warning viewers against the desperate lengths to which the most unpatriotic Northerners seemed willing to go to avoid serving in the military. (*Library of Congress*)

(fig. 52) was copyrighted on December 15, 1863; probably inspired by the season, the print provided an image of hope for temporary reunion in time for the Christmas holiday.

This genre proved especially applicable after Appomattox. Soon after the war's end, the *Philadelphia Inquirer* offered its subscribers "presentation" copies of W. T. Harding's *The Soldiers Return to His Home* (fig. 53), in which the returned veteran is more voluble than his predecessor in Currier and Ives's 1863 print. Here the soldier

THE UNION VOLUNTEER.

HOME FROM THE WAR.

Figure 52. Currier and Ives, *The Union Volunteer. / Home from the War.* New York, 1863. Hand-colored lithograph, 13¾ × 17¼ inches. An expanded, indoor version of the embrace depicted in Currier and Ives's three-character 1861 print, *Home from the War* (see fig. 44), this lavish lithograph brought the returning veteran back into the cathedral of American life, the family parlor. Wife, children, and mother rush to greet him; the ornate, cluttered setting looks inviting and comforting, and the books on the table near the window hold the promise of the leisure and self-improvement this soldier surely deserves. (*Library of Congress*)

gestures broadly, happily sharing war stories with his wife, children, and parents, all seated peacefully once again before the family hearth beneath framed prints of Abraham Lincoln and Ulysses S. Grant. The situation was much the same, down to the expansive gestures and enraptured family audience, in *How We Won the Battle*, published by Bradley and Company of Philadelphia after a painting by Christian Schussele. Here the sun shines with symbolic brightness from the modest parlor window, but the look of concern on the faces of the wife and father suggests that this family harbors no illusions about the perils of peace, even though their hero has survived the perils of war.

THE SOLDIERS RETURN TO HIS HOME,
PRESENTATION PLATE OF THE PHILADELPHIA INQUIRER JANUARY, 1866

Figure 53. [Anton] Hohenstein, *The Soldiers Return to His Home. / Presentation Plate of the Philadelphia Inquirer January, 1866.* Signed, lower left, "Hohenstein." Published by W. T. Harding, Philadelphia, 1866. Lithograph, 18¾ × 24⅛ inches. As his enraptured family listens intently, a returned veteran regales wife, children, and parents with war stories in this lithograph issued as a premium for readers of the pro-Republican newspaper, the *Philadelphia Inquirer.* The soldier has been wounded—note the crutch leaning against the fireplace at right—but he shows no lack of vigor as he reminisces. Patriotic portraits of Lincoln and Grant stare down from the wall. If the print bore a resemblance to group portraits of the Lincoln family that appeared after his assassination in 1865, there is good reason: lithographer Hohenstein had issued a number of them, in one of which Lincoln's son, Tad, was depicted precisely like the young man in this scene at left. (*The Lincoln Museum*)

Though executed with at least as much craft, *Home from Andersonville* (fig. 54), engraved by William Sartain of Philadelphia, was a flawed image. The print portrayed a soldier, head swathed in bandages, who has fallen into a chair at home, where he is being embraced by his grateful wife. Their infant child rests contentedly in a cradle nearby. The soldier has survived the most notorious of all the war's prison camps, where 13,000 captured Union men died of sickness or starvation. The problem with this print is that its central figure, the soldier, is anything but

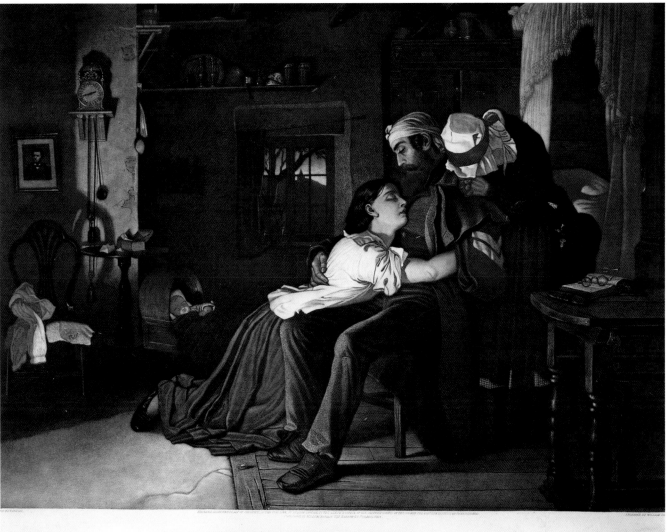

Figure 54. William Sartain, after a painting by Joseph Noel Paton, *Home from Andersonville.* / *"Blessed Are They that Suffer for Righteousness Sake."* Philadelphia, 1866. Mezzotint engraving, 13⅞ × 19½ inches. Repatriated Andersonville prisoners were, in reality, horrifically emaciated, quite unlike the robust survivor portrayed here. His well-fed appearance is attributable to the fact that engraver Sartain modeled the print after an 1856 English painting that depicted the return of a Scots Fusilier guard from brief service in the Crimean War. Photographs were at the time amply documenting the horrors of the Confederacy's most notorious prison camp, but atrocity pictures were not suitable for family parlors; print buyers evidently preferred romanticized views that emphasized family reunion, not individual suffering. (*The Lincoln Museum*)

starved. He is too beefy to be among the Andersonville survivors, harrowing photographs of whom were being circulated at the time to an appropriately appalled North. But atrocity pictures of skeletal survivors were not suitable for display in family homes or veterans' halls, and the Sartain print may have been issued to qualify for honored places on the walls of both. Surely only those who boasted extensive knowledge of British art would have recognized that the reason this supposed Andersonville survivor looked so well fed is that his figure—the entire scene, in fact—

had been borrowed from an engraving of British artist Joseph Noel Paton's earlier picture of an earlier, far briefer war, *Return from the Crimea*.[31]

In their true, harrowing condition, Andersonville survivors were quite the opposite of ideal central characters for Civil War reunion prints. Captain Henry Wirz, the commander of Andersonville, would be tried, convicted, and hanged. Maimed and sickly veterans struggled to survive in a peacetime Union that must have seemed to them as daunting as the battlefield. But on the parlor walls of American homes, Union veterans were miraculously restored to health and broken family circles were made whole. The "house" was no longer divided, and domestic prints of the war behind the lines had illustrated the slow march toward reunification. They proved perfect, if roseate, responses to the urgent recommendations of author Clarence Cook, who, in his influential 1878 book, *The House Beautiful*, called on ordinary Americans to "admit the ornaments of life," among which "pictures" and "engravings" were cited as "chief nourishers of life's feast."[32]

Prints by no means exhausted the possibilities for attractive subjects that lay behind the lines. The body of prints depicting Civil War America is hardly comprehensive. Depictions of the scenes behind the lines emphasized the patriotic, sentimental, and volunteeristic; little attention was paid to the industrial, mechanical, and coercive.[33] While the typical opening chapter of twentieth-century histories of the war deals with the relative advantages enjoyed by the North over the South, emphasizing Union economic and material superiority in railroad miles, manufacturing capacity, and sheer wealth, these were not factors much celebrated in the nineteenth-century North's visual image of the war.

Railroading had already proved a popular subject for prints. Currier and Ives issued at least forty-eight railroad images over the years. The majority appeared in the 1870s and 1880s, and those issued during the Civil War, like *The "Lightning Express" Leaving the Junction*, issued in 1863, seemed oblivious to the military uses to which such vehicles were then being put. One searches in vain for depictions of troop trains (what one Rhode Island soldier described as "the cars . . . carrying their living freight") or, for that matter, depictions of the military railroads themselves. Victory may have ridden the rails in fact, but in the Northern visual image of the conflict, victory rode horses and marched.[34]

Outdoor photography of the war placed more emphasis on railroads and engineering, bridges and trestles. The most likely reason is that such photography was commissioned by organizations under the War Department that had a professional interest in military technology. Carefully identified and preserved, they occupy a disproportionate share of the surviving archive of images taken out-of-doors during the war. But the photographers' choice of subject by no means reflects the popular perception of the conflict, or even the nature of the conflict itself, which in many ways really did boil down in the end to hard marching and horseback riding.[35]

The accumulation of supplies for the mass armies of the war also constituted a favorite subject for Civil War photographers. But perhaps this focus arose from the fact that camera operators were limited, as the printmakers were not, by a medium that could not depict moving subjects. The print artists were limited only by their imaginations, and they gave the American people what the people wanted: depictions of the action, the heroic contests, the battles, and, to some extent, a more placid, less organized life behind the lines than really existed in the North between 1861 and 1865.

The effect of this buildup of supplies on the people back home was not as great as the photographic record might suggest, nor was there government propaganda to heighten awareness of this effort. Methods of controlling the economy were generally confined to market forces—indeed, to put it more directly, the economy was not much controlled at all in the North. (It was a different story in the Confederacy, which required considerable coercion and expropriation to bring about its minor miracle of war production.)[36] The Union government, innocent of any notions of propaganda beyond political electioneering and Thanksgiving proclamations, did not blanket the country with posters urging conservation of food and fuel, investment in war bonds, or hard work in the factory to produce goods for the war. There was none of the organized effort America employed to illustrate patriotism for its citizens during World War I and World War II. In the 1860s, it seemed, patriotism could be safely assumed to prevail; it did not need much encouragement.

In short, there was no real notion of "home front" during the Civil War; there was only "home," and that, rather than some militarized, propagandized, and coerced version of it, was what the printmakers offered their customers.

Twilight of the Wooden Ships

4

Technology and Tradition in Navy Prints

Nathaniel Hawthorne followed the events of the Civil War closely and commented on them with a certain dyspeptic tone, in keeping with his lack of enthusiasm for the Republican administration in Washington. Where others saw glorious feats of arms, he was as likely to find somber meanings. In the case of the famed naval battle between ironclads, the Union *Monitor* and the Confederate *Virginia* (constructed from the sunken *Merrimac* of the prewar navy, and often called by its original name), Hawthorne said that the *Monitor* "could not be called a vessel at all; it was a machine." The writer seemed at once to sense that the emergence of such naval technology signaled the end of a romantic era in the image of war at sea. "All the pomp and splendor of naval warfare are gone by," he observed. "Henceforth there must come up a race of engineermen and smoke-blackened cannoneers . . . and even heroism—so deadly a gripe [*sic*] is Science laying on our noble possibilities—will become a quality of very minor importance."[1]

Heroism and glorious feats of arms were the principal subjects of popular prints of the Civil War, and one finds in them quite a different outlook from Hawthorne's. But the ironclad naval vessels devised during the Civil War did look like harbingers of an ugly industrialism to come, and one might think that printmakers had difficulty making them fit the simple need for glory and patriotism. Certainly collectors and connoisseurs since that time have shunned Civil War naval subjects. Naval prints of the Civil War are twice removed from genuine respect. First, the prestige in collecting naval prints attaches to images from the age of sail, especially from the War of 1812. Second, the navy's role in the Civil War was, by almost any reckoning, of less importance than the army's.

The most celebrated Union naval achievement of the war, the construction of the *Monitor* and its successful battle against the *Virginia*, did not lend itself easily to a lingering romantic aesthetic: the *Monitor* was an ugly machine and a relentless reminder of industrialism. The myth of American identity—as opposed to its increasingly smokestack-studded reality—resisted identification with machine technology.

Similarly, the navy's greatest sustained contribution to Union victory, the blockade, was a matter of patient vigilance rather than vivid dramatic event or action and was never successfully symbolized in pictorial imagery. There was no naval Gettysburg, no "turning point" when the blockade tightened from ineffective to strangling. Two key naval actions, the passage of the forts at Vicksburg and the Battle of New Orleans, occurred in the dark of night, and that did not make the printmakers' task any easier.

But printmakers, many of them located in port cities like Boston, New York, and Philadelphia, did follow the action of the Union navy, and their prints have been unfairly neglected. An excellent example of the little-celebrated achievement of the naval printmakers is the pair of lithographs of the inland naval war, *The Mississippi in Time of Peace* and *The Mississippi in Time of War* (figs. 55, 56). Currier and Ives copyrighted both images on March 16, 1865, about a month before Appomattox. These two large prints, carefully crafted by Frances Flora Bond "Fanny" Palmer, paid an unacknowledged debt to the greatest of America's river painters, George Caleb Bingham, whose *Jolly Flat Boat Men* surely inspired the figures atop the flatboat in Palmer's "peace" scene.[2]

Palmer must have looked upon her task primarily as a challenge of genre—how to capture the essence of the war on the rivers. She decided to make the prints symbolic of that warfare; she did not opt for scenes from a particular battle or location. Palmer turned for inspiration to Bingham's eyewitness views of the great river, for she lived in New York and Brooklyn after her 1844 immigration from England to America and never saw the Mississippi herself.[3]

In contrast with the sunrise of enterprise, commerce, and freewheeling activity on the river depicted in the "peace" print, the companion image featured the symbolic nighttime of war, with its fiery destruction of a paddle-wheel steamer, its half-sunken flatboat, and the dark hulk of a Union gunboat bringing retributive destruction to the ultimate symbol of the slaveocracy, the plantation house with its neoclassical columns (on shore at the viewer's left). In other words, the viewer beholds in *The Mississippi in Time of War* an ugly ironclad Union machine, the product of an advanced industrial economy, destroying the Southern plantation society. Together, the two prints conveyed a moral that secessionists were meant never to forget.

No patriotic publisher was eager to depict as an actual event the shelling of a helpless private dwelling by an ugly, bullying ironclad monster under an American flag. As an event, it might have qualified as an atrocity, not something to be celebrated in parlor images, but a scandal to be covered up or explained away. Palmer offered art more than commerce—or at least a more artistic sort of commerce than Currier and Ives's customary political and Civil War prints represented.[4]

Currier and Ives's achievement in these prints was substantially a product of tradition. Viewed without its title, *The Mississippi in Time of Peace* is simply a steamboating print. Mississippi River life and the lure of the steamboats came to be a staple of the Currier and Ives portfolio: the firm produced some thirty steamboating prints over the years. The first of these, also the work of Fanny Palmer (using as inspiration this time not George Caleb Bingham but H. D. Manning), called *A Midnight Race on the Mississippi*, was published on the eve of war in 1860. The commercial result must have proved happy for Currier and Ives, for the firm continued to publish Mississippi riverboating prints through the war and well after it, and that first steamboating print remains to this day among the most sought-after of Currier and Ives lithographs.

The Mississippi River provided both a readily recognizable landscape and victories for the Union navy, a change from the defeats of the Army of the Potomac in the first two years of the war. From the beginning, the Union inland river fleet proved a success story, combining innovation, engineering, and rapid production under nearly impossible deadlines. Once on the waters it seemed to sweep the rebel defenses out of its way. To follow the headlines down the rivers—and Currier and Ives always followed the headlines in the war—was to follow a steady string of Union victories.

Yet another tradition dictated Currier and Ives's attention to the works of the Union river fleet in the West: the subject of fire. Whereas *The Mississippi in Time of Peace* was basically a steamboating print, *The Mississippi in Time of War* was basically a disaster print, the sort of picture of a conflagration that originally made the Currier firm successful and famous. (A landmark of the firm's earliest fame was the *Awful Conflagration of the Steam Boat "Lexington" in Long Island Sound on Monday Eveg Jany. 13th 1840*, of which the many blazing Civil War ships decades later were direct descendants.)

An old hand at Currier and Ives, Palmer created many of the works that made the firm famous. Besides the pathbreaking steamboat print, she was responsible for such landmark lithographs as the hunting scene *Wild Duck Shooting*; one of the pioneering railroad prints, *American Express Train* (also produced during the Civil War); part of the nostalgic pastoral *Life in the Country* series (also of Civil War vintage); and, after the war, important images of westering America including *Across the Continent: Westward the Course of Empire Takes Its Way*.[5]

In her early fifties at the time of the war, Palmer had reached a peak of skill as a popular image maker when she executed the two Mississippi River scenes. She clearly had the overall artistic or decorative effect of her two works in mind when she approached the task, for the prints work best as a pair, hung side by side, with the mantle of moss-draped trees forming a proscenium curtain pulled aside to the left and right to offer the viewer the contrasting moral tableaus of American river life.[6]

Fanny Palmer barely missed becoming the most important popular image maker of the Civil War. She was strategically placed at the prolific Currier and Ives firm, she was at the height of her powers, and she was adaptable as an artist. But Fanny Palmer was reputedly never very accomplished in producing the human form in art. Ultimately, the Civil War proved to be decided by its land battles, and these, with their masses of heroic infantrymen, were apparently a closed book to Palmer.

Figure 55. Currier and Ives, after Frances Palmer, *The Mississippi in Time of Peace*. New York, 1865. Hand-colored lithograph, 18¼ × 27¾ inches. Because steamboats could go up and down river, they largely replaced flatboats in Mississippi River commerce, but Palmer nostalgically telescoped the technological eras on the river in this steamboating print, which alludes only indirectly to the Civil War in its title. Other steamboating prints, produced in peacetime, did not invoke the patriotic theme present here in the pictorial display of three United States flags. (*The Harry T. Peters Collection, Museum of the City of New York*)

But she did well with naval warfare, and it is a sign of the longtime neglect of women artists in the nineteenth century and of the tendency to stereotype warfare as a province of male interest alone that her achievement as a war artist has not heretofore been noticed.[7] Palmer produced a substantial part of Currier and Ives's creditable coverage of the naval war, particularly the war on the inland waterways. Thanks in part to Palmer, the firm's most solid achievement as a popular chronicler of the Civil War came in its thorough and vivid coverage of the war on inland waters. Its reporting was prompt—*Adm. Porter's Fleet Running the Rebel Blockade of the Mississippi at Vicksburg*, for example, was copyrighted on May 18, 1863, barely a month after the event it portrayed—and the naval images are generally of higher quality than the military ones, especially the small-folio military prints.[8]

One sign of the care taken by Currier and Ives in creating its naval prints is that the firm produced three depictions of the action at Island No. 10 (see fig. 57). Two were virtually identical, with minor changes in naval architecture made in the sec-

Figure 56. Currier and Ives, after Frances Palmer, *The Mississippi in Time of War*. New York, 1865. Hand-colored lithograph, 18¼ × 27¾ inches. Palmer completed her pair of prints by transforming her Mississippi steamboating image into a fire-disaster print—another popular genre in Currier and Ives images in peace or war. In doing so she created a mythic evocation of the conquering of the plantation regime by the naval machines of the United States. The river gunboat pictured resembles one of the vessels of the ironclad fleet rapidly built in Missouri at the beginning of the war that later dominated the rivers of the South (Paul H. Silverstone, *Warships of the Civil War Navies* [Annapolis, Md.: Naval Institute Press, 1989], 151–53). (*The Harry T. Peters Collection, Museum of the City of New York*)

ond version.[9] The prints nevertheless fell short of historical accuracy. They exaggerated the effectiveness of the mortar boats, which appeared to fire on the enemy from cover while the enemy could not fire back. Actually, the naval bombardment of Island No. 10 ultimately proved ineffective, and the mortar fire from the novel craft depicted along the shore was annoying without being destructive. Andrew Foote, who was commanding the river fleet, conducted the bombardment from too distant a range, having been made cautious by damaging fire directed at the Union gunboats at Fort Donelson earlier. Finally, a bold commander, Captain Henry Walke, ran the *Carondelet* past the Confederate batteries at night and essentially turned the rebel flank. With the protection of the *Carondelet* and another Union gunboat that ran the gauntlet later, Union infantry forces crossed the river and laid siege to the Confederate island.[10]

Testimony about the accuracy of one of Currier and Ives's Island No. 10 lithographs came from Captain Walke himself. As a naval artist too (his sketches had formed the basis of a famous Mexican War naval portfolio years earlier, and after the Civil War he illustrated David Dixon Porter's *Naval History of the Civil War*), Walke took natural interest in the pictures of actions in which he was a participant. An opinionated officer whose contentious memoirs were written to set the record straight about his accomplishments during the war, Walke commented acidly about one of the scenes:

Reporters, politicians, artists and lithographers were sometimes employed with much pains and expense, that they should magnify the actions of our fleet and the deeds of our warriors, pretty much in proportion to the personal influence or inducements offered. Some of the pictures, in particular, are good specimens of this artifice and humbug; among them being one purporting to represent this

Figure 57. Currier and Ives, *Bombardment and Capture of Island "Number Ten." / On the Mississippi River, April 7th 1862, by the Gunboat and Mortar Fleet under Command of Com. A. H. Foote . . . .* New York, 1862. Hand-colored lithograph, 16 × 22½ inches. As Captain Henry Walke bitterly pointed out, at the time of the fall of Island No. 10, the *Carondelet* and *Pittsburg* (shown in the print at left center) were twenty miles away, *below* the Confederate fortifications. These two gunboats and a landing force under General John Pope forced the surrender of the Confederates. (*The Harry T. Peters Collection, Museum of the City of New York*)

bombardment of Island No. 10, under which it surrendered on the 7th of April, 1862. The picture is intended as a complete bird's-eye view—twenty-two and a half inches by sixteen inches—in very brilliant colors, in which, however, the artists and artificers have, at great pains, succeeded in misrepresenting the so-called capture of the island; but no such scene, or anything like it, occurred there. Gunboats and mortars present are portrayed . . . as all firing at once; and all the gunboats, except the "Taylor" and "Lexington," are steaming rapidly down upon the island (which, by the way, has come up to meet them about two miles from its usual position, and is very considerably elongated), and all the Confederate batteries blazing away at a frightful rate. The picture is entitled—"Bombardment and capture of Island No. 10 on the Mississippi river, April 7th, 1862, by the gunboats and mortar fleet under command of Commodore Foote . . ."

In the construction of the picture the flag steamer "Benton," the most formidable gunboat, has the post of honor, of course. This picture is such a remarkable illustration of the above-mentioned works, that they all appear to have been designed by the same clique of artists. The true position of our gunboats on this occasion, in relation to each other, was nearly *the reverse* of this representation; the "Carondelet" and "Pittsburg" being then down the river, twenty miles below Island No. 10, and having, with our army, under General Pope, actually gained the victory twelve hours previous to the surrender of the island to Commodore Foote. But here these gunboats are placed prominently in the rear.[11]

We have never found any evidence that prints depicting the Union war effort were commissioned or influenced for the sake of heroic reputation, and such origins seem unlikely given their commercial source. Unlike most paintings, popular prints ordinarily originated with business firms attempting to maximize profits and not with patrons attempting to create image or prestige. Certainly, influencing image content in popular prints for the sake of personal reputation was not a common occurrence, as Walke might lead us to believe. Nevertheless, Walke's informed view of the Currier and Ives print of Island No. 10 provides rare insight into the inaccuracies perhaps inevitable in depicting combat scenes.

Though possibly accurate in criticizing details, Walke underestimated Currier and Ives's overall achievement. For one thing, the firm's prints helped assure and perpetuate the patriotic fame of the bombardment and capture of Island No. 10, an action otherwise likely to have been forgotten, coming in the wake of Grant's victory at Fort Donelson and being a small battle compared to the Battle of New Orleans, fought around the same time. The printmakers' depiction of the scenic bend in the river and of the peculiar river craft involved in the campaign was crucial to lending the action a distinct presence in American memory. Moreover, the general ability of the student of river campaigns to visualize the nature of the battles and sieges on inland waters owes much to these and other early river war prints.[12]

Currier and Ives's coverage of the naval war formed part of an established marine tradition at the firm, which had its headquarters only blocks from one of the busiest ports in the world. Its lithographers had been covering the exploits of the clipper ships with a series of now famous prints published in the early and mid-1850s. Currier and Ives capitalized on the epoch-making confrontation of the *Monitor* and *Virginia*, the headline-producing sinking of the *Alabama* by the *Kearsarge*, and other Civil War naval events. Yet these works did not capture the nature of the combat as well as the firm's river scenes did. The ocean offered no distinctive sense of place for the actions, and the wooden vessels, screw steamers for oceangoing warfare, offered little novelty and could barely be distinguished from earlier naval ships. The famous ironclads that fought at Hampton Roads did not lend themselves to representation in a visually striking print until Julian O. Davidson, a marine painter, tackled the difficult subject in the 1880s for chromolithographer Louis Prang.

The challenge of portraying the ironclads was obvious. When Hardin Littlepage, a midshipman on the Confederate ram *Virginia*, gazed out at the *Minnesota* and the rest of the Union's blockading vessels in Hampton Roads, Virginia, on the morning of March 9, 1862, he saw what he thought was the boiler from one of the wooden steamers sitting on a raft awaiting repair. That was in fact his first glimpse of the USS *Monitor*.[13]

The new ironclads were not picturesque. They may have fit a later era's hardened attitude toward products of industrialization. The 1891 print of *The First Encounter of Iron-Clads*, published by the Calvert Litho. Company of Detroit and issued as a premium by the McCormick Harvesting Machine Company, carried this caption: "This fight settled the fate of the 'Wooden Walls' of the world and taught all nations, that the Warship of the future must be like the McCormick Harvester-Machine of Steel."[14] The Civil War ships were clad in iron, not steel, but the point was otherwise correct.

Ultimately there was no avoiding the challenge, because nearly everyone knew immediately that the battle between the *Monitor* and the *Virginia* marked a milestone in naval history—"the inauguration of a new system of naval warfare," as one print caption put it.[15] It was the first combat between ironclad vessels. The *Monitor* saved the Union cause at sea, and its technological precocity gave America prestige abroad. It offered the world the first important American, as opposed to European, naval battle. Picturesque or ugly, this combat could not be ignored, and neither marine painters nor popular printmakers would neglect the subject. Far from it, for they poured forth a mass of images inspired by the combat at Hampton Roads.

In later years, scholars considerably reduced the significance of the battle, which had been exaggerated by proud Northerners. As historian James P. Baxter pointed out, over 100 ironclad ships were already under construction throughout the world by the time the *Monitor* and *Virginia* fought. Historian William N. Still has recently suggested that the battle offered symbols of the new era but did not bring the new era into being or notably influence naval construction elsewhere in the world afterward. Neither the Union nor the Confederate vessel, for all their ingenious qualities, offered a solution to the challenge of making heavy ironclads capable of steaming the oceans. They were virtually invulnerable to shot and shell, but they could not go to sea. They were best suited to harbor defense.[16]

Nevertheless, the country—and the world—took immediate notice of the battle, and Currier and Ives employed Fanny Palmer to capture the dramatic ironclad combat. She was credited as "artist" of the lithograph *Terrific Combat between the "Monitor" 2 Guns and "Merrimac" 10 Guns. / In Hampton Roads, March 9th 1862* (fig. 58), the firm's large-folio print of the historic encounter. A lengthy caption described the combat as "The First Fight between Iron Clad Ships of War . . . In which the little 'Monitor' whipped the 'Merrimac' and the whole 'School' of Rebel Steamers." Almost two-thirds of the image consisted of sky, pierced only by a plume of smoke, the Confederate flags on the *Merrimac*, and tiny masts and flags in the background. The unimaginative composition balanced the dueling ironclads in the foreground, flanked by wooden ships in the distance on either side of the print and by American flags to the left and right on the encompassing shorelines in the background. The best part of the print by far was the artfully drawn water. The Confederate vessel, much of it obscured by smoke, was crudely delineated, seamless and boltless, without much attention to detail; Palmer probably had few sources to aid her in sketching this heretofore secret weapon of the Confederacy. Had she had the benefit, as later artists did, of the article on the battle written by John Taylor Wood, a lieutenant on board the *Virginia*, she would have known, at least, that "both ends of the [*Virginia's*] shield were rounded."[17]

Currier and Ives exemplified an exaggerated patriotism, as one commentator has observed: after all, the *Virginia* was certainly not "crippled" (as the caption of the small-folio version of the print put it) and in fact sailed away to worry Union commanders for weeks to come; the ship was not "whipped" within any reasonable meaning of the word. The other Confederate vessels that sailed out with the *Virginia* were hardly imposing enough to call a "fleet" and were no match for the big Union vessels stationed at Hampton Roads.[18]

Currier and Ives devoted four prints to the battle itself and one to the preliminary combat of the *Virginia* the day before. Lee and Walker of Philadelphia quickly issued a sheet music cover for a "Monitor Grand March" (fig. 59). Other printmakers made contributions as well, even into the twentieth century (fig. 60). Ugly or not, the *Monitor*, the *Virginia*, and many other Civil War ironclads churned across the walls of American parlors. Such popular works of art perhaps implicitly welcomed and celebrated technology. The purchasers of prints may well have held less complicated attitudes toward technology than marine painters.

But only one print explicitly celebrated the technological feat of devising and producing these modern ironclad warships, a lithograph by Endicott and Company of New York entitled *The First Naval Conflict between Iron Clad Vessels. / In Hampton Roads, March 9th 1862* (fig. 61). The central image offered a composition familiar from Palmer's print, but the vignettes around the border of the battle image cele-

THE FIRST FIGHT BETWEEN IRON CLAD SHIPS OF WAR.

TERRIFIC COMBAT BETWEEN THE "MONITOR" 2 GUNS & "MERRIMAC" 10 GUNS.

IN HAMPTON ROADS, MARCH 9TH 1862.

In which the little "Monitor" whipped the "Merrimac" and the whole "School" of Rebel Steamers.

Figure 58. Currier and Ives, *The First Fight between Iron Clad Ships of War. / Terrific Combat between the "Monitor" 2 Guns and "Merrimac" 10 Guns. / In Hampton Roads, March 9th 1862. / In which the little "Monitor" whipped the "Merrimac" and the whole "School" of Rebel Steamers.* New York, 1862. Lithograph, 7⅝ × 12⅝ inches. Patriotic exaggeration characterized the caption of Currier and Ives's print, along with a David and Goliath conception of the contest. As the curators of the famous Beverley R. Robinson Collection of naval prints at Annapolis expressed it, the caption exaggerated "not only the results of the action but the Confederate strength." The Confederate ship was driven off and kept from sinking the wooden blockading fleet, but it was hardly "whipped," and the Union fleet present outgunned the "school" of rebel steamers 219 to 15. The *Merrimac* had a 3,200-ton burden compared to the *Monitor*'s 776; it was heavier largely because of the huge casemate holding the guns in broadside. Overall, of course, the David and Goliath proportions for the navies of the Union and Confederacy ran quite the other way: the Confederacy began the war with no navy, no shipyards, and few sailors. Its achievements, helping to revolutionize naval technology with ironclads and naval mines, were considerable. (*Currier and Ives Navy: Lithographs from the Beverley R. Robinson Collection* [Annapolis, Md.: U.S. Naval Academy Museum, 1983], 70; Silverstone, *Warships of the Civil War Navies*, 4, 202.) (*The Lincoln Museum*)

brated technological innovation. At the top was a portrait of John Ericsson, whose brainchild, more than any other single person's, the *Monitor* was. The inventor's image was balanced at the right by a depiction of a "Caloric Engine."

Ericsson, the inventor, became more famous than the man who actually commanded the vessel in battle, John Worden, whose portrait does not appear in any of the eleven vignettes around the border of the Endicott print. Thus technology, as Hawthorne gloomily predicted, definitely triumphed over heroism. Indeed, such

Plate 1. L[ouis]. Rosenthal, after William Winner, *Raising the Flag May 1861, / From the Original Picture by Winner.*
Published by Charles Desilver, Philadelphia, ca. 1864. Hand-colored engraving, 22½ × 26¾ inches. As Union troops march
toward the defense of the Capitol in the background and a knot of cheering sailors, led by drummer boys, emerges from
the right foreground, an exuberant group of young people—perhaps designed to represent the national future—raises a
huge American flag in salute to the "Defenders of the Union," to whom the print is dedicated. Symbolic storm clouds darken
the skies, but the Capitol remains in a radiant glow, the flag billows majestically, and the scene is suggestively framed by two
Clark Mills heroic bronze sculptures of the military heroes of earlier wars, Andrew Jackson (left) and George Washington
(center). The print is meant to assure viewers that the flag, the symbol of the Union, will be preserved for the next generation.
Engraver Rosenthal did make one error in the composition: in creating a scene that was meant to depict a rally the month
after the surrender of Fort Sumter, he included a Capitol dome that was not completed until three years later.
(*Library of Congress*)

THE DEFENDERS OF THE UNION.

Plate 2. Sarony, Major and Knapp. *The Defenders of the Union.* New York, 1861. Hand-colored lithograph, 17 × 25½ inches. The future and the past of the Union high command—George B. McClellan and Winfield Scott—sit on opposite sides of a council of war in this tribute to the early military heroes of the North. The younger general was not unaware of their sharply differing images. "It made me feel a little strangely last evening when I went in to the Presdt's with the old General leaning on me," he confided boastfully in August 1861, "the old veteran (Scott) & his young successor; I could see that many marked the contrast." Within a month, however, he was declaring Scott "the great obstacle . . . a *dotard* or a *traitor!* I can't tell which." McClellan would soon succeed him. (Stephen W. Sears, ed., *The Civil War Papers of George B. McClellan: Selected Correspondence, 1860–1865* [New York: Ticknor and Fields, 1989], 50, 79, 81.) Portrayed here, from left to right, are McClellan, Silas H. Stringham, Irvin McDowell, Franz Sigel, John E. Wool, John A. Dix, Nathaniel Banks, Samuel P. Heintzelman, Scott, Robert Anderson, John C. Frémont, and Benjamin F. Butler. This print was republished as a *carte-de-visite* photograph by M. Knoedler in 1862. (*Anne S. K. Brown Military Collection, Brown University*)

THE GUARD HOUSE.

Plate 3. L[ouis]. Prang and Company, after Winslow Homer. *The Guard House.*
Signed in stone, bottom, "WH." Boston, 1861. Chromolithograph, 4 × 2⅜ inches.
Soldiers convicted of drunkenness in camp are made to stand atop barrels, heavy logs
on their shoulders, as punishment for their crime. In 1863 Homer adapted this comic
print into a formal painting he called *Punishment for Intoxication*, focusing on the
bearded man with the feathered cap. (*The Metropolitan Museum of Art*)

Plate 4. Thomas Nast, untitled drawing in pencil, ink, and wash, ca. 1861–62. Nast preserved this model for a Civil War print—few of which survive from any painter or printmaker of the Civil War era—in his personal scrapbook. (*John Hay Library, Brown University*)

THE DOMESTIC BLOCKADE.

Plate 5. Currier and Ives, after a drawing by Thomas Nast, *The Domestic Blockade*. Signed, lower right, "Th. Nast 3/62." New York, 1862. Hand-colored lithograph, 24⅓ × 18⅓ inches. A servant wields a broom as a weapon in an attempt to regain her territory, the family kitchen, in this home-front lithograph based on Thomas Nast's rough sketch. To defend their newly acquired position, the determined-looking little boy and his amused sister have piled tubs, basins, baskets, and chairs into a fortification, aiming at potential invaders a row of empty bottles positioned to resemble field artillery. The Little Zouave of this lithograph, together with his flag-waving sister, symbolized the understandable mimicry of real war by children whose fathers had gone off to fight for the Union. The year after this print was published, artist Nast copyrighted a *carte-de-visite* copy of the lithograph, designed for family photograph albums. (*The Lincoln Museum*)

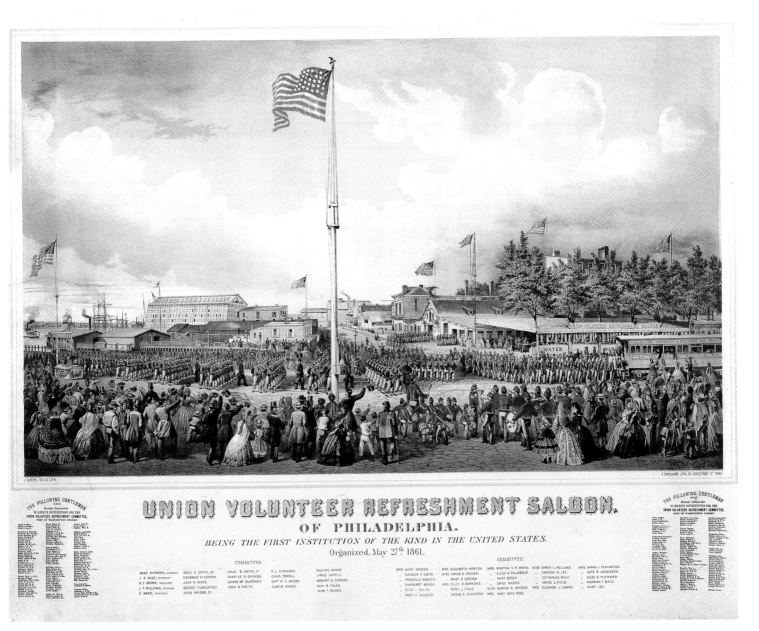

UNION VOLUNTEER REFRESHMENT SALOON.

OF PHILADELPHIA.

BEING THE FIRST INSTITUTION OF THE KIND IN THE UNITED STATES.

Organized, May 27th. 1861.

COMMITTEE.

ARAD BARROWS, CHAIRMAN	ISAAC B. SMITH, Sr.	ISAAC B. SMITH, Jr.	D. L. FLANAGAN.
J. B. WADE, SECRETARY	ERASMUS W. COOPER.	CHARLES B. GRIEVES.	CHRIS. POWELL.
B. S. BROWN, TREASURER	JOHN W. HICKS.	JAMES MC GLATHERY	CAPT W. S. MASON.
J. T. WILLIAMS, STEWARD	GEORGE FLOMERFELT	JOHN B. SMITH.	CURTIS MYERS.
E. WARD, PHYSICIAN	JOHN KRIDER, Sr.		

RICHARD SHARP.			
JAMES CARBELL			
ROBERT R. CORSON			
SAML B. FALES.			
JOHN T. WILSON.			

COMMITTEE.

MRS. MARY GROVER.	MRS. ELIZABETH HORTON	MRS. MARTHA V. R. WARD.	MISS SARAH L. HOLLAND.	MRS. SARAH J. PEMINGTON.
" MARIAH P. SMITH.	MISS ANNIE B. GROVER.	" ELIZA A. RELMBOLD	" AMANDA M. LEE.	" KATE B. ANDERSON.
" PRISCILLA GROVER	" MARY D. GROVER	" MARY GREEN.	" CATHARINE BAILY.	" ELIZA G. PLUMMER.
" MARGARET BOYER	MRS. ELLEN B. BARROWS.	" EMILY MASON	" ANNIE L. FIELD.	" HANNAH F. BAILY.
" ELIZA J. SMITH.	" MARY L. FIELD.	MISS MARTHA B. KRIDER	MRS. ELEANOR J. LOWRY.	" MARY LEE.
" MARY A. CASSEDY.	" ANNIE A. ELKINTON	MRS. MARY DAVIS WADE.		

Plate 6. J[ames]. Queen, *Union Volunteer Refreshment Saloon. / Of Philadelphia. / Being the First Institution of the Kind in the United States. / Organized May 27th. 1861.* Published by T. Sinclair, Philadelphia, 1861. Hand-colored lithograph, 16¼ × 26¾ inches. Printmaker Queen employed nearly a bird's-eye perspective to suggest the impressive numbers of Union soldiers who were welcomed and fed at Philadelphia's Refreshment Saloon in the spring of 1861. Gaily attired marching bands play in the foreground, and spectators cheer enthusiastically, as lines of soldiers file from the docks at left toward the troop trains at right that will take them south to the defense of Washington. The slant-roofed building just behind the train station is the Refreshment Saloon itself, which offered both food and drink (note the "water" sign visible at right). Over the next four years, the saloon—the forerunner of the USO canteens of World War II—served 600,000 meals and provided space for thousands of soldiers to write letters home. Lithographer Queen also created *Philadelphia Zouave Corps Passing Independence Hall*, a print of the city's Zouaves on their way to the war. (Alvin Robert Kantor and Marjorie Sered Kantor, *Sanitary Fairs: A Philatelic and Historical Study of Civil War Benevolence* [Glencoe, Ill.: SF Publishing, 1992], 144–245.) (*The Philadelphia Print Shop*)

Plate 7. L. Prang and Company, after Julian Oliver Davidson, *The "Monitor and Merrimac": The First Fight between Ironclads.* Boston, 1886. Chromolithograph, 15 × 22 inches. As carefully researched as any depiction of the historic naval battle at Hampton Roads, Davidson's image for the ambitious Prang series of Civil War chromos added drama by adopting a near waterline view of the famous vessels, abandoning the bird's-eye perspective more typical of popular prints (and adopted by Davidson himself for the model he produced for Prang's chromo of the Battle of Mobile Bay [see plate 8]). (*The Lincoln Museum*)

Plate 8. L. Prang and Company, after Julian Oliver Davidson, *Battle of Mobile Bay*. Boston, 1886. Chromolithograph, 15 × 22 inches. This well-researched chromo was issued with a detailed key to help viewers identify the nineteen vessels portrayed—and explain six more "concealed by smoke"—in its dramatic evocation of the celebrated battle of August 5, 1864. Comparison of the subtle coloration of the water with the more simplistic approach to depicting a river in Fanny Palmer's work (see figs. 55 and 56) suggests the higher artistic aspirations of Louis Prang's "war pictures" of land and sea battles. (*The Lincoln Museum*)

Arise Beloved Mother

Plate 9. Joseph E. Baker, *Arise Beloved Mother*. Published by J. H. Bufford, Boston, 1864. Lithograph, 14 × 25 inches. A uniformed George B. McClellan and his vice presidential running mate, George H. Pendleton, help lift Columbia, the symbol of American liberty, from the rubble of war in this rare campaign print. The Democratic nominee for president gestures toward the U.S. Capitol in the distance, before which a farmer plows his fields, suggesting the restoration of peace. The dead bodies at right are meant to demonstrate the terrible toll of the war from which McClellan will presumably rescue the country. Shackles are symbolically broken on Columbia's wrists, but there is no visual reference here to the emancipated slaves, whose freedom under a McClellan administration was not guaranteed. (*Photograph courtesy the David J. and Janice L. Frent Collection*)

Major General Grant

Plate 10. J[oseph]. E. Baker, *Major General Grant*. Signed, lower left, "J. E. Baker." Published by J. H. Bufford, Boston, 1863. Hand-colored lithograph, 20¼ × 17¼ inches. One of the earliest and most dramatic of all large-size print tributes to Ulysses S. Grant, this vivid lithograph portrayed the general as the quintessential aristocratic field commander, complete with plumed hat and saber, personally rallying his men against the enemy in the distance. Such heroic, but unlikely, portraiture antedated the later development of what historian John Y. Simon has called the "popular image of a man in a plain and rumpled uniform, chewing on a cigar, seated on a stump and whittling" (John Y. Simon, introduction to *U. S. Grant: The Man and the Image*, by James G. Barber [Washington, D.C.: National Portrait Gallery, 1985], 19). At Shiloh, Grant did make a dramatic appearance on the field on the second day of fighting. "I gathered up a couple of regiments," Grant recalled, ". . . formed them in line of battle, and marched them forward, going in front myself" (Ulysses S. Grant, *Personal Memoirs*, 2 vols. [New York: Charles W. Webster and Company, 1892], 1:350–51). The print celebrated Grant's capture of Vicksburg in July 1863; the huge explosion in the background likely represents the famous mine explosion at Vicksburg. But Grant captured that city by siege, not by assault led on horseback. (*Anne S. K. Brown Military Collection, Brown University*)

DONELSON, SHILOH,
VICKSBURG,
CHATTANOOGA

FAC-SIMILE OF THE CELEBRATED ANTROBUS PORTRAIT OF GENERAL U.S.GRANT PAINTED ON THE BATTLE FIELD OF CHATTANOOGA 1863-4.
A SOUVENIR OF THE GREAT PAST
RESPECTFULLY DEDICATED TO THE GRAND ARMY OF THE REPUBLIC

Plate 11. W. J. Morgan and Company, after John Antrobus, *Facsimile of the Celebrated Antrobus Painting of General Ulysses S. Grant Painted on the Battlefield of Chattanooga 1863–64.* Copyrighted by W. Steele, Cleveland, 1888. Chromolithograph, 30½ × 24 inches. Subtitled "a souvenir of the Great Past," this popular print adaptation of a canvas painted from life was "respectfully dedicated to the Grand Army of the Republic," the huge veterans' organization whose 400,000 members doubtless seemed a rich potential audience for such a chromo. Twenty-three years after the end of the Civil War, a decade after serving two terms as president of the United States, Grant remained in popular prints not a civilian magistrate, but a perpetually uniformed war hero. The *Chicago Tribune* had described the wartime portrait that inspired this print as "a great historical painting" (P. J. Staudenraus, *Mr. Lincoln's Washington: Selections from the Writings of Noah Brooks, Civil War Correspondent* [New York: Thomas Yoseloff, 1967], 289). (*Library of Congress*)

Plate 12. L. Prang and Company, after Thure de Thulstrup, *Battle of Atlanta* (also known as *Siege of Atlanta*). Boston, 1888. Chromolithograph, 15 × 22 inches. One of Prang's "aquarelle facsimile prints" of the Civil War, a justly famous series of chromos based on specially commissioned watercolors, this scene immortalized the moment when General William T. Sherman and his staff looked at the besieged city of Atlanta for the last time before beginning their fateful March to the Sea. (See figs. 117 and 118 for detail and photographic source.) "An unusual feeling of exhilaration seemed to pervade all minds," Sherman recalled—a quote reprinted in the printmaker's advertising brochure for the chromo. (*The Lincoln Museum*)

THE FALL OF RICHMOND, V.ª ON THE NIGHT OF APRIL 2.ᴰ 1865.

This strong hold the Capital City of the Confederacy, was evacuated by the Rebels in consequence of the defeat at 'Five Forks' of the Army of Northern Virginia under Lee, and capture of the South side Rail-Road by Gen.ˡ Grant._ Before abandoning the City, the Rebels set fire to it, destroying a vast amount of property; and the conflagration continued until it was subdued by the Union troops on the following morning.

Plate 13. Currier and Ives, *The Fall of Richmond, Va. on the Night of April 2nd 1865.* New York, 1865. Hand-colored lithograph, 16 × 22¼ inches. The Virginia State House, like a Greek temple, dominates the skyline in this justifiably famous print of the Confederate capital engulfed in flames. To the left is the spire of St. Paul's Church, where Jefferson Davis learned while attending services that he must abandon Richmond that day. The railroad bridge over which Davis escaped stands behind the Mayo Bridge in the foreground. Currier and Ives also issued a small-folio version of this large print, and then a revision with several alterations in the carriages and people fleeing across the bridge in the foreground. (*Library of Congress*)

APRIL 12 1864, UNION. (MAJ. BOOTH, (COM. COLORED T. 262 (MAJ. BRADFORD) W. T. 276 & CIV., 350 K₞, 60 W₞ & 164 MIS. .CONF. (GEN. FORREST.) 20 K₞ & 60 W₞. COPYRIGHTED 1892 BY KURZ & ALLISON. 76 & 78 WABASH AVE., CHICAGO

THE FORT PILLOW MASSACRE.

Plate 14. Kurz and Allison, *The Fort Pillow Massacre.* Chicago, 1892. Chromolithograph, 18 × 22 inches. Kurz and Allison's habit of printing casualty figures in the margins of their battle prints takes on special poignancy in this image, which depicts the massacre of African Americans by Confederate forces under General Nathan Bedford Forrest on April 12, 1864. Forrest's forces were said to have slaughtered black soldiers after they surrendered, but the vignettes here show his soldiers killing unarmed women as well. This is the only print in the series to feature the Confederate flag in the prominent center of the image—here consecrating the murderous behavior of Forrest's troops. (*The Lincoln Museum*)

Plate 15. L. Prang and Company, after Thure de Thulstrup, *Battle of Chattanooga*. Boston, 1886. Chromolithograph, 15 × 22 inches. Standing boldly against the horizon on Orchard Knob, General Ulysses S. Grant (left background, center of group) is flanked by Generals Gordon Granger (left) and George H. Thomas (right) as they watch the field where Union troops overrun Confederate defenses at the base of Missionary Ridge in Chattanooga, Tennessee, on November 25, 1863. Prang's advertising promotion for the chromo emphasized "the compact form of General Grant lifting his field glass to his eye" and "the heroic proportions of General Thomas, then newly christened the 'Rock of Chicamauga [*sic*]'" (*Text to Number Seven of Prang's War Pictures*, advertising brochures in the Thomas J. Watson Library, The Metropolitan Museum of Art, 8–9). Although an eastern printmaker, Prang included this western scene among the first of his eighteen war chromos. (*The Lincoln Museum*)

Plate 16. L. Prang and Company, after Thure de Thulstrup, *Sheridan's Ride.* Boston, 1886. Chromolithograph, 15 × 22 inches. Advertised as a depiction of "The Home Stretch" of General Philip H. Sheridan's celebrated ride from Winchester, Virginia, at the Battle of Cedar Creek on October 19, 1864, this was one of two chromos of the eighteen-print Prang series devoted to Sheridan's exploits in 1864, suggesting how high his reputation remained two decades after the war. But the print suffers from some errors of detail: the general waved no flag that day, only his own hat, on his inspiring gallop to rally his troops, and, bearded at the time, he did not much resemble the carefully mustachioed gentleman shown here. But at least one veteran of that exhilarating day complimented artist Thulstrup on his Sheridan compositions, telling him he had "attained an exceptional degree of realism" (*Text to Number Three of Prang's War Pictures*, 8, 19). (*Library of Congress*)

Plate 17. L. Prang and Company, after Thure de Thulstrup, *Battle of Allatoona Pass.* Boston, 1887. Chromolithograph, 15 × 22 inches. Confederate forces attack the vital Federal supply depot at Allatoona in northwestern Georgia, well behind Sherman's lines after the fall of Atlanta, but before his March to the Sea. From high atop Kennesaw Mountain on the clear morning of October 5, 1864, Sherman was able "to see the smoke of battle about Allatoona, and hear the faint reverberations of the cannon." He looked on in "painful suspense," he recalled, until he saw the smoke slowly clear and received word around 4 P.M. that the Union post had held its ground. An evangelical hymn writer of the time popularized the phrase "Hold the Fort" in a work allegedly based on Sherman's words to the Union commander. (William Tecumseh Sherman, *Memoirs* [1875; reprint, New York: Library of America, 1990], 2:147; *Text to Number Nine of Prang's War Pictures,* 30.) In this chromo, the dramatic story unfolds from the point of view not of the commanding general, but of the fighting men rising to Sherman's challenge and defending their position. At this moment, the small garrison leaps over breastworks, charges with bayonets and clubbed muskets, and drives the Confederates down the hill. (*The Lincoln Museum*)

Plate 18. [Printmaker unknown], *Freedom to the Slaves*. Lithograph, 9 × 11 inches. As a regiment of "colored troops" marches off to glory in the background, a white recruiter calls on newly emancipated slaves—shown here kneeling and half-clothed—to join the Union army in order to guarantee their freedom. In the right foreground, a white soldier removes shackles from a slave's arms, while another slave gathers a serpent, a frequently employed symbol of rebellion, in a discarded Confederate flag. Meanwhile, as the American flag waves proudly, blacks are shown in a future characterized by land tilling, public school attendance, and churches. Note the triad of American flags: the battle flag carried by departing troops at right, the flag flying over the peaceful school at left, and, crowning all, the flag at center around which blacks are asked to rally to win the war. (*William A. Gladstone Collection*)

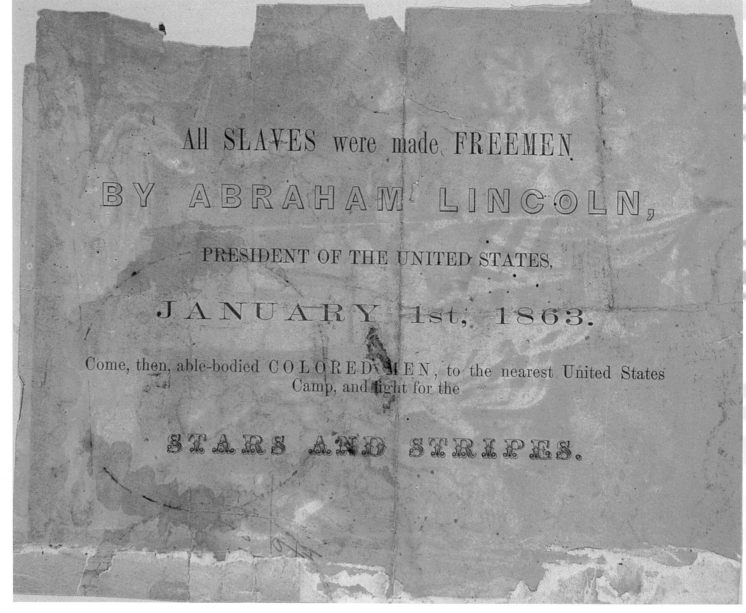

Plate 19. Message on the reverse side of the recruiting handbill, *Freedom to the Slaves* (plate 18). (*William A. Gladstone Collection*)

COME AND JOIN US BROTHERS.

PUBLISHED BY THE SUPERVISORY COMMITTEE FOR RECRUITING COLORED REGIMENTS
1210 CHESTNUT ST. PHILADELPHIA.

P. S. Duval & Son, Lith. Cor 5th & Minor St. Phil.

Plate 20. P[ierre]. S. Duval, *Come and Join Us Brothers.* Published by the Supervisory Committee for Recruiting Colored Regiments, Philadelphia, ca. 1863–65. Chromolithograph, 13¾ × 17⅞ inches. Eighteen determined African American soldiers, together with their own drummer boy, fix their stares at potential "colored" volunteers in this post-emancipation recruiting poster. The success of black troops in battle gave lie to the libel that they could not be trusted to bear arms. A second version of this print was retitled *United States Soldiers at Camp "William Penn" Philadelphia, Pa.* (*Chicago Historical Society*)

RGE of the 54 MASS.(COL'D) REG'T JULY 18 1863. UNION (GEN. GILLMORE, COM.) LOSS - GEN. STRONG, COL'S SHAW, CHATFIELD, PUTNAM KR GEN. SEYMORE W'D. 1200 331 KF & WY. CON'F. (FALL BEAUREGARD, COM.) LOSS: 14 OF'S. & 300 SOL.   COPYRIGHTED 1890 BY KURZ & ALLISON. ART PUBLISHERS, 76 & 78 WABASH AVE., CHIC

STORMING FORT WAGNER.

Plate 21. Kurz and Allison, *Storming Fort Wagner*, Chicago, 1890. Chromolithograph, 22 × 28 inches. The famous series of Kurz and Allison chromos devoted several titles to the experiences of black troops: the massacre at Fort Pillow, the Battle of Olustee, the Battle of Nashville, and this famous depiction of the martyrdom of the Fifty-fourth Massachusetts at Battery Wagner in South Carolina. In all the chromos the American flag figured prominently, crowning the bravery and sacrifice of black troops, just as the banner had once dominated prints suggesting defiance in the wake of the outbreak of rebellion. Such prints strongly suggested that patriotism was now a commodity to which both races could aspire. (*The Lincoln Museum*)

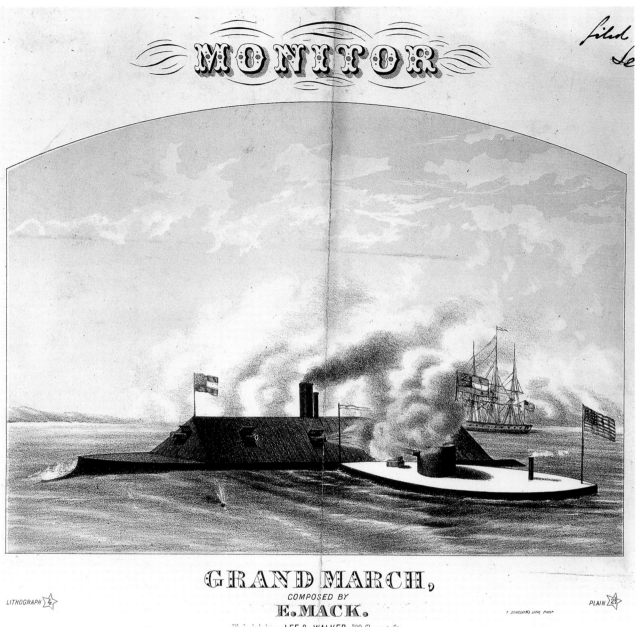

Figure 59. [Printmaker unknown], "Monitor Grand March." Composed by E. Mack. Lithographed sheet music cover, 7 × 9⅞ inches. Published by Lee and Walker, Philadelphia, 1862. The print owed a debt to the common source of Fanny Palmer's image for Currier and Ives and of Endicott's image of the battle, here reversed. The music, as the star system of pricing visible in the lower margins indicated, sold for a higher price with a lithographed cover. (*Library of Congress*)

an outlook continues to dominate our conception of the naval history of the Civil War. James McPherson's *Battle Cry of Freedom*, for example, devotes a page to Ericsson and calls him a "genius"; Worden's name is not mentioned anywhere in the book, though the battle at Hampton Roads is reported in detail. Describing a similarly important land action without mentioning the commander of the victorious side would be unlikely.[19]

Most prints merely reported the technologically significant Union naval victory,

LAST OF THE WOODEN NAVY.

BATTLE BETWEEN THE MERRIMAC (VIRGINIA) AND THE U.S. FLEET
IN HAMPTON ROADS, MARCH 8, 1862.

Figure 60. A. B. Graham Company, after W[illiam]. B. Matthews, *Last of the Wooden Navy. / Battle between the Merrimac (Virginia) and the U.S. Fleet / In Hampton Roads, March 8, 1862.* Photogravure, Washington, D.C., 1907. Nostalgia for the days of sail rather than patriotism was the purpose of this late-industrial-age print. It capitalized on the traditional image of the receding sailing vessel juxtaposed with the machine steaming ahead—toward the twentieth century. (*Special Collections, University of Georgia Libraries*)

but some, particularly those based on the works of marine painters, contained a note of nostalgia for the passing of the wooden ships. In these, the wooden ships recede toward the horizon as the ironclad steams forward. Among the best to employ this symbolic device were prints that appeared in the 1880s, and probably the best among those were the works of marine painter Julian O. Davidson. "The principal illustrations of the naval engagements published in the 'Century' war papers during the past two years are by Davidson," chromolithographer Louis Prang boasted about his favorite marine artist.[20]

Davidson's depiction of the Hampton Roads battle for the Prang series of Civil War chromolithographs (plate 7) added to technical skill in depicting maritime scenes considerable compositional power. The print's visual impact derives from its composition, essentially a black and white diagonal, with the villain of the piece, the *Virginia*, on the viewer's left, a dark hulk belching black smoke that obscures the light of day. The *Monitor*, on the right side of the image, occupies the light triangle, and its cannon fires with a cloud of virtuous white smoke.

Prang and Company issued six prints of naval engagements from the Civil War, half the number of its depictions of land battles. The firm published chromolithographs of the *Capture of New Orleans, Monitor & Merrimac, Battle of Mobile Bay, Kear-*

sarge & Alabama, Battle of Port Hudson, and *Capture of Fort Fisher.* The last named depicted sailors attacking a fort on shore, and the *Kearsarge* image showed action on deck.

If print purchasers read the company promotional literature, they found that the *Monitor* and *Virginia* image emphasized historical authenticity based on interviews with Ericsson, sailors, and witnesses. Historically accurate illustration was difficult in this instance, because both ships were destroyed not long after the battle, the *Virginia* blown up by the Confederates themselves to avoid capture and the unseaworthy *Monitor* sunk in a gale. For its part, the patriotically pro-Northern Prang company, without actually invoking biblical imagery, described the action in David and Goliath terms, with "the little Monitor" harrying the slower Confederate vessel, which looked like "some huge marine monster," with the thrust and parry strokes of a "duellist" or "gladiator." The brochure gleaned many of its facts from the article on the battle by Union turret gunnery officer S. Dana Greene that had appeared in the Battles and Leaders series in *Century* magazine. The brochure, unlike the print, described the unseen heroism of the sailors toiling in the engine room and manning the guns, but in the last sentence it celebrated "the little Monitor, this production of Ericsson's genius, which rendered useless the existing war-ships of Europe and America and revolutionized the building of navies forever." In sharp contrast to the practice in describing land battles in the Prang series, no mention was made in the brochure of the names of the commanders of the *Monitor* or the *Virginia.*[21]

J. O. Davidson employed diagonal composition for another successful print in the Prang series, *Battle of Mobile Bay* (plate 8). Altogether different in point of view, the Mobile Bay chromo employs a bird's-eye perspective, but Davidson put the Union fleet on one diagonal and the Confederate fleet, steaming out to intercept it, on another. He chose the dramatic moment in the action when the lead monitor *Tecumseh* struck a mine (called a "torpedo" during the Civil War) and quickly sank with most hands on board. The confusion following that harrowing event led to Admiral Farragut's famous exhortation: "Damn the torpedoes. Full speed ahead."

If Davidson served Prang well, so too did Prang serve Davidson. The billows of smoke from the cannon fire, the dingy clouds overhead, the different colors of the water in the bay and farther out at sea, and the red brick of the masonry walls of Fort Morgan all benefited from Prang's attention to color in the chromolithograph. Like the prints of land battles in the series, the naval prints owed much to a post-photographic view of art. In his depiction of the Battle of Fort Fisher, Davidson portrayed the assault by a naval landing party, taking a point of view roughly from behind the Confederate position. The most prominent feature of the print is a carefully delineated Armstrong cannon, a huge seacoast battery fixture capable of throwing a giant 150-pound projectile. There were two reasons for fixing his focus on the great cannon. First, the gun was a notorious import from Great Britain, and thus, like most American naval artists of the period, Davidson kept up an anti-British theme.

Figure 61. Endicott and Company, after Charles Parsons, *The First Naval Conflict between Iron Clad Vessels. / In Hampton Roads, March 9th 1862.* Copyrighted by S. A. Lotridge, New York, 1862. Lithograph, 13½ × 21 inches. Celebrating the inventor Ericsson and his technological innovations in the *Monitor*, rather than the prowess of the naval commander Worden and his crew, this print accurately captured the image of the battle that would thereafter dominate the literature of the Civil War. The David-Goliath proportions of the contest seem exaggerated by the rather diminutive *Monitor* depicted in the main image. Interior views of ships in popular prints were rare. (*The Old Print Shop, New York*)

Second, and more important, as the text accompanying the image stated, the Armstrong gun "was photographed as it stood in the traverse when captured."[22]

Where the ironclads were concerned, the printmakers readily celebrated technology and left heroism out of the picture. The historians often followed in their wake, but navy men naturally took a more balanced approach. The lively chapter on the battle at Hampton Roads in Admiral David Dixon Porter's *Naval History of the Civil War*, for example, included portrait illustrations of the commanders of the ironclads and discussions of their tactics in the battle. Porter made clear the importance of command in naval warfare by his patriotic assessment of the battle:

There is glory enough in this fact for the little "Monitor" without claiming more for her. She saved not only the squadron, but the honor of the nation, and her gallant commander is fully entitled to all the honors he received. Had he not been disabled at such an inopportune moment [Worden was blinded by a hit on the pilot house late in the action] he would, in our opinion, have compelled the

"Merrimac" to surrender; for the tide was ebbing and in another hour the "Merrimac" could not have maneuvered and would have grounded; the "Monitor" then could have taken position under the iron-clad's stern and knocked her frame in.[23]

The purely technical image of the Civil War navy came from Endicott and Company, the firm whose lithograph so successfully presented the technological view of the success of Ericsson's *Monitor*. The firm's two- and three-stone lithographs were among the finest naval prints of the Civil War. By the time George Endicott established a partnership with the New York lithographer Moses Swett in 1830, opening for business on Nassau and Spruce Streets, Endicott had already been in the print-publishing business a full two years, practically from the dawn of the lithographic art itself. By 1852 the firm was specializing in marine subjects.[24] Endicott's sons, William and Francis, now ran the business and advertised "Particular Attention Paid to the illustration of Steamboats, Steamships . . . &c."

Naturally, the Endicotts specialized in naval scenes during the Civil War. The greatest limitation on the firm's considerable skills stemmed from its chosen subject matter, for to depict the proudest achievements of the United States Navy and of the shipbuilding industry of New York was to focus on ironclad monitors. This development in marine architecture was covered well. At one point during the war, a new list of titles from the company featured "Fine Colored Prints, Published and for Sale by Endicott & Co., Lithographers in every Branch of the Art," all available "to be sent by Mail, securely Rolled and postage paid, on receipt of price." The offerings included thirty-eight 19-by-30-inch lithographs of "U.S. Monitors, at $1.50 each" and eight prints of "U.S. Iron Clads," from the *Agamenticus* to the *Tonawanda*, at two dollars each, as well as nine 20-by-33-inch prints of Union monitors—the *Canonicus, Mahopac, Oneota, Tecumseh, Tippecanoe, Saugus, Manhattan, Catawba,* and *Manayunk,* "in storm"—for two dollars each. The old navy figured in the offerings as well: twenty-nine "U.S. Gun-Boats," at one dollar for plain prints and two dollars for "extra colored" prints, and eight 2-by-3-foot "U.S. Screw Sloops, at $2.00 each." The long list of "Miscellaneous Prints" all boasted a naval theme, including prints of Russian and Italian frigates, the bombardment of Fort Fisher, ironclads being tossed in gales, the launching of a warship from the Continental Works, the battle between the *Monitor* and *Virginia* (now only fifty cents), and prints of steamboats, ferry boats, and steamships.[25]

As subjects of marine art, monitors proved trying. The original *Monitor*, which gave the class of vessels their generic designation, had only eighteen inches of freeboard—the distance between the upper deck and the waterline.[26] Sitting low in the water was a key to their combat success, for they offered no broadside target and much of their machinery was protected below the waterline; in rough waters, parts of the deck sat *below* the water. Above sea level, there was little else to depict except the cylindrical metal turret or turrets holding the vessels' modest broadsides of one or two guns. Monitors did not look very impressive in prints or in person. Admiral Porter described the original as looking "more like a large floating buoy than a man-of-war."[27]

Ocean-going monitors generally sported a tall smoke funnel that was removed in battle. Except for the smoothly cylindrical gun turret and the funnel, not always present, the artist was lucky to be presented a flag, a vent or two, a railing, or a pilot house above the waterline to offer some identifiable profile on these extremely low-silhouetted vessels.[28]

Endicott's waterline silhouette views of monitors were therefore starkly minimal in appearance. The printmakers also offered a depiction of storm-tossed monitors at sea. Such images—suggesting the ship of state in troubled waters—were most appropriate to Civil War marine art. But monitors, however fearsome they might have been in combat, lacked dramatic presence as representations of the mighty ship of state. Their decks awash in the stormy seas and their low profiles failing to thrust above the horizon line of the pictures, the monitors tended to play second fiddle to the sea itself. Besides, seaworthiness was the monitors' key problem, and such prints suggested their vulnerability rather than their invincibility. After December 31, 1862, they served as reminders of how the original *Monitor* was lost—in rough seas.

There can be no doubt about what audience the firm aimed to attract with such depictions: the crews of the very ships and the veterans of the naval war themselves. A letter written to an unknown Union naval officer two days after the surrender at Appomattox reveals the marketing strategy. The company gamely renewed an apparently unfruitful effort to sell a "Chromo Lithograph of the Bombardment of Fort Fisher." Obviously concerned about their stock of war prints illustrating a war now apparently over, the firm offered inducements to the potential purchasers who had once sailed the seas: "We send you a sample copy by to days mail and as your vessel occupies quite a prominent place in it we think the officers and crew would like to have some copies[.] If you will make out a list of those who want them and send the money to us with the addresses to which the copies are to be sent we will allow you an extra copy for every five names you obtain and will send them safely post paid by the following mail."[29]

Most naval prints suffer from one deficiency that military prints also share: they were best at rendering vivid impressions of great events of the war—a battle, a siege, a dramatic moment in a naval action—but they could not accurately depict a campaign. In the case of naval history even more than military history, this inadequacy led to the failure to report what was by most accounts the navy's greatest contribution to the victory of the North: the blockade.

There appears to be but one popular print depicting any episode of the naval blockade of the Confederate coast. The American lithographers' neglect of the blockade constitutes nothing less than a failure of imagination caused by the commercial motives of the print publishing industry. Battles and other dramatic events made headlines; the blockade generally did not. It was simply there, each day, patiently growing tighter. The printmakers had no patience themselves: they had achieved commercial success as illustrators of headline-making news, and they apparently scanned the newspapers of the day for inspiration.

The naval printmakers also failed to democratize their subject matter. Focusing on the common soldier eventually became one of the greatest achievements of the military prints, but the naval ones never did so.[30] Only two prints depicted combat on the deck of a naval vessel. Technology triumphed in the naval images, rather than human valor.

Printmakers devoted only a few portrait prints to naval commanders—most notably Admiral Farragut—though nothing in proportion to their achievements. One exception, however, is a masterpiece of Civil War art: the untitled engraved adaptation of William Heysham Overend's great Civil War painting, *An August Morning with Farragut: The Battle of Mobile Bay, August 5, 1864* (fig. 62), arguably the best naval painting inspired by the war. The print version was first published in London in September 1884 by the Fine Art Society and copyrighted by Max Jacoby and Company.

Overend chose to depict sailors in combat, something rarely done. He also democratized naval art by putting the focus on the common sailors, who are accurately depicted, from the unique reality of integrated service (black and white enlisted men served together only in the navy, not in the army) to portrait likenesses of the *Hartford*'s crew. The depictions of Farragut and the other officers on the poop deck were portrait likenesses, copied from or based on photographs, some of them made in New Orleans where the *Hartford* docked for a time after the Battle of Mobile Bay. Thus Lieutenant Commander John G. Watson stands with a pistol ready to shoot any Confederate marine who might draw a bead on Farragut, who watches the battle in exposed position from the rigging of the *Hartford*. What is unusual are the portrait likenesses of the common sailors: Overend copied the helmsmen's likenesses from a photograph taken in New Orleans, and Joseph Tessier and John McFarland thus stand at the wheel in as scrupulous portraiture as Watson and the admiral himself.[31]

Overend's artistic genius impelled him to choose to depict combat between a wooden ship and an ironclad—the Confederate ram *Tennessee*—in a battle won by the wooden vessel (with the help of the rest of Farragut's fleet, which included ironclad monitors, as J. O. Davidson's depiction of the battle for Prang revealed). In the painting and in the print based on it, heroism thus triumphed over the machine; had Overend included other ironclads, the painting would have been but another image marking the passing of the wooden ships. Instead, the Union sailors stare down the monster bravely, and only one shrinks from the task. The drama of struggle between brave and sweating men of flesh and blood, on the one hand, and the gray and inhuman machine, on the other, was the stuff of myth in a society coping with industrialization and the rapidly expanding factory system.

As this print, with its aging admiral and its aging wooden warship, demonstrated, the nineteenth century did not unanimously embrace the intrusion of the machine

Figure 62. Max Jacoby and Company, after William Heysham Overend, for the Fine Art Society, [*An August Morning with Farragut: The Battle of Mobile Bay, August 5, 1864*]. London, 1884. Within the traditional organizational design of military sociology, with the flag and officers at the top of a pyramid and common enlisted men at the bottom, artist Overend created perhaps the most influential naval image of the Civil War. The late-industrial-era image depicts heroic men locked in life-and-death struggle with a faceless machine. Only one sailor cringes from the contest. (*Library of Congress*)

age on the battlefield. When a Confederate innovation, the sea mine (or "torpedo"), was used, it was widely condemned by Union sailors as a cowardly and inhuman form of warfare. In his official report after the battle, the captain and commanding officer of the *Brooklyn*, James Alden, referred to the sinking of the *Tecumseh* by one of these torpedoes as "assassination in its worst form." After the Battle of Mobile Bay, Farragut, writing in the third person, congratulated his men "for their gallant conduct during the fight of yesterday. It has never been his good fortune to see men do their duty with more courage and cheerfulness, for although they knew that the enemy was prepared with all devilish means for our destruction, and though they witnessed the almost instantaneous annihilation of our gallant companions in the *Tecumseh*, by a torpedo, . . . still there were no evidences of hesitation in following their commander in chief through the line of torpedoes and obstructions." The notable word in Farragut's commendation was "devilish." Farragut wrote feelingly of the terrors of the new naval combat. In a report on the battle he commented on the nerve-racking nature of fighting against inhuman machines: "Regular discipline will bring men to any amount of endurance, but there is a natural fear of hidden dangers, particularly when so awfully destructive of human life as the torpedo, which requires more than discipline to overcome."[32]

Admiral Farragut, although regarded by most authorities as the greatest naval figure of the war on either side, was a traditional sailor. He did not much like ironclads and rarely said anything glowing about them. In his after-battle report on Mobile Bay he mentioned the shaping of part of the action by "our ironclads, from their slow speed and bad steering." When asked to report on ironclads later for Secretary of the Navy Gideon Welles, he wrote grudgingly, "The monitors are no doubt most valuable vessels in smooth water, and ironclads are indispensable so long as our enemies have them." Off the record, he made his preference for the antique wooden ships plainer. "Why, if a shell strikes the side of the *Hartford*," he said, "it goes clean through unless somebody happens to be directly in the path, there is no damage, excepting a couple of easily plugged holes. But when a shell makes its way into one of those 'damned teakettles' it can't get out again. It sputters around inside doing all kinds of mischief." The admiral put his money where his mouth was: he made a wooden ship, not an ironclad monitor, his flagship.[33]

Farragut might be called a naval fundamentalist who believed more in heroism than in machines. He lectured the secretary of the navy on the point in November 1864: "Permit me to say that I think the world is sadly mistaken when it supposes that battles are won by this or that kind of vessel. . . . The best gun and the best vessel should certainly be chosen, but the victory three times out of four depends on those who fight them."

Like most Civil War officers of high rank, Farragut could not in good conscience recognize the dictates of the "modern style of command," as historian John Keegan terms it. He felt obligated to expose himself to the same dangers the common sailors faced. Thus he hung out over the *Tennessee* from his perch in the rigging at Mobile Bay, exposing himself to danger so great that common sailors rushed to tie him to the rigging and Watson drew his pistol, to try to protect him from marine sharpshooters. In his official report to the Navy Department, Farragut explained his reluctant decision to let the *Brooklyn* lead the way into the Confederate harbor instead of his flagship, the *Hartford*:

It was only at the urgent request of the captains and commanding officers that I yielded to the *Brooklyn* being the leading ship of the line, as she had four chase guns and an ingenious arrangement for picking up torpedoes, and because, in their judgment, the flagship ought not to be too much exposed. This I believe to be an error, for apart from the fact that exposure is one of the penalties of rank in the Navy, it will always be the aim of the enemy to destroy the flagship.

"Exposure is one of the penalties of rank" was the credo of courage of the Civil War officer on land or sea. It risked needless death, but it was rewarded by some print-makers, who, like the press of the day, recognized "that bluff, persistent, daring recklessness . . . makes the hero."[34]

In his own mind, Farragut the traditionalist soon transformed the victory at Mobile Bay into a triumph over the bullying and insidious new naval architecture. Note this passage from his reply to the secretary of the navy's letter commending him for the victory. The secretary had bitterly criticized the commander of the Confederate ram *Tennessee*, Admiral Franklin Buchanan, a former U.S. naval officer who had chosen to go with the South in the war. Farragut replied:

> [Buchanan], though a rebel and a traitor to the Government that had raised and educated him, had always been considered one of its ablest officers, and no one knew him better or appreciated his capacity more highly than myself, and, I may add, felt more proud of overcoming him in such a contest, if for no other reason than to prove to the world that ramming and sinking a helpless frigate at her anchor is a very different affair from ramming steamers when handled by officers of good capacity.

What the great victory at Mobile Bay boiled down to in this analysis was ultimate revenge for the sinking of the frigate *Congress* by the cowardly ironclad monster *Virginia*—and proof that officers could best technology. Of course, a realistically unheroic view of the sinking of the *Congress* was voiced by Professor James Russell Soley of the United States Naval Academy after the war: "Nothing shows more clearly the persistence of old traditions than the presence of these helpless vessels in so dangerous a neighborhood." The old wooden sailing ships, Soley commented, were "of no value for modern warfare."[35]

When it comes to depictions of the men who served under the officers, the record is deplorably bare aside from Overend's masterful effort. This seems odd, for it would have proved simple and economical for Currier and Ives to adapt one of its batch of sentimental genre prints from the 1840s—*The Sailor's Return* or *The Sailor's Adieu*—to Civil War times by adding a smoke funnel to the vessel depicted in the background and perhaps updating the sailor's uniform a bit. That was never done, nor did Currier and Ives or other printmakers come up with depictions of the shipboard life of common sailors of the Civil War. They remained—in prints—the most unsung of heroes.[36]

Slow and Steady Wins the Race

The 1864 Presidential Campaign in the Graphic Arts

Recalling the first Lincoln campaign for the presidency in 1860, the great New York photographer Mathew Brady, who was as skillful at self-promotion as he was at posing his subjects, boasted that the famous portrait he made of Lincoln on the day he delivered his Cooper Union address in New York had proven nothing less than "the means of his election" that year. The witness who reported this observation, himself a painter and thus similarly inclined to emphasize the prestige of images, agreed: "The effect of such influences, though silent, is powerful."[1]

The quote has often been cited to emphasize the role photography played in the 1860 race, indeed, the increasingly important place all photographs held in political campaigns beginning in the mid-nineteenth century. But what Brady conveniently ignored when he lavished credit on his own medium was that engraved and lithographed adaptations of that photograph, not the original itself, had played the biggest role in the 1860 campaign. By the year of Lincoln's election, print portraits had long since achieved a status in the American home analogous to that of religious icons of old, occupying honored places in family parlors in an age in which politics was respected and political heroes revered. And because photographs themselves could not yet be reproduced for newspapers, popular prints still held sway as the pictorial objects of mass distribution in election campaigns.[2]

Unfortunately, because the influence of pictures was, as the artist said, "silent," we cannot always infer the convictions attached to the images. Political prints did not cater to the sophisticate. An anecdote told in a speech in New York in 1862 provides a cautionary tale. The speaker, a refugee Presbyterian minister from Mississippi given prominence on the platform to reveal the cruelties of the Confederates toward their Unionist dissenters and to show that Southern Unionists wanted slavery abolished as much as Northern antislavery crusaders did, held bitter memories of his treatment at the hands of poor white Mississippians. He related this story to make his point about them:

Let me tell you that the slaves are more intelligent than the poor whites in the South. Why I went into a house not three months ago, and there was a lady belonging to this class of sand-hillers, and I remarked by way of passing the time, that there was a picture of the Presidents. "Yes," said she; "them's the Picters of the Presidents, and some of 'em must be gittin' mighty old by this time, if they ain't dead." [Prolonged laughter] I remarked, in addition, that that one at the head was Gen. Washington. "Yes," said she, "I've heern of him ever since I was a gal; I wonder if he's dead yet."[3]

Unlike Washington, Lincoln was all but unknown when he first ran for president, and printmakers deserve considerable credit for introducing his hitherto unknown appearance to educated and ill-informed Americans alike in 1860. They produced an extraordinary array of images, both favorable and unfavorable: portraits, cartoons, and posters that helped define his early image as the honest railsplitter and flatboatman whose rise personified the American dream. One would have expected a similar flurry of graphic images to emanate from the election that took place four years later—a virtual referendum, as Lincoln might have put it, on "the momentous issue of civil war." But on one level, such was not the case.[4]

It is perplexing that the pictorial record of the 1864 race seems at first glance so much sparser than that of 1860. The 1864 race was, after all, crucial. No nation gripped by rebellion had ever scheduled a democratic election. But Lincoln insisted that the will of the people, "constitutionally expressed, is the ultimate law for all," adding: "If they should deliberately resolve to have immediate peace even at the loss of their country, and their liberty, I know not the power or the right to resist them. It is their own business, and they must do as they please." The election, Lincoln believed, was a "necessity." As he expressed it, with evident relief, once the voters had reelected him, "We can not have free government without elections; and if the rebellion could force us to forego, or postpone a national election, it might fairly claim to have already conquered and ruined us."[5]

Political parties ignored any constraints that civil war might impose on politics and ran the usual, boisterous political campaign familiar at election season in America, and in America only, from 1840 on. Torch-lit parades, fireworks, pig roasts, marching bands, floats, and glee clubs did their customary partisan duty, and with the usual result: enormous numbers of voters turned out in most states, more even than cast ballots in the phenomenal election of 1860. Such campaigns always inspired badges, banners, and buttons—and 1864 was no exception—but why did the 1864 campaign seem to inspire fewer pictures than the campaign of four years before?[6]

For one thing, the faces of Abraham Lincoln and his Democratic challenger, General George B. McClellan, were familiar by 1864, reducing demand for the kind of straightforward portraits that had been needed to introduce Lincoln and his rival candidates, Stephen A. Douglas, John C. Breckinridge, and John Bell, four years earlier. Yet Lincoln prints from 1860 showed him without whiskers, and McClellan's image to date was decidedly military. There were compelling reasons to offer revised versions of both likenesses.

Nor had war brought a hushed tone or particularly respectful attitude toward either President Lincoln or General McClellan in 1864. Any glance at the scurrilous abuse common in speeches and newspapers that year surely dashes that notion—and the printmakers would go on to produce many irreverent cartoons as well. It is possible that threat of censorship or arrest, under conditions of wartime security, inhibited antigovernment image makers from venting their wrath pictorially against the president, but the abuse that made it into print despite the precarious state of press freedom lends little support to such speculation. Prints had been performing yeoman service introducing the military heroes of the day to the American public; why had the printmakers somehow chosen to eschew the traditional political purpose of their images?

The relative dearth of 1864 campaign prints may have been attributable in part to growing competition from photography. By 1864 thousands of *cartes-de-visite* photographs of Lincoln had been produced, sold, and preserved in "family" albums, and there was little reason to remain unaware of the appearance of the country's bearded leader. There was no shortage of McClellan photographic portraits in the public domain, either. Well before he was nominated by the Democrats in August, McClellan was one of the most frequently photographed celebrities in America. And like Lincoln, he had also become familiar to patrons of engravings and lithographs, in the general's case through both portraits and battle scenes.[7]

There were other factors at work inhibiting the production of prints bearing captions that defined their subjects as "candidates." Freshly analyzed, these factors do more than explain the absence of campaign prints; they suggest instead that there were more campaign prints than have previously been acknowledged. Many have simply gone undesignated as such. Some of the newsworthy battle prints that celebrated Union triumphs that election year—for example, the engravings and lithographs of the capture of Atlanta and the sinking of the CSS *Alabama* by the USS *Kearsarge* off the coast of Cherbourg, France—cheered voters in the Union at moments of deep public dissatisfaction with the war effort.

The victory of the *Kearsarge* in particular provoked "great rejoicing throughout the country" when news of its June 19 triumph reached the North. Secretary of the Navy Gideon Welles, who astutely observed in his diary that such victories tended to have "a party-political influence . . . not gratifying to the opponents of the administration," thought the sinking of the *Alabama* particularly heartening to the North. As he put it at the time, it was "universally and justly conceded a triumph over England as well as the Rebels." The capture of Atlanta on September 1 similarly inspired Currier and Ives, E. B. and E. C. Kellogg, and other printmakers to issue celebratory depictions of that highly significant event. The only surprise is that this timely Federal success did not generate even more. (The fight in distant Cherbourg

opposite

Figure 63.
L. Lipman,
*Emancipation
Proclamation.*
Published by
Martin and Judson,
Madison, Wisconsin,
1864. Lithographed
broadside, 26¾ ×
20¾ inches.
Although Lincoln
composed the
document in
the formulaic
language of official
proclamation-
making, laced
throughout with
pettifogging legalese,
America's print-
makers at first
reverently rendered
his words in a sort of
copperplate script.
The decorative
border vignettes
contrasted the harsh
life of slavery with
the life of freedom to
come. The slavery
vignettes came
straight from the
abolitionist lexicon
of horrors: frequent
application of the
cat-o-nine-tails
(making no excep-
tion of women),
families separated
by slave auctions,
and the rigors of
herding along the
interstate slave trail.
By contrast, these
Yankee lithographers
imagined a peaceful
post-emancipation
life of Franklinesque
savings of earnings,
cheerful school days,
and a cozy domestic
life. (*The Lincoln
Museum*)

was depicted more often than the fight in crucial Georgia. One Union Party ballot ticket issued in California featured a blue-tinted wood engraving of that faraway naval engagement.)[8]

There was no shortage of more overtly political printmaking. Many print tributes to the single greatest act of Lincoln's presidency, the Emancipation Proclamation, appeared in 1864 The proclamation was one of the achievements, after all, on which Lincoln based his campaign for reelection. According to bibliographer Charles Eberstadt, who in 1950 located fifty-two separate printings of the document (many elaborately illustrated), seven editions were published in 1862, seventeen in 1863, and seventeen more in 1864. The motivation seems clear: 1862 was the year Lincoln issued the preliminary proclamation; 1863 was the newsworthy "year of ju-bilee" when the final proclamation took effect; and 1864 was a presidential election year, which likely explains the continued healthy output (fig. 63).[9]

The abundance of these tributes undoubtedly served to limit the need for other Lincoln campaign prints. More to the point, they *were* campaign prints, for by 1864 emancipation was not only news, it had become an issue. It was surely difficult for printmakers to create symbols of emancipation that did not include a depiction of the people being freed, but because of pervasive white racism, blacks could not often be subjects for commercially viable popular prints designed for white audi-ences. Thus the earliest prints noting the advent of the historic proclamation relied mainly on attractive renderings of the actual text of the document.

The crucial place the Emancipation Proclamation held in that bitterly disputed election campaign was evident as well in the message of an 1863 lithographed car-toon entitled *Breaking that Backbone*, in which the rebellion was symbolized by a fanged, hideous beast with an arched back. The cartoon suggested that General Henry W. Halleck could not break the backbone of rebellion with "skill," Secretary of War Edwin M. Stanton could not break it with the "draft," and McClellan could not break it with "strategy." All were shown wielding Lincolnesque railsplitter's mauls, which proved unequal to the task. Only the old Railsplitter himself carried a tool capable of breaking the backbone of the Confederacy—an axe labeled "Eman-cipation Proclamation." As Lincoln confides to his secretary of war, "I'm afraid this axe of mine is the only thing that will fetch him." Many printmakers obviously thought that he was right.[10]

The 1864 election prints have never been systematically counted or closely stud-ied. They appear to have been nearly as plentiful as the prints of four years earlier, and sometimes more vicious: personal, mean-spirited, cruel, race-baiting, and divi-sive. A full year before Lincoln was assassinated at the hands of John Wilkes Booth, he suffered character assassination at the hands of America's engravers and lithog-raphers. But so did McClellan.

Because printmakers have left us almost no business records and their products were largely greeted without formal reviews in literature or the press—and even without much notice by the very people pictured in the prints—it is rarely possible

to describe the number produced or sold. The variety of images may give an illusion of the quantity of images produced for a campaign; it is ultimately impossible to tell. It is quite possible that the variety of images prompted by the unprecedented four-way race for the White House in 1860 gives the illusion of greater quantity.

To be sure, the 1864 campaign inspired some straightforward campaign banners as well. The Currier and Ives lithography firm covered the race with party-blind commercial zeal, publishing a *Grand National Democratic Banner* (fig. 64) that was almost indistinguishable from its *Grand National Union Banner for 1864* (fig. 65) and was similar as well to the *Grand Banner of the Radical Democracy* (fig. 66), published for John C. Frémont's brief third-party candidacy. Currier and Ives had created a boilerplate design for which party standard-bearers could be lithographed to order.

An early historian of the 1864 campaign suggested that whenever Lincoln was assailed that year by unflattering pictures, "the Republican Party answered promptly with the aid of Currier & Ives." But there is no evidence to suggest that the Republicans assisted printmakers in conjuring up rebuttals, or that Currier and Ives conspired with Lincoln's party to respond to pictorial attacks. Political images in the 1860s were created from the bottom up—invented and supplied by artists and their publishers, then sold to interested customers—and not from the candidates and officeholders down, as most campaign-generated graphics are created today. For Currier and Ives, like other Northern printmakers, the 1864 campaign invited commercial opportunity, not political commitment. Far from favoring Republicans, Currier and Ives subtitled one of its 1864 prints of McClellan "the people's choice for Seventeenth President of the United States."[11]

Somehow the publishers moved in step with the politicians. Whereas, for instance, Lincoln's candidacy had inspired illustrated sheet music covers during the "hurrah" campaign of 1860, his face seems to have decorated none at all in the more issues-oriented campaign of 1864. His opponent, on the other hand, was portrayed on the cover of a flattering "McClellan Schottisch[e]." But the sheet music, published by Ehrgott, Forbriger and Company of Cincinnati, was the only example located for this book.

At least as often as in 1860, however, the 1864 race inspired separate-sheet display cartoons: thought-provoking, witty, but often cruel lampoons that struck hard at the most divisive political and personal issues of 1864. In these cartoons one can see illustrated vividly the raw toughness of the campaign as well as the skill of the artists who covered it. Political caricatures were included in—but not confined to—illustrated weekly newspapers, to be glanced at briefly and then discarded when the next edition came off the press; such cartoons appeared almost exclusively in the larger metropolitan weeklies of New York and Boston. Lithographers also published election-season cartoons as separate-sheet display prints to be circulated in bulk by political activists across the country. Unfortunately, no evidence has yet come to light to illuminate the mystery of precisely how and where these cartoon

PUBLISHED BY CURRIER & IVES,   Entered according to act of Congress, in the year 1864, by Currier & Ives, in the Clerk's Office of the District Court of the United States, for the Southern District of N.Y.   152 NASSAU ST, NEW YORK

GRAND NATIONAL DEMOCRATIC BANNER.

PEACE! UNION! AND VICTORY!

TEMPLE OF LIBERTY.

ABRAHAM LINCOLN.

ANDREW JOHNSON.

PUBLISHED BY CURRIER & IVES,   Entered according to Act of Congress in the year 1864 by Currier & Ives, in the Clerks Office of the District Court of the United States, for the Southern District of N.Y.   152 NASSAU ST NEW YORK.

GRAND, NATIONAL UNION BANNER FOR 1864.

LIBERTY, UNION AND VICTORY.

prints were used. Surely they were not the stuff for family parlors—imagine Winfield Scott "waiting for a movement" in a Victorian parlor! But they may have decorated Union League clubs, Democratic clubs, and partisan newspaper offices. At least we know that political cartoons were advertised in the newspapers for bulk sale throughout the North.

The military man now running on a peace platform made for one obvious target; rarer was the Democratic view of McClellan as maligned war hero. In the only known such print (fig. 67), he was depicted as a modern version of the Roman commander Belisarius. Belisarius had triumphed in battle, only to be sent into later action by Emperor Justinian without proper support (McClellan believed that Lincoln had similarly undercut him during the Peninsula Campaign) and ultimately replaced by an inferior commander (just as Lincoln had replaced McClellan with John Pope). In case viewers of the day did not know enough ancient history to get the idea, the McClellan figure explains: "After the First Battle of Bull Run, I reorganized your shattered forces. After the second, I saved your menaced Capitol. I sit by the wayside waiting for justice from the people. Shall I have it?"

In most campaign cartoons, justice was denied George B. McClellan. Printmakers, like pamphleteers, typically preferred exhuming and dissecting McClellan's military record until they had reduced him in print to a coward and drunkard. Thus McClellan's campaign failed spectacularly. The point of nominating what we now call "Eisenhower candidates"—popular military heroes as presidential standard-bearers—was to take the focus off divisive issues and bask in military glory. In McClellan's case, the strategy backfired and his military record became a major issue in and of itself.

A few years earlier, the ambitious "Young Napoleon" had proudly posed in the photographer's studio armed with binoculars, the "weapon" required of modern major generals compelled by the scale of Civil War engagements to scan huge, panoramic battlefields to direct troops. Now printmakers could employ a variation on the seemingly innocuous prop to revive the old rumors that McClellan had retreated to a safe gunboat during the 1862 Battle of Malvern Hill (fig. 68), content

---

opposite
Figure 65. Currier and Ives, *Grand National Union Banner for 1864. / Liberty, Union and Victory*. New York, 1864. Lithograph, 12½ × 8¾ inches. For the renamed Republican Party of 1864's presidential election campaign, Currier and Ives offered companion portraits of the Lincoln-Johnson "National Union" ticket. This time the archaic symbolism—a farmer plowing a field—was exhumed directly from a print that the same firm had issued to portray Martin Van Buren and Charles Francis Adams in its *Grand Democratic Free Soil Banner* for the campaign of 1848. Even then it might have been considered outdated: the man-and-plow image was last important in 1840, when Whig supporters of William Henry Harrison, a former general, invoked the Cincinnatus image of the military hero returned to his farm. The only difference between Currier and Ives's 1848 print and this 1864 version, aside from the replacement of candidates' portraits, was the substitution for an olive branch held in the eagle's mouth in the original with a small streamer that resembled a serpent. (Bernard F. Reilly Jr., *American Political Prints, 1766–1876: Catalog of the Collections in the Library of Congress* [Boston: G. K. Hall, 1991], 280–81.) (*The Lincoln Museum*)

GEN! JOHN C. FREMONT.
FOR PRESIDENT.

GEN! JOHN COCHRANE,
FOR VICE PRESIDENT.

PUBLISHED BY CURRIER & IVES.   Entered according to act of Congress, in the year 1864, by Currier & Ives, in the Clerk's Office of the District Court of the United States for the Southern District of New York.   152 NASSAU S! NEW YORK

GRAND BANNER OF THE RADICAL DEMOCRACY,
FOR 1864.

THE MODERN BELISARIUS.

McClellan.—AFTER THE FIRST BATTLE OF BULL RUN, I RE-ORGANIZED YOUR SHATTERED FORCES; AFTER THE SECOND, I SAVED YOUR MENACED CAPITOL: I SIT BY THE WAYSIDE WAITING FOR JUSTICE FROM THE PEOPLE. SHALL I HAVE IT?

Figure 67. [Printmaker unknown], *The Modern Belisarius*, 1864. Wood engraving, 10½ × 15 inches. The unknown artist of this print managed to create an affecting image of McClellan as the modern analog of the Roman general Belisarius, who repeatedly saved his country only to have its jealous sovereign thrust him aside afterward. The mixture of melancholy and determination in this portrait seems appropriate, but the artist may have erred, from a purely visual standpoint, in depicting the general "sitting by the wayside," in the words he used in the caption, since a reputation for inaction dogged McClellan, and he might have benefited from more energetic poses in the sympathetic prints issued during the presidential campaign. (*The Lincoln Museum*)

opposite
Figure 66. Currier and Ives, *Grand Banner of the Radical Democracy, / For 1864*. New York, 1864. Lithograph, 12½ × 8¾ inches. The rarest of the 1864 Currier and Ives campaign posters, this example featured John C. Frémont and John Cochrane, candidates who withdrew from the race in September. The artists seem to have been struck symbolically dumb in representing this ticket and invoked no images at all in the flag-festooned field below the portraits save for the rather obliquely suggested cornucopias that support the roundel portraits of the candidates. Above, the traditional American eagle, this time carrying a stars-and-stripes shield, emerges from darkened clouds, suggesting that the Frémont-Cochrane ticket offered bright hopes for the Union's emergence from the storm clouds of war. (*Library of Congress*)

to observe the action through field glasses while his troops fell on the distant shore. In the caption to this Currier and Ives print, McClellan was the discredited "gunboat candidate" for president, substituting telescope for sword to his eternal shame and disgrace.

An anonymous printmaker made McClellan's battlefield performance appear even more reprehensible. *Head Quarters at Harrison's Landing / "See evidence before Committee on conduct of the War"* portrayed the general lounging on the deck of a gunboat. Armed only with a glass of champagne, his sword lying useless at his side, he appeared indifferent to the battle raging on the shore. Currier and Ives drove the same point home with a stinging comparison to McClellan's eventual successor, Ulysses S. Grant, in *The Old Bull Dog on the Right Track* (see fig. 87). In this cartoon, Lincoln tells "Little Mac" he is confident that General Grant will be quite capable of finishing off the pack of curs "that chased you aboard the gunboat two years ago." "Little Mac" was made in such prints to look very little indeed.

But Currier and Ives assailed both candidates, confident of finding buyers from both political parties. *The True Issue or "Thats Whats the Matter"* (fig. 69), for example, showed Lincoln and Jefferson Davis tearing apart a symbolic map of the United States, Lincoln insisting, "No peace without abolition," and Davis, "No peace without separation." Here McClellan emerged as the hero, restraining each sectional president while nobly insisting: "The Union must be preserved at all hazards!" At least one Boston printmaker, J. H. Bufford, suggested in *Arise Beloved Mother* (plate 9) that the George B. McClellan–George H. Pendleton ticket represented the only path to the restoration of peace.

Most lithographed cartoons that year were harsher. By and large, they fell into three distinct categories: criticisms of McClellan's war record, comparisons between the Republican and Democratic platforms (usually presented in two separate images, side by side, on a single sheet), and attacks on alleged Republican beliefs in race-mixing.

The novelty of a military man—in the printmakers' usual view, a uniformed general—preaching peace proved all but irresistible to cartoonists, particularly once opponents digested the Democratic platform, which resolved "that immediate efforts be made for a cessation of hostilities, with a view of an ultimate convention of the States, or other peaceable means, to the end that, at the earliest practicable moment, peace may be restored" on the basis of a Federal Union of the States. McClellan attempted to retreat from this resolution with his letter accepting the nomination, which stated: "I . . . could not look in the face of my gallant comrades of the Army & Navy, who have survived so many bloody battles, and tell them . . . that we had abandoned that Union for which we had so often periled our lives."[12]

But his opponents fought hard to keep McClellan tied to the peace plank, and printmakers fed off the issue imaginatively, making ramshackle wooden platforms a key emblem of their cartoons, lambasting McClellan for using his acceptance letter to have it both ways on the peace issue, or creating dual-image prints that compared

Lincoln and the Republican platform to McClellan and that of the Democrats. A typical lithograph, *Little Mac's Double Feat of Equitation*, published in Providence, Rhode Island, portrayed him as a circus acrobat literally stretched to the limit atop two horses representing the divergent views of the Chicago platform and the Chicago nominee's letter of acceptance. The image of the straddling acrobat was

THE GUNBOAT CANDIDATE
AT THE BATTLE OF MALVERN HILL.

Figure 68. Currier and Ives, *The Gunboat Candidate / At the Battle of Malvern Hill.* New York, 1864. Lithograph, 10⅙ × 13¼ inches. Republicans repeatedly charged McClellan with physical cowardice. The usual assertion was that he had remained aboard the gunboat *Galena* while his army fought the Battle of Malvern Hill, Virginia, in 1862. In fact, McClellan had set out on the *Galena* before the battle began to inspect a possible fallback position for his army, which he thought exhausted. The seeming defeatism of the gunboat trip, combined with the risk he took in leaving his troops exposed to attack in his absence, led partisan journalists and other enemies to criticize the general bitterly. Here, in a cartoon probably drawn by Currier and Ives artist Louis Maurer, the story was transformed into one illustrating physical cowardice. McClellan perches on a saddle (he had achieved earlier fame for inventing a saddle that bore his name) balanced on the ship's boom, peering at the action with a telescope. As the battle rages, McClellan can only declare: "Fight on my brave Soldiers and push the enemy to the wall, from this spanker boom your beloved general looks down upon you." (Stephen W. Sears, *George B. McClellan: The Young Napoleon* [New York: Ticknor and Fields, 1988], 220–21; Stephen W. Sears, ed., *The Civil War Papers of George B. McClellan: Selected Correspondence, 1860–1865* [New York: Ticknor and Fields, 1989], 568.) (*Library of Congress*)

echoed in New York printmaker T. W. Strong's *Little Mac, in his Great Two Horse Act, In the Presidential Canvass of 1864*, showing McClellan split between war and peace, as Lincoln reminds his opponent: "You tried to ride them two hosses on the Peninsula for two years Mac but it wouldn't work." Looking on forlornly was a caricatured Irishman. Lithographed cartoons featured such figures to frighten Americans away from the Democrats as the party of Catholics and immigrants, and now they took on an image of threatening brutality because of the prominent role played by Irish laborers in the horrifying New York City draft riots of the previous year. As a result of

Figure 69. Currier and Ives, *The True Issue or "Thats Whats the Matter."* New York, 1864. Lithograph, 10½ × 12¾ inches. Though senior partner Nathaniel Currier was "a Republican in politics," according to his obituary, his presses routinely published both pro- and anti-Lincoln cartoons; printmaking firms were businesses and not political organizations (*New York Times*, November 22, 1888). This simple and effective pro-McClellan cartoon captured the "true issue" for some Americans: preservation of the Union. The common Democratic view was that Republican insistence on emancipation kept the Confederates resisting, but the anonymous cartoonist here took a view that the extremist leaders on both sides, Lincoln (left) and his Confederate counterpart, Jefferson Davis (right), perpetuated the war with their unreasonable political demands and thereby threatened the survival of the Union. Davis's tattered trouser legs had by 1864 become a standard symbol of the economic inefficiency of the Southern slave economy. The haste with which cartoons were prepared for political campaigns is apparent here in the poor proofreading: the artist misspelled "Pennsylvaina" and "Minasota," and the latter contained a reversed "N." (*The Lincoln Museum*)

the draft riots, Irishmen became as familiar a staple of anti-Democratic campaign prints in 1864 as blacks had been in the anti-Republican prints of 1860.[13]

Slow and Steady / Wins the Race (fig. 70) was yet another variation on the "straddling two horses at once" theme, showing Lincoln astride a noble "Union Roadster" and waving an American flag whose pole is surmounted by a liberty cap, symbolizing the emancipation of slaves. McClellan, meanwhile, was shown balanced precariously between mounts—one labeled "Brag and Bluster," the other, a jackass, identified as "Fawn and Cringe"—both being whipped on by the "Ohio Clown," running

Figure 70. [Printmaker Unknown], *Slow and Steady / Wins the Race*, 1864. Lithograph, 12 × 18¼ inches. Of all the hasty works of America's commercial lithographers, probably none bore the telltale marks of rushing to market more than political cartoons. Their artists were not faced with the daily or weekly deadlines confronting the modern newspaper cartoonist, but they nonetheless had to work quickly to capitalize on the rather brief season of interest in the presidential campaign, for after election day their prints surely became worthless. Though this print bears evidence of such haste—the egregious proofreading error of dropping an "n" in the caption, "The Uion Roadster"—it also boasts compelling, if occasionally bizarre, imagery. The figure of Lincoln (looking almost nothing like the original) rides to victory with a liberty cap on his flagpole. McClellan straddles a "Brag and Bluster" war horse and a "Fawn and Cringe" "Peace Donkey," which bucks under the weight of the rebel war debt. A jester identified as the "Ohio Clown," perhaps meant to be McClellan's running mate, Ohioan George H. Pendleton, whips the "ugly beast" forward. Lincoln comments on an old joke he heard out West, and McClellan declares he has seen "many a Clown ride two horses that never saw West-Point." Less explainable is the Jewish immigrant in the carriage in the right background, who observes the horse race and concludes: "By mine Faders Abraham, Isaac, and Jacob, I peleif de Old Abe will win!" (*Lilly Library, Indiana University*)

mate George Pendleton, who carries a banner pleading: "Peace, Peace, Anything for Peace."

A favorite artistic weapon in the printmakers' arsenal was the Democratic platform itself, which was invariably depicted literally—as a pile of rotten wood pieced together to make a rickety platform. Currier and Ives's print, *The Chicago Platform and Candidate* (fig. 71), portrayed McClellan as two-faced. He tells peace Democrats, represented by a stereotypical Irishman, that he stands firmly on the peace plank, but he urges a soldier to refer instead to his acceptance letter. As for the flimsy-looking platform, it is feebly supported by an unholy quartet: antiwar New York City mayor Fernando Wood, Clement L. Vallandigham, Jefferson Davis, and a figure identified as "Jeff's Friend"—Satan himself. Currier and Ives's *"Your Plan and Mine"* (fig. 72) showed a McClellan prepared to sell free blacks back into slavery, while Lincoln endorses the use of African American troops to put the national bayonet to traitor Jefferson Davis.

Printmakers produced such comparisons unrelentingly, frequently using the two-panel cartoon to suggest the virtues of one candidate and the vices of the other. In *Democracy* by Louis Prang of Boston, this took the form of a reference to an earlier Democrat and general, Andrew Jackson, who had fought against disunion treachery by John C. Calhoun in the nullification crisis; thirty years later his party's nominee, McClellan, abandons the Democracy's once-stalwart Unionism and cringes atop his controversial platform, olive branch in hand, ready to make peace at any price with Jefferson Davis. As printmaker M. W. Siebert of New York saw it in *Union and Liberty! and Union and Slavery* (fig. 73), the race had come down to a choice between free labor under Lincoln and slavery under McClellan, in collaboration with Davis.

Emerging in many of these 1864 cartoons was a new symbolic formula. In 1860 the cartoonists had perfected an essential anti-Lincoln image featuring such props as a log rail, the lurking figure of publisher Horace Greeley, and an African American. Together they symbolized Lincoln's popular nickname ("The Railsplitter"), the allegedly lunatic reform impulse of the Republican Party, and the purportedly dangerous social threat that lay behind it, racial equality. No such symbolic formula had been developed for Lincoln's three opponents that year. But in 1864 the cartoonists could concentrate on only two men in opposition, and they developed a similar visual vocabulary of denunciation for the Democrats.

The most important innovation was an analog to the threatening black man, which the cartoonists found in the Irish American. As readily recognizable physically as the African American because of years of English anti-Irish caricature, the Irishman grew in symbolic power from the mere dupe of the Democratic bosses, led to the polls and colonized in close electoral districts, to a great and violent social threat after the New York City draft riots of 1863. From that emerged the image of a brutal and slow-witted Democratic thug.[14]

Cartoonists inserted the new figure to good effect but never brought all their

Figure 71. Currier and Ives, *The Chicago Platform and Candidate.* New York, 1864. Lithograph, 11 × 15¾ inches. Probably drawn by Louis Maurer, this print prominently featured the most recent entry into the cartoonists' lexicon of ethnic stereotyping, the simian Irish voter (right). A legacy of the previous summer's draft riots in New York City, and of the pro-Republican pictorial coverage of them in *Harper's Weekly*, the Irish Democrat was now depicted as a brutish and violent bigot. Here he wields a club as he vows to vote for McClellan if he stands firm for "killing the Nagurs." The two-faced candidate—one eye on his racist supporter, the other on a Union veteran he attempts to woo with his letter of acceptance criticizing the party's peace plank—is about to collapse through the rotting boards of the Democratic platform. This print was copyrighted on October 3, 1864, giving it about a month of circulation among Lincoln supporters before election day. (*The Lincoln Museum*)

anti-McClellan symbols together in one simple and powerful image. The rickety planks of the 1864 Democratic platform emerged as successors to the ubiquitous log rails visible in so many 1860 anti-Lincoln cartoons, and Jefferson Davis and Clement Laird Vallandigham were used to represent the political lunatic fringe in much the same way Greeley had been used in the 1860 cartoons. In the end, the short campaign season of 1864 may have snuffed out the creative impulses emerging in the anti-McClellan cartoons. The late August nomination seems to have left too little time for the images to develop fully.

The emergence of the two-panel lithographic cartoon in 1864 marked the ad-

Figure 72. Currier and Ives, *"Your Plan and Mine."* New York, 1864. Lithograph, 8¾ × 12¾ inches. In a particularly brutal attack on the Democratic platform and candidate, George B. McClellan is shown proffering an olive branch to Jefferson Davis as they conspire in the bloody subjugation of an African American who has already fought for his country. Lincoln, by contrast, is shown forcing on a beaten Davis "unconditional submission to the government and laws." To the old stereotype of Davis as the Southern planters' leader, with his tattered trouser legs (symbolizing the economic inefficiency of the slave system) and Bowie knife (symbolizing the violence on which the slave system ultimately rested), Currier and Ives's artist added an image rather new in 1864: a sympathetic African American (far right). Amidst the fierce brandishing of knives and bayonets, the cartoon also carried an unusually forgiving message in Lincoln's word balloon—"The great and magnanimous Nation that I represent have no desire for revenge upon you," he declares to Davis. Hanging Jeff Davis from a sour apple tree was the more customary message delivered at this level of political discourse. This print was copyrighted on September 28, 1864. (*Library of Congress*)

vent of a sharply issue-oriented campaign. The heavy black line down the middle of each such cartoon stands to this day as a sign and symbol of the irreconcilable platforms of the Republican (Union) Party and the Democrats in that historic canvass. The two parties were never clearer about drawing a line between themselves. The format had not been a feature of the cartoons of 1860, with four presidential candidates to contend with, nor of previous elections with only two.

McClellan escaped one likely criticism from the cartoonists. Generals running for president were vulnerable to depiction as potential dictators, but Republicans had long since settled on a different strategy for opposing McClellan, and cartoon-

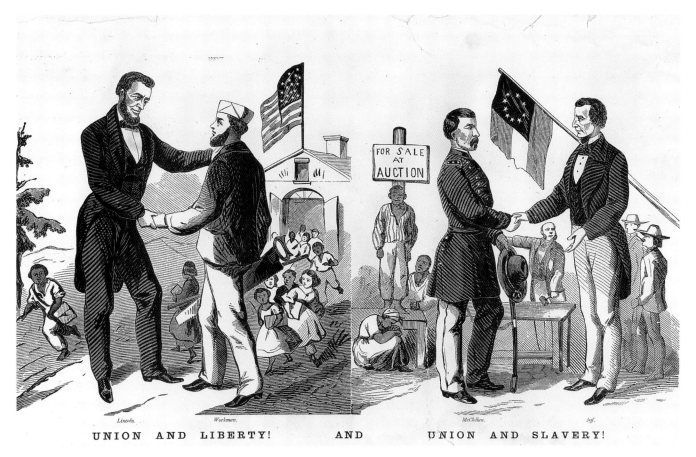

UNION AND LIBERTY!   AND   UNION AND SLAVERY!

Figure 73. [Artist unknown], *Union and Liberty! and Union and Slavery!* Published by M. W. Siebert, New York, 1864. Wood engraving, 10⅝ × 20¼ inches. Embodying a rare appeal to working-class voters, the anonymous artist of this engraving, in one of the two-panel, good-and-bad cartoons common in this election, held up a vision of racial harmony in the nation's schools. Jefferson Davis and George B. McClellan shake hands on perpetuating slavery, with its auctioning of human beings and separation of husband and wife by sale (note the weeping slave wife in the center foreground). Lincoln, by contrast, shakes hands with the common laborer carrying a carpenter's saw, as black and white children dance merrily out of a school-house. For all its apparent good intentions, the print may well have offended potential Lincoln supporters who believed that their candidate favored emancipation but not necessarily racial equality, a notion Lincoln himself did little to alter. (*The Abraham Lincoln Museum, Lincoln Memorial University*)

ists would follow their lead. They portrayed McClellan as cowardly and lacking in forcefulness, with none of the "By the Eternal, I take the responsibility" independence of that earlier general, Andrew Jackson. McClellan might be depicted as a political acrobat riding two horses, balancing his own pro-war beliefs against the platform's peace plank, but he would never be depicted as a tyrannical man on horseback. The Republicans were bent on giving the general a cowardly and weak image incompatible with a Caesar, and printmakers sensed this and provided its illustration.

Thus the shovel rather than the saber came to figure prominently in anti-McClellan cartoons. One such print (fig. 74) showed him trying to reach the White House by digging. Columbia, hovering above a graveyard of visible skeletons, declares: "I once entrusted my fate to you but you betrayed me; you tampered with my foe; you allowed, for his benefit, these my Children to die. . . . You shall rise no more to any position to do me harm; you shall dig your own grave and be forgotten forever!" As usual, such images were rooted to some degree in actual experience. In the Peninsula Campaign of the summer of 1862, McClellan had besieged Yorktown, digging elaborate trenches before the Confederate fortifications, only to have the greatly outnumbered enemy slip away one night. His approach to Richmond was thus delayed by a month, time perhaps crucial for the preparation of the defenses of the Confederate capital.

As much as any single figure, New York journalist George Wilkes transformed the Yorktown siege from military event to political symbol. The editor of *Wilkes' Spirit of the Times*, a "sporting" (horse-racing) newspaper, Wilkes switched from McClellan supporter to McClellan hater. He followed the Republican criticism of McClellan in Congress, where Senator Benjamin F. Wade accused the general of being for "digging and not for fighting." In a widely circulated editorial of August 4, 1862, published again in 1863 as part of a pamphlet called *McClellan: From Ball's Bluff to Antietam*, Wilkes wrote of the Yorktown campaign: "Instead of taking the meagre city by assault, and giving the North and East an opportunity to square accounts of glory with the West, his bloodless strategy was again put in play, and he distributed the shovel instead of drawing forth the sword." After the Seven Days' battles, too, Wilkes alleged, McClellan would "relinquish the musket for the spade." Wilkes then jeered at the young general's bombastic dispatch after the campaign, in which he asked, "May I be permitted to allow my troops to inscribe YORKTOWN on their banners, as other generals have done?"[15]

A year later these anecdotes resurfaced in bruisingly cruel Republican stump speeches in the presidential election campaign. Senator Wade, for example, spoke in New York at Mozart Hall in late October, reviewing McClellan's entire military career. There is not a hint of the man on horseback in this oration. Instead, there was only the coward and traitor (Wade repeatedly used the very words). Of the Yorktown campaign, the senator declared: "The rebels knew how rapidly the Yankees would fall before the miasma of the swamps, and were glad to let them dig in quiet."[16]

Senator Wade knew the theme well, for he had helped to develop it more than a year earlier when the Republicans were building their case against the likely Democratic nominee. As a member of the Joint Committee on the Conduct of the War, the Ohio senator had watched McClellan avoid an answer to the question of whether he had sat safely at the rear on a gunboat while his troops fought the Battle of Malvern Hill miles away on shore. McClellan told the hostile congressional committee that he could not remember.[17]

Only when events heated up for the campaign of 1864 did McClellan explain the gunboat story to Democrat Reverdy Johnson of Maryland:

It is entirely untrue that I was on a gun boat during the battle of Malvern Hill. In the morning, after having arranged the lines of battle & made every preparation I went on a gun boat with Capt Rodgers to do what I did not wish to trust anyone

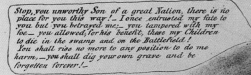

Stop, you unworthy Son of a great Nation, there is no place for you this way!— I once entrusted my fate to you but you betrayed me;— you tampered with my foe— you allowed, for his benefit, these my Children to die in the swamp and on the Battlefield! You shall rise no more to any position to do me harm,— you shall dig your own grave and be forgotten forever!—

LITTLE MAC TRYING TO DIG HIS WAY TO THE WHITE HOUSE BUT IS FRIGHTENED BY SPIRITUAL MANIFESTATIONS.—

Figure 74. [Printmaker unknown], *Little Mac Trying to Dig His Way to the White House / But Is Frightened by Spiritual Manifestations,* ca. 1864. Lithograph, 10½ × 15 inches. A traditional cartoon situation—a candidate trying to tunnel his way to the White House—became especially appropriate in McClellan's case when the shovel replaced the saber as a symbol of his military leadership. Note once again the general's body leaning away from challenge. McClellan's notorious affinity for digging trenches to win battles leads him to attempt tunneling under the White House, looming in the shadows at right, but on his way he uncovers the grotesque skeletal remains of battlefield casualties. The figure of Liberty, brandishing a sword, appears to denounce McClellan as an "unworthy Son of a great Nation." (*The Lincoln Museum*)

else—i.e. examine the final position to which the Army was to fall back. I returned immediately and was with Genl Porter near the left of the line before the enemy made his first attack, nor did I leave the land during the continuance of the battle. You will find the whole story in my report. I can conscientiously say that during the whole Seven Days my personal movements were made in accordance solely with my sense of duty—that I went wherever I thought my presence as the Comdr was of most benefit to my Army.[18]

But it was too late for explanations. The damage was done, and it was as great as that caused by Lincoln's sneaking into Washington incognito in 1861 or asking for a tune to be sung on a battlefield in 1862.

Wade flogged McClellan mercilessly. Apparently picking up on Wilkes's account of Yorktown, the Ohio senator thundered that McClellan "begged the privilege of inscribing 'Yorktown' upon the banners of our brave soldiers! Great God! These soldiers would have scorned to disgrace themselves by any such description." More withering scorn followed in the account of Malvern Hill. "A general," Wade told the cheering and jeering crowd at Mozart Hall, "who was not a coward, would have now led his soldiers and triumphed with them or died in his tracks. Our forces concentrated at Malvern Hill. Gen. McClellan simply rode along the lines of the army half an hour before the battle commenced, and then withdrew with his staff on board a gunboat. . . . There he was, on a gunboat, amidst his wine and cigars, giving no attention to the operations in the field."[19]

The Democrats should have anticipated and answered the gunboat charge more forcefully. Modern readers should not overlook an important phenomenon at work here: the Republicans proved eager to subject McClellan's war record to scrutiny and spent much of the campaign doing so, supplying in speeches like Wade's a sort of anti–campaign biography. Customarily, with military-hero candidates, the general's own party loved to dwell on the heroic record from military history—Harrison at Tippecanoe, for example, or Jackson at New Orleans—while ignoring the substantive issues in the canvass. Such would not be the case in McClellan's campaign.

The treatment of McClellan in the election campaign points to the source of the heroic ideal that doomed many Civil War generals to risk death unnecessarily. Politicians demanded that the generals triumph literally at the head of their troops or, as Wade put it, "die in their tracks." But, as Keegan has shown, modern warfare required that commanders stay in the rear, coordinating the movements of huge armies over vast terrain. Printmakers had helped create the image of McClellan personally leading his troops, and now they would help erase it. The politicians and cartoonists did little to preserve the lives of the common soldiers, either, when they branded the shovel a coward's tool.[20]

The campaign of lithographed cartoons heated up in earnest in late September. According to the incomplete regional copyright records, most of Currier and Ives's campaign caricatures were issued in the fall, because the Democrats did not hold their convention and nominate McClellan until late August. *Your Plan and Mine*, the comparison of the two platforms, was registered on September 28. The two-faced McClellan of *The Chicago Platform* was registered on October 3, a lithograph depicting McClellan and Pendleton as the Siamese twins was copyrighted on October 5, and the pro-McClellan print, *The True Issue*, on October 6. One of the firm's anti-Lincoln prints, an indictment of the federal monetary system entitled *Running the Machine*, was registered even later, on October 15. Such images had no commercial viability after election day, and apparently the lithographers could make money off the prints in a mere month of sales.[21]

All told, Lincoln was attacked in 1864 as often and as scathingly as McClellan, and often by the same printmakers. As frequently as McClellan was burdened with such derisive emblems as shovels, binoculars, olive branches, and the wood of rotten platform planks, Lincoln was depicted along with personal symbols of his own that were similarly designed to elicit sneering denigration. His increasingly well-known affection for humor, for example, endearing as it is to modern Americans, would be used against him as showing him unfit for the job of president.

The creator of one such cartoon portrayed Lincoln vulgarly requesting a comic song on a battlefield still littered with the dead and wounded soldiers of Antietam. This cartoon, rooted in the pro-McClellan *New York World*, maintained that Lincoln had asked a boon companion to sing comic songs while visiting the site of the bloody battle. Lincoln had in fact asked for a sad song on the way home from this undoubtedly depressing visit. The *World's* version so infuriated the usually thick-skinned president that he prepared a written response, although, in the end, he chose not to send it. The 1864 cartoon showed Lincoln clutching a Scottish cap, an oblique reference to the earlier, equally exaggerated report that he had so disguised himself to pass through Baltimore in 1861. With its images of suffering soldiers gazing helplessly as the indifferent commander in chief asks for music, the print gave Lincoln a truly diabolic image and was likely designed not only to assail Lincoln's character generally, but specifically to injure his chances of winning the votes of those who had lost relatives in battle.[22]

Americans knew by 1864 that Lincoln not only liked to laugh, but also liked Shakespeare, and in one campaign print, his opponent was shown playing the gravedigger's scene from *Hamlet*, with Lincoln as Yorick's unearthed skull, appropriately eulogized by McClellan for the benefit of "Horatio"—in this case Democratic New York governor Horatio Seymour—as "a fellow of infinite jest." But there was more to this particular print than meets the eye. Placing McClellan in a graveyard, even one from literature, might call to the thoughtful viewer's mind the battlefield casualties for which he was responsible, although it might remind viewers, too, of Lincoln's allegedly scandalous behavior on the corpse-riddled battlefield of Antietam. Moreover, portraying McClellan as Hamlet-like—slow to make decisions—might remind voters of his sluggish, indecisive 1862 campaign against Richmond.

To a reflective observer, the image might prove confusing, but on the whole it was a strong piece of work, uncluttered and with reference to well-known traits and tastes of the president. At the same time, the appearance of the actual gravedigger as the stereotypical Irishman alerts us that the Republicans succeeded in reviving and expanding a new and embarrassing symbol, unrelated to McClellan's personal record, into the 1864 campaign: the Irish American draft rioter. They did not fully develop this image, which carried with it the lingering appeal to all the anti-Catholic voters who had swarmed into the Republican ranks between 1856 and 1860, turning John C. Frémont's defeat into Lincoln's victory. The Republicans' failure to pursue so useful an idea may be explained by that fact that, unlike the McClellanesque Yorktown shovel and the Malvern Hill gunboat and wine, it may have been prepared in case the Democratic nominee turned out to be Horatio Seymour, the governor of New York, whose famous "Friends" speech, aimed at calming the draft rioters, was tortured by Republicans into a show of complicity with them.[23]

The field was eventually crowded with anti-Lincoln images. They were typified by Currier and Ives's *Abraham's Dream,* which showed the sleeping president's worst nightmare: the goddess of Liberty chasing him from the White House as a smartly uniformed McClellan ascends its steps. But many of the other anti-Lincoln prints focused on race. The newest word in the nation's political vocabulary, "miscegenation," meaning interracial marriage and replacing the old term, "amalgamation," had been introduced in an anonymously written tract as a prank to embarrass gullible Republicans.[24] The pamphlet, issued in New York, recommended as a solution to what was then called the race question the blending of the races by intermarriage, then widely regarded as an outrageous idea. The authors attempted to get prominent antislavery supporters to endorse the tract. It fooled some and doubtless stirred racial hatred among many white Northerners with passages predicting racial integration:

> It is idle to maintain that this present war is not a war for the negro. It is a war for the negro. Not simply for his personal rights or his physical freedom—it is a war, if you please, of amalgamation, so called—a war of looking, as its final fruit, to the blending of the white and the black. All attempts to end it without a recognition of the political, civil, and social rights of the negro will only lead to still bloodier battles in the future.

The real power of such hoaxes lay below the level of humor in the simmering, secret fears of white Northerners. Now insecure white voters found their concerns venomously illustrated in images that typically portrayed African Americans dressed in fine clothes, parading scandalously in full equality with whites, and featured captions that identified such scenes as "what we are to expect" from Lincoln's second term. "What we are to expect" occasionally ventured into hitherto taboo territory: the implicit threat of cross-racial sexual relations, illustrated in provocative images designed to strike fear in the hearts of jealous white men and their supposedly endangered ladies.[25]

No print publisher played the race card more blatantly in 1864 than the New York firm of Bromley and Company. Bromley issued a book full of irreverent Lincoln stories and crude caricatures written by the fictional "Major Jack Downing," the character that had been invented during the Jacksonian era by satirist Seba Smith. Bromley also offered a "Badge of Liberty" in the form of a highly polished Copperhead pin (made of copper, of course), "suitable for ladies or gentlemen, who are fearless enough to declare their devotion to Free Speech, Free Press, and the Rights of White Men." The firm completed its catalog with a series of four separate-sheet anti-Lincoln cartoons, three of which focused on race. Bromley promoted all its wares in an advertisement (fig. 75) that portrayed Lincoln declaring in the bottom left panel: "That is what I call goin' to the bottom of a subject."

The Bromley prints appear to have been but one element of a virtual interlocking directory of anti-Lincoln publishing activity in New York City. Bromley and Company had John F. Feeks and Company as its "General Agent" in 1864, and the same Feeks was responsible for publishing a considerable amount of anti-Lincoln literature that year, including *Abraham Africanus I: His Secret Life, as Revealed under the Mesmeric Influence* and *Lincolniana; or the Humors of Uncle Abe. Second Joe Miller. "That Reminds Me of a Little Story."* The third edition of the Bromley-Feeks *Letters of Major*

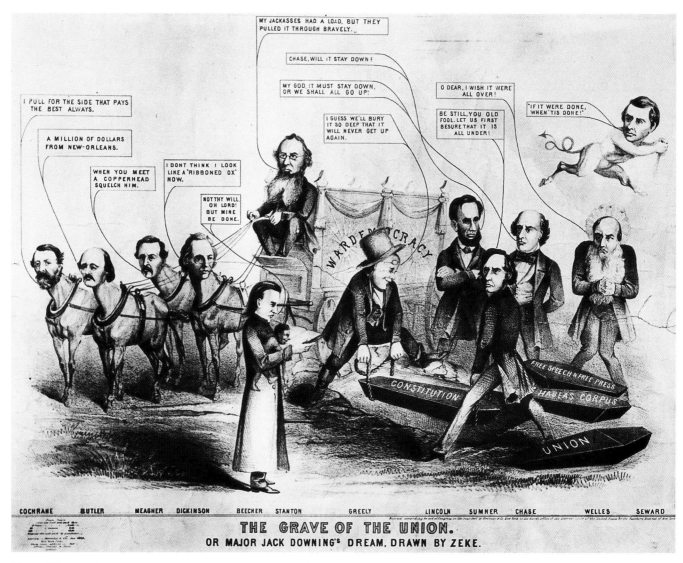

Figure 76. Bromley and Company, *The Grave of the Union. / Or Major Jack Downing's Dream, Drawn by Zeke.* New York, 1864. Lithograph, 15½ × 19¼ inches. "Irresistibly comic and amusing," according to Bromley and Company's advertisement (see fig. 75), this print, designed to lambaste the president for suspending civil liberties during the Civil War, depicted Lincoln and his administration preparing to bury the Constitution in a grave already occupied by a coffin labeled "Union." The hearse has been pulled by four "jackasses"—pro-war Democrats including General Benjamin F. Butler—and is driven by Secretary of War Stanton. Horace Greeley leads the burial party, declaring, "I guess we'll bury it so deep that it will never get up again." Abolitionist Senator Charles Sumner warns, "Be still, you old fool. Let us first be sure that it is all under!" Present to pronounce religious rites is Rev. Henry Ward Beecher, cradling a black baby. And President Lincoln asks, "Will it stay down?" The overall vision was described as a dream by the comic character Jack Downing, a device dropped from subsequent pictures in the Bromley series. (*Library of Congress*)

Jack Downing, of the Downingville Militia was meanwhile published by the firm of Van Evrie, Horton and Company. Feeks also published *The Lincoln Catechism Wherein the Eccentricities and Beauties of Despotism Are Fully Set Forth*, with a woodcut of an African American featured on the title page. Finally, John Van Evrie, publisher of the racist *New York Weekly Day-Book*, wrote *Subgenation: The Theory of the Normal Relation of the Races; an Answer to "Miscegenation."* Only *What Miscegenation Is! And What We Are To Expect Now that Mr. Lincoln is Re-elected*, by L. Seaman, among the known campaign

Figure 77. Broml[e]y and Company, *Miscegenation / Or the Millennium of Abolitionism*. New York, 1864. Lithograph, 14 × 20⅛ inches. Perhaps the most famous of the four "political caricatures" issued by the Bromley firm, this print was designed as a "capital hit upon the new plank in the Republican platform," according to the Downing advertisement, which added, "It represents society as it is to be in the era of 'equality and fraternity,'" a thinly veiled comparison to the chaos that followed empowerment of the citizenry in postrevolutionary France. "No description can do justice to the hits contained in this picture," boasted the ad, which lauded this and the previous caricature as "excellent campaign documents." The print envisioned the "abolitionist millennium" suggested by the newly coined term for racial intermarriage. Horace Greeley still holds center stage as the symbol of crank racial reform in the Republican Party, a role he had played in 1860 (here he describes the scene as a "political and social Paradise"), but he is joined in this image by a personality new to the hated symbols of abolitionism, Senator Charles Sumner of Massachusetts, who made several such appearances in 1864 campaign cartoons. Among the sentiments expressed by those who look on as Lincoln doffs his hat to a mixed-race couple (left) is that of an Irish woman wheeling a black child. She cries: "And it is to drag naggur babies that I left old Ireland!" This image was likely designed as well to woo Irish voters to the Democrats, just as brutish caricatures of Irish men in pro-Lincoln prints were calculated to frighten voters opposed to immigration. (*Library of Congress*)

pamphlets that baited the race issue, was published outside the Bromley–Feeks–Van Evrie axis. The intense identification with the racial issue thus did not have a broad publishing base but stemmed rather from a narrow source in New York.

Bromley's large prints (roughly 16 by 19 inches) were priced at twenty-five cents each, sixteen dollars per hundred, suggesting that they were designed for bulk distribution to Democratic clubs. Since they were issued in collaboration with the *New York World* and other anti-Lincoln organs, they were the closest thing we have to "official" campaign graphics in an era in which such pictures were derived or created by commercial publishers, not political organizations. *The Grave of the Union* (fig. 76) was the first in the series of cluttered images. In Bromley's own description, "This . . . comic and amusing . . . picture shows at a glance the entire object and design of the Abolition . . . party. Ben Butler . . . Horace Greeley . . . Stanton, Chase, Seward, Sumner, Welles, Beecher . . . rejoicing over the grave of the Union." Lincoln himself presided over the burial of the "Constitution, the Union, Habeas Corpus, Free Speech, and Free Press."[26]

To publisher Bromley, the new Union Party platform calling for a constitutional amendment abolishing slavery everywhere was above all an invitation to race-mixing, or at least an opportunity to capitalize on such fears with provocative pictures. Perhaps the most demagogic of his responses was *Miscegenation / Or the Millennium of Abolitionism* (fig. 77). It showed that familiar figure from 1860 Lincoln cartoons, Horace Greeley, happily "eating ice-cream with a female African" of monstrous physique, declaring that society at last had reached absolute perfection." Lincoln was shown proudly greeting a mixed-race couple as "intimate friends," words that must have seemed explosively shocking to a preponderantly racist white electorate in 1864. Bromley's advertisement for this print highlighted images of "Lincoln, Sumner, Greeley . . . and a large number of 'colored ladies and gentlemen,' with white drivers and servants, showing what society is to be in the Millennium of Abolitionism."[27]

Another advertisement for the print ran on July 9 in John Van Evrie's negrophobic *New York Weekly Day-Book* (a newspaper that until 1863 had blatantly called itself *The Caucasian*), recommending that the picture "ought to be circulated far and wide as a campaign document." On pages that bore the headlined reminder, "White Men Must Rule America," ran a complete description of the miscegenation print, described as a "capital hit upon the new plank in the Republican platform." Here, the advertisement maintained, was a true picture of "society as it is to be in the era of 'Equality and Fraternity'":

Sumner is introducing a strapping "colored lady" to the President. A young woman (white) is being kissed by a big buck nigger, while a lady lecturer supposed to be "The inspired Maid" [the Republican orator Anna Dickinson] sits upon the knee of a sable brother urging him to come to her lectures, while Greeley, in the very height of ecstatic employment, is eating ice-cream with a female African of monstrous physique, declaring that society at last had reached ab-

THE ABOLITION CATASTROPHE,
Or the November Smash-up.

Figure 78. Bromley and Company, *The Abolition Catastrophe. / Or the November Smash-up.* New York, 1864. Lithograph, 15½ × 19⅛ inches. Over-eager to offer purchasers as many "hits" as possible against the Republicans, the anonymous artist of this third in Bromley's four-cartoon series succeeded only in making the result cluttered and unfocused. It was designed to suggest that support for abolitionism would lead to disaster for both Lincoln's candidacy and for the Union itself. In its omnibus references to political issues, it also included unusual comment on foreign policy, the feared Mexican venture of Napoleon III and its violation of the Monroe Doctrine. Note the train carrying McClellan safely to the White House at top. These prints proved somewhat more expensive than those offered in the Downing advertisement: they sold for sixteen cents each if purchased in quantities of 100. (*Library of Congress*)

solute perfection. In the background is a carriage, negroes inside, with white drivers and footmen; a white servant girl drawing a nigger baby, and a newly arrived German surveying the whole scene exclaiming, "Mine Got, vot a guntry! Vot a beeples!"[28]

The third in the Bromley series, *The Abolition Catastrophe* (fig. 78), warned of a "November smash-up" on the rock pile of emancipation, public debt, confiscation, and the draft should Lincoln be reelected. McClellan and Pendleton safely pilot the

Union train to the White House, above the wreck, as the general shouts down to the capsizing Lincoln: "Wouldn't you like to swap horses now?" The ridiculous president can only reply, "This reminds me of a. . . ." Giving full credit for the Republican wreck to McClellan, a passenger on board the Democrats' sturdy train rejoices: "Little Mac is the boy to smash up all the Miscegenationists."

Finally came *The Miscegenation Ball* (fig. 79), purporting to illustrate a scandalous

Figure 79. Kimmel and Forster, *The Miscegenation Ball*. Signed, lower right, "Thomas [?]." Published by Bromley and Company, New York, 1864. Lithograph, 16⅛ × 20⅓ inches. The largest of the four Bromley caricatures, and the only one credited to printmakers Kimmel and Forster of New York, this was also the subtlest effort of the series. It purported to portray an event that had actually occurred, according to the extended caption, at the Lincoln Central Campaign Club in New York on September 23, 1864. The anti-Lincoln *New York World* had alleged that Lincoln supporters, among them "prominent men," had danced openly with black women at a scandalous "negro ball." According to the printmakers' interpretation, those who sat out the dance behaved even more outrageously: they can be seen embracing and kissing on the benches at right. The revelers dance beneath a portrait of Lincoln in the background and a sign that declares "Universal Freedom" to be the promise of the administration. The onlookers peering through the skylight above are intended to represent the witnesses who reported the scene to the newspapers. This superior print was evidently a work for hire; less than a year later, the same lithographers, Kimmel and Forster, would issue a series of flattering portraits lauding Lincoln as one of "Columbia's noblest sons." (*Library of Congress*)

scene that had occurred at the Lincoln Central Campaign Club on Broadway and Twenty-third Street. "No sooner were the formal proceedings and speeches hurried through with," the caption alleged, "than the room was cleared for a 'negro ball,' which then and there took place!" The story continued that while some members of the "Central Lincoln Club" left "before the mystical and circling rites of languishing glance and mazy dance commenced . . . many remained." "This fact we certify," it continued, basing its charge on a September 23, 1864, report in the *New York World*, "that on the floor during the progress of the ball were many of the accredited leaders of the Black Republican party, thus testifying their faith." What really lay at the bottom of this allegation remains unknown.

As the Bromley series and the many Currier and Ives cartoons suggest, campaign prints of 1864 generally avoided identifying strengths and virtues, instead accentuating the negative: Lincoln's alleged secret plans for race mixing and tasteless sense of humor; McClellan's supposed cowardice, ineptitude, and hypocrisy. Picture publishers alarmed voters far more often than they inspired them in 1864. The celebratory side of the print business was represented by engraved and lithographed portraiture—of McClellan the commander, of Lincoln the Emancipator—reminding voters of successes all but ignored by the cartoons. It now seems clear that because so many portraits, Emancipation Proclamation tributes, and battle scenes appeared (or remained on view) in 1864, campaign graphics that year may well have been as plentiful as those issued in 1860. A full effort at producing campaign ephemera and literature fits with the strong result, an enormous turnout of voters in most states.

As usual, the demand for campaign prints ended quite suddenly. On November 26, 1864, less than three weeks after the election that returned Lincoln to the White House, *Harper's Weekly* published an advertisement from a disappointed Democrat now desperate to unload suddenly outdated stock. Under the headline "Lincoln and McClellan" came the following offering to readers of the *New York World*, which had conspired in the production of so much anti-Lincoln imagery of the 1864 campaign:

> A fine engraving of the two on one plate, will be sent, free, on receipt of two three-cent postage stamps to pay postage, to every reader of THE WORLD. The same engraving can not be bought for one dollar. We send them free.
> —Dr. W. R. Merwin & Co., New York[29]

No record exists of how many readers responded, or how many free prints were distributed. As the Union moved closer and closer to victory, few pictures must have seemed more irrelevant, and they have remained so until now. But in their time such prints not only chronicled the dark side of one of American history's most important elections, they likely played a part in arousing Americans to an unmatched level of political excitement and involvement.

The Real Men of the War

Print Portraits of the Victors

*I have been importuned from many quarters for my likeness, autographs, and biography.
I have managed to fend off all parties and hope to do so till the end of the war. I don't
want to rise to be notorious, for the reason that a mere slip or Accident may let me fall,
and I don't care about falling so far as most of the temporary heroes of the war. The real
men of the war will be determined by the closing scenes, and then the army will determine
the questions. Newspaper puffs and self-written biographies will then be ridiculous caricatures. Already has time marked this progress and indicated this conclusion. [General
William T. Sherman, December 30, 1863][1]*

On the subject of fame, General Sherman, who desired only the genuine and lasting kind, possessed profound insight. Proving the truth of his words, the beautiful
old engraved and lithographed portraits of George B. McClellan today have the effect principally of marking how far that general ultimately fell from public grace.
The "real men of the war" proved to be Ulysses S. Grant, William T. Sherman, David
G. Farragut, and Philip H. Sheridan. Their military and naval exploits prompted extensive celebration in battle scenes. But of all the victors, only Grant gained the
number and variety of portrait tributes that his achievements deserved.

Honor was assured to Grant's willing lieutenant, the intense Sherman, only in
September 1864, when the city of Atlanta fell to his army. It came even later for the
young and irascible Irish bachelor, Philip Sheridan, with his famous ride to victory
at Cedar Creek in October 1864—also while he reported to Grant as his superior.
Sheridan's image appeared on the cover of *Harper's Weekly* following his dramatic
ride, and he went on to inspire several subsequently issued prints (see plate 16)
and sheet music covers, including an equestrian portrait by Currier and Ives. Yet,
inexplicably, an effort to stimulate audience interest in a chromolithograph of artist-
poet Thomas Buchanan Read's well-received painting, *Sheridan's Ride*, ended without
success. Although a sales pamphlet promised a print "equal to the best of the chromos now in the market," a print that would be "furnished mounted (together with

a fac-simile autograph copy of Read's Poem) to subscribers at the low cost of $10," the project was apparently abandoned; no copy of the chromo has been located.[2]

As for Farragut, despite brilliant victories to his credit in independent commands from the fall of New Orleans in 1862 almost to the war's end, he was an admiral, and most people realized then what historians have confirmed since: that the Civil War was won on land. By war's end, a revealing advertisement in *Harper's Weekly* would promise subscribers to a proposed home for the orphans of deceased Union soldiers a free 20-by-25-inch engraving of "President Lincoln, Lieut. Gen. Grant, Gen. Sherman [and] Sheridan"—the real heroes of the war.[3]

"The Old Bull Dog"

In Civil War military portraiture, Ulysses S. Grant eventually reigned supreme. The reasons for his unparalleled place in Civil War iconography are obvious. Grant enjoyed celebrity status beginning with his victory at Fort Donelson in early 1862 and genuinely heroic stature from the 1863 fall of Vicksburg on. He rose to command all the Union armies for the last year of fighting, accepted the surrender of Robert E. Lee's Army of Northern Virginia, and then was twice elected president (many people wanted him to run for a third time). His long years of prominence provided ample opportunities to brush off wartime engraver's plates and lithographic stones, or to create new ones, to provide pictures for the old general's political admirers.

But Grant's journey to pictorial fame was neither swift nor straight. Printmakers were at first challenged to locate models from photographs or illustrated newspapers. A bias toward the eastern theater of the war, whose major cities housed the great printmaking firms, also slowed the production of prints of westerners like Grant. A dedication to timely publication complicated these problems and diminished accuracy and creativity.

Lack of photographic models posed the initial impediment. Grant had long since dispersed his Mexican War daguerreotypes to various relatives. (Not until the 1880s did engraver Alexander Hay Ritchie obtain one to use as a model for a frontispiece portrait in the first volume of Grant's memoirs.)[4] The first photographs of Grant as a Civil War officer, taken in October 1861 in Cairo, Illinois, show a proud new officer wearing his regulation colonel's uniform, complete with a hat decorated with ostrich feathers, and holding his dress sword in his lap. Thus accoutred, he seems to the modern viewer quite unlike the "rough-and-ready" general who took inspiration from his disheveled old Mexican War commanding general, Zachary Taylor. But the most unusual feature of this first photograph was that Grant wore an unfamiliar-looking long beard, squared off at the bottom. Grant's son, Frederick, who judged the photograph "a remarkably good picture of General Grant as he looked at that time," explained that "during the time that he was serving in Missouri he did not trim his beard nor did he do so on being stationed at Cairo."[5]

Grant dispersed copies of the new picture to family and friends as personal mementos, without an eye to wider fame. The pose was soon rendered obsolete by no less influential an adviser than the general's wife. Soon after commanding troops none too successfully at his first fight, the Battle of Belmont, Missouri, on November 7, 1861, the general sent for Mrs. Grant. Appalled by her husband's changed appearance, Julia Dent Grant told the general bluntly that "she did not like the length of his beard." Grant soon had the offending beard shaved close. In February 1862 the general won attention by capturing Forts Henry and Donelson. Then, in April, he gained more notice by giving the Union a costly but much-needed victory at the Battle of Shiloh. Such events were bound to create a public curiosity about the man, and journalists, photographers, and printmakers rushed to satisfy it.[6]

The Cairo pose, however, did not provide the inspiration for the media, for in sending copies to his wife, sister, aunt, and uncles, Grant had apparently depleted the ready supply. Instead, some printmakers adapted photographs of a man who looked like Grant—or, apparently, as Grant looked before Julia made him trim his long beard. As explained by Grant's aide, Horace Porter, "Some of the earliest pictures purporting to be photographs of him had been manufactured when he was at the distant front, never stopping in one place long enough to be 'focused.' The practicers of that art which is the chief solace of the vain, nothing daunted, photographed a burly beef contractor at the rear, and spread the pictures broadcast as the determined but rather robust features of the coming hero." According to one historian, the lookalike was even named Grant—William Grant—and his picture had been taken in Cairo, the same town in which the general had posed, at around the very same time. The combination of coincidence and resemblance conspired for a time to confuse both image makers and their public.[7]

Horace Porter told his amusing anecdote from memories of events twenty years in the past. Moreover, they were memories of hearsay: Porter did not himself lay eyes on Grant until October 23, 1863, more than a year and a half after Shiloh, and did not join the general's staff until April 1864. No doubt Grant's officers found the case of mistaken identity funny and told humorous stories that became considerably embroidered over time, and Porter believed the embroidery. It was a minor matter anyway, and as an author of a memoir of service with Grant on his decisive late campaigns, Porter would probably not bother to check such an anecdote.[8]

Credit for producing what was probably the first print portrait of Grant—even if it was William and not Ulysses who wound up being portrayed—belongs to J. L. Magee of Philadelphia, who copyrighted a small, full-length lithograph, *Major Gen. Grant, The Hero of Fort Donelson*, on March 22, 1862. Engraver J. C. Buttre of New York followed with his own adaptation of the same erroneous model. His engraved portrait (fig. 80) likely also appeared in mid-1862, probably not long after Grant's Shiloh victory. But Grant was not yet quite so famous that his admirers knew that he boasted far more hair on his head than the subject of Buttre's engraving, or that his eyes were lighter colored and set closer together.[9]

Eng^d by J.C. Buttre.

U. S. Grant

MAJ. GEN. ULYSSES S. GRANT.

Figure 80. J[ohn]. C. Buttre,
Maj. Gen. Ulysses S. Grant. New York,
ca. 1862. Engraving, 12 × 9½ inches.
A spurious photograph of Grant—actually
showing an Illinois beef contractor possibly
named William Grant—inspired this
early print, versions of which remained in
circulation even after the general achieved
fame. *Frank Leslie's Illustrated Newspaper*
published occasional portraits based on the
same photo for two years, and until 1864
Harper's Weekly based its Grant portraits
exclusively on the spurious photograph.
(John Y. Simon, introduction to *U. S. Grant:
The Man and the Image*, by James G. Barber
[Washington, D.C.: National Portrait Gallery,
1985], 18–19, 34–35.) (*National Portrait
Gallery*)

For at least a year, *Frank Leslie's Illustrated Newspaper* persisted in publishing wood-cut adaptations of both the authentic but outdated Cairo photograph and the beef contractor photograph. An anonymous *Leslie's* artist also contributed a separate-sheet woodcut (fig. 81), which featured a Grant portrait—along with other generals—based on the genuine but out-of-date photograph of Grant in his plumed hat. *Harper's Weekly* seemed to prefer the beef contractor model, and as late as February 4, 1864, featured a woodcut of a Thomas Nast portrait showing a long-bearded Grant who now bore little resemblance to the original.

The New York firm of Caldwell and Company was able to market an even more improbable likeness, an earnest but somewhat stilted equestrian lithograph, *Maj. Gen. Ulysses S[.] Grant* (fig. 82). In the print, Grant not only sports his Cairo beard but wears a grand uniform unlike any that he donned in the field: the modest os-trich feathers of his dress hat have been replaced by the plumed hat of a cavalier, and epaulets uncharacteristically adorn his shoulders. He wears a variation on his Cairo sash at the waist, and his tiny hands fill long gloves that daintily grip the reins of his horse. The appearance of undisturbed tents in the background of the scene suggest the printmaker was ignorant of reports that Union troops at Shiloh had been surprised by Confederate attackers while they slept.

War correspondent Sylvanus Cadwallader—not always the most reliable source of information about Grant—insisted that as late as November 1863, soon after the siege of Chattanooga, even Grant's own soldiers remained unsure about their commander's true appearance. On his first day in camp, Cadwallader noticed a photographer's tent, "surrounded by a crowd of soldiers." He approached it to investigate and discovered an entrepreneur hawking "Grant" pictures:

> The operator was selling photos from the last negative ever taken of Gen. Grant (as he asserted) at fifty cents each nearly as fast as he could make change. A glance showed me that they were not photos of Grant from any negative, but really those of some (to me) unknown general officer. The rascal had sold many hundreds of them as genuine, life-like pictures of Gen. Grant. As very few soldiers in that army had ever seen Grant, the imposture was easy. I exposed the fraud promptly. The money was refunded to every purchaser present, and a file of soldiers sent to prevent his being thrown into the river by the swindled and infuriated men.[10]

If we are to believe Cadwallader's observations, Grant remained an elusive figure for his men for the simple reason that he was rarely among them. Appearing on the field during a battle, Grant was not, admitted his telegraph operator, Samuel H. Beckwith, "what would be called an imposing figure," although he was a "first class horseman." But it was understandable that printmakers made his appearance rather grand. Frank G. Chapman had filed a report from the Shiloh battlefield for the *New York Herald* alleging that Grant had saved the second day at Shiloh by appearing on the field on horseback. According to the *Herald*, "Grant rode to the left . . . and then ordered a charge across the field, himself leading, as he brandished his sword and waved them on to the crowning victory, while cannon balls were falling like hail around him." This was inspiring battlefield leadership indeed. But an Ohio newspaper promptly dismissed the report as "pure romance," adding that Grant not only did not lead the charge (General William Nelson had done so), he did not even order it (Buell got the credit). "Grant," the editorial insisted, "was not seen on the left wing during the day and in fact had no business there."[11]

Whatever the truth about Grant's behavior, his image as equestrian field commander lived on in prints. Joseph E. Baker's handsome colored lithograph for John H. Bufford of Boston (plate 10), for example, showed him not only leading a charge astride his black horse, but wearing a plumed hat and brandishing his saber. No doubt his aide, General Horace Porter, had such images in mind when he complained: "He was pictured in the popular mind as striding about in the most approved swash-buckler style of melodrama." As Porter put it, "There were then few correct portraits of him in circulation."[12]

In battle Grant performed his most important functions behind the lines, issuing orders and surveying the field of battle. He was, as John Keegan suggests, among the first of the modern generals in style, from his clothing to his occupations on the battlefield to the kind of warfare he waged. Eventually several artists so depicted

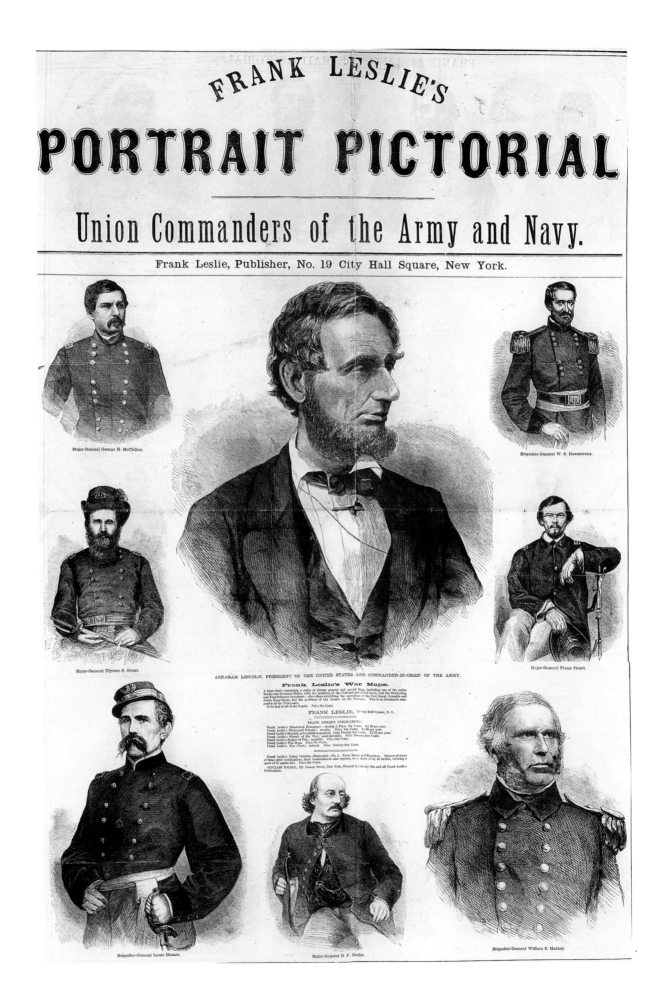

FRANK LESLIE'S
PORTRAIT PICTORIAL

Union Commanders of the Army and Navy.

Frank Leslie, Publisher, No. 19 City Hall Square, New York.

Major-General George B. McClellan.

Brigadier-General W. S. Rosencrans.

Major-General Ulysses S. Grant.

ABRAHAM LINCOLN, PRESIDENT OF THE UNITED STATES AND COMMANDER-IN-CHIEF OF THE ARMY.

Major-General Franz Sigel.

Frank Leslie's War Maps.

A large sheet, containing a series of sixteen general and special Maps, including one of the entire Border and Southern States, with the positions of the National and Rebel forces, and the Blockading and Expeditionary squadrons; also others exhibiting the operations of the Port Royal, Burnside and Butler Expeditions, and the positions of the Armies on the Potomac. This is an invaluable companion to the Newspaper.
To be had at all News Depots. Price Six Cents.

FRANK LESLIE, 19 City Hall Square, N. Y.

FRANK LESLIE'S PUBLICATIONS:

Frank Leslie's Illustrated Newspaper ; weekly.] Price Six Cents. $2.50 per year.
Frank Leslie's Illustrated Zeitung ; weekly. Price Six Cents. $1.00 per year.
Frank Leslie's Monthly [a beautiful magazine]. Price Twenty-five Cents. $2.50 per year.
Frank Leslie's History of the War; semi-monthly. Price Twenty-five Cents.
Frank Leslie's Budget of Fun ; monthly. Price Six Cents.
Frank Leslie's War Maps. Price Six Cents.
Frank Leslie's War Chart ; colored. Price Twenty-five Cents.

Frank Leslie's Union Victories Illustrated.—No 1. Forts Henry and Donelson. Sixteen pictures of these rebel fortifications, their bombardment and capture, on a sheet 33 by 46 inches, covering a space of 21 square feet. Price Six Cents.
SINCLAIR TOUSEY, 121 Nassau Street, New York, General Agents for this and all Frank Leslie's Publications.

Brigadier-General Louis Blenker.

Major-General B. F. Butler.

Brigadier-General William S. Harney.

him. But in some of the first prints issued to confirm, and also take advantage of, his growing fame, Grant was placed into the mise-en-scène of traditional military portraiture.[13]

The proper distance between the habitually cool, relentless commander and his men was strikingly achieved by John Sartain in a mezzotint (fig. 83) published in 1864. Here Grant merely holds the reins of an ideal white charger (of Grant's best-known real horses, Cincinnati was black and Egypt was brown). The white horse and awkward pose betrayed the print's frugal origins in an outdated plate showing General Zachary Taylor in the same setting and in a nearly identical pose (fig. 84). To update the pose, Sartain burnished out the portrait of Taylor, replaced it with one of Grant, altered the uniform, made some other minor changes, and reissued the sixteen-year-old portrait as new.

Sartain's brother William used the same bit of artistic deception years later. He issued a handsome equestrian print (fig. 85) after the war, showing an imposing Grant reining in his foaming horse as he surveys a battlefield triumph, a soldier cheering him on. The print proved to be a copy of an 1863 engraving by A. B. Walter that originally depicted not Grant but George B. McClellan (fig. 86). Thus Grant superseded McClellan both in command and in iconography.

As late as March 1864, when Grant arrived in Washington for his first meeting with Abraham Lincoln, many Americans, even those residing in the nation's capital, evidently did not yet know what the Union army's greatest hero looked like. According to Horace Porter, the front desk clerk at Willard's Hotel failed to recognize Grant and assigned the uncomplaining general a nondescript room on the establishment's top floor. Only when the dusty-looking little man had signed the register "U. S. Grant & Son—Galena, Illinois" did the startled and apologetic clerk reassign Grant to the best suite in the house.[14]

---

opposite
Figure 81. [Artist(s) unknown], *Frank Leslie's Portrait Pictorial / Union Commanders of the Army and Navy.* Published by Frank Leslie, New York, ca. 1862. Wood engraving, 33 × 23 inches. This large patriotic poster offered depictions of seven early Union military heroes, grouped around a central portrait of the commander in chief. All of the images had appeared previously, but separately, on the pages of *Frank Leslie's Illustrated Newspaper.* Evidently the artists had encountered difficulty obtaining current models of the celebrities: they based Lincoln's likeness on an old, beardless 1860 campaign photograph, with whiskers superimposed to update it, and modeled General Benjamin F. Butler's portrait (bottom center) on a civilian photograph (the general appears in mufti). For Grant (center left), the engraver relied on the photograph made in Cairo, Illinois, in October 1861. Grant wears the regulation feathers in his hat and carries his sword in his lap. Ironically, the resulting portrait made him appear a more dashing and romantic figure than such officers as George B. McClellan (upper left), and Franz Sigel (center right, with his name misspelled), who usually outdistanced the plain-dressing Grant in accoutrements. The advertising copy below Lincoln's portrait reveals that Leslie's publishing operation was engaged in the display print business in 1862, offering, as an "invaluable companion to the Newspaper," sixteen war maps, along with the first edition of a proposed series entitled *Frank Leslie's Union Victories Illustrated* (a 33-by-46-inch sheet, for six cents, featuring sixteen pictures of Forts Henry and Donelson, the scenes of Grant's first great triumphs). (*National Portrait Gallery*)

Figure 82. Caldwell and Company, *Maj. Gen. Ulysses S[.] Grant.* New York, ca. 1862. Hand-colored lithograph, 14¾ × 10 inches. To concoct this fanciful equestrian portrait, the Caldwell firm imposed an exaggerated dress uniform on an adaptation of the engraving of the Grant lookalike published in *Harper's Weekly* and placed the resulting portrait atop a stock picture of a military horse. Such early images, rushed to market to meet public interest in the emerging hero from the West, sacrificed accuracy in depiction for speed in production. The haste in composition is suggested in the carelessly sketched camp background, which owes much to traditional military portraiture, and the incongruous cannonball in the foreground of the camp (rather than on the battlefield). The importance of patriotism is evident in the rendering of the flag as the most boldly delineated item in the background. (*The Lincoln Museum*)

PUB? BY CALDWELL & C⁰ 82 CEDAR ST N.Y.

MAJ.GEN.ULYSSES S GRANT.

It took printmakers, too, some time to assign preeminence to Grant. Currier and Ives, that bellwether of printmaking trends, did issue a number of portraits, but the earlier ones are undated, and a far greater number seem to have come off the presses in 1884 and 1885—long after the war, and even Grant's presidency, had ended. The image of "Grant in Peace," in the words of the title to one such postwar print, seems to have inspired as many prints as did Grant in war. Any attempt to understand Grant iconography is complicated by his two presidential campaigns, both of which capitalized on his military fame. Many undated portraits can at best be narrowed to the eight-year span between 1864 and 1872.

Grant's image grew formidable enough to be used to help Abraham Lincoln in his bid for reelection in 1864. Having disdained interest in a presidential draft himself, Grant now assumed a clearly subordinate role but nevertheless became one of Lincoln's strongest weapons, his bulldog reputation a convincing counterpoint to the Democratic platform's peace plank. Thus Currier and Ives's campaign cartoon, *The Old Bull Dog on the Right Track* (fig. 87), showed a nervous Democratic candidate, George B. McClellan, begging Lincoln to call off the huge, bearded dog perched stubbornly on the railroad tracks to Richmond. "I think it's best to give the old bull dog full swing to go in and finish them," Lincoln replies. His "bulldog," who wears three stars on his shoulders and a collar labeled "Lieutenant General"—the only Grantian prop he lacks is a cigar—gazes confidently toward the Confederate capital and assures the characters in the print (and through them, the war-weary voters of 1864): "I'm bound to take it."

The next year, 1865, marked a watershed for the Grant image. It had taken four years for printmakers to catch up to Grant's unparalleled successes in both theaters of the war, not to mention the rudiments of his appearance. Once Grant overpowered the Army of Northern Virginia, they made up for lost time. No single event of Ulysses S. Grant's life inspired more prints than the surrender he accepted at Appomattox on April 9, 1865.[15]

Some of these proved balms for Grant's image, reinforcing his modesty by showing him in an unadorned uniform, in stark contrast to Lee, who was magnificent in full dress, with a gleaming sword at his side. As Sylvanus Cadwallader had observed of Grant: "His clothing was unexceptionable in quality and condition . . . his manner of wearing it was scarcely up to military requirements. . . . His overcoat was generally the army blue of regulation pattern no wise differing from those of officers or privates, with nothing on it to distinguish him or denote rank."[16]

Grant's plain appearance at Appomattox was more a happy accident than a matter of conscious image making. Given the choice, he would have dressed otherwise; Cadwallader insisted that Grant did possess finery "for state occasions." He had, for example, been given a magnificent dress uniform by "some New York friends" in late 1864 or early 1865, prompting a rather maudlin Grant to lament: "There have been times in my life when the gift of an overcoat would have been an act of charity. No one gave it to me when I needed it. Now when I am able to pay for all I need,

Figure 83. John Sartain, *Lieut. General U. S. Grant.* Published by William Smith, Philadelphia, 1864. Mezzotint engraving, 20⅞ × 15¾ inches. Probably inspired by Grant's promotion to lieutenant general in early 1864, this battlefield portrait tries to capture Grant's bulldog determination: he holds the reins of a white horse, a classic symbol of military art, while the weaponry at his feet bolsters the image of Grant the resolute commander. In reality, the pose was an updated version of an older engraving of Mexican War hero Zachary Taylor (see fig. 84), with Grant's face, based on a current photograph, superimposed and the uniform altered. Soldiers in the background of the Taylor print, wearing Mexican War–style hats, are replaced here by men in the kepis of the 1860s. But Sartain did not replace the outmoded split-trail cannon at lower right with the one-piece trail typical of the Civil War. He also failed to burnish out all of Taylor's scabbard, leaving a ghost image in this print. (*The Lincoln Museum*)

LIEUT. GENERAL U. S. GRANT.

MAJOR-GENERAL ZACHARY TAYLOR.

PRESIDENT OF THE UNITED STATES.

Figure 84.
John Sartain, *Major-General Zachary Taylor. / President of the United States.* Published by William Smith, Philadelphia, 1848. Mezzotint engraving, 20⅞ × 15¾ inches. Although dated 1848, this print was probably updated in 1849 when Taylor entered the White House—hence its subtitle. Taylor had been made major general in 1846, and the following year he defeated Santa Anna at the Battle of Buena Vista. But Taylor died barely a year into his term as president, and demand for this heroic image had likely long ended when, some fifteen years later, the still-thriving Sartain printmaking firm dusted off the old plate on which it had been engraved, burnished out the figure of Taylor, and replaced it with that of a new rough and ready hero, Ulysses S. Grant, an appropriate choice since Grant admired Taylor. (*Library of Congress*)

ULYSSES S. GRANT.

Figure 85. William Sartain, after Christian Schussele, *Ulysses S. Grant*. Philadelphia, 1892. Engraving, 24 × 19 inches. Signed in plate, lower left, "C. Schussele." Galloping across a battlefield on a foaming black charger, Grant is greeted by an enthusiastic soldier as staff officers in the background direct Union artillery. The pose was taken entirely from an earlier oil painting, and subsequently issued popular print (see fig. 86), of General George B. McClellan. (*Library of Congress*)

Figure 86. A[dam]. B. Walter, after Christian Schussele, *Maj. Gen. Geo. B. McClellan / On the Battle Field of Antietam*. Philadelphia, 1863. Engraving, 24 × 19 inches. Signed in plate, lower left, "C. Schussele, / 1863." The original image from which Sartain pirated his postwar Grant equestrian pose (see fig. 85), this engraving presented a heroic view of "The Young Napoleon" at Antietam— a site at which Grant never fought. (*The Lincoln Museum*)

such gifts are continually thrust upon me." More important, Grant knew precisely when propriety dictated that he wear such attire. "It is safe to say that no one ever saw him with his coat buttoned up to his chin," Cadwallader admitted, quickly adding, "except on ceremonial occasions." Surely no "ceremonial occasion" ever loomed larger on Grant's horizon than Appomattox.[17]

The explanation for the carelessness that some would celebrate as a virtue when his plain style collided dramatically with Lee's splendor at Appomattox was that Grant indeed planned to wear his best uniform that day, but his best clothes did not arrive in time to be donned for the surrender ceremony. Grant had no choice but to garb himself in "the uniform of a private with the straps of a Lieutenant-General." His trousers were tucked into "ordinary top boots," his aide Horace Porter remembered, and his "single-breasted blouse of dark-blue flannel" was "unbuttoned in front." As Grant admitted, "In my rough travelling suit I must have contrasted very strangely with a man so handsomely dressed." A legend was born because a trunk was late.[18]

That unhappy circumstance did not stop several printmakers, however, from portraying Grant as every inch the equal of his foe—not only militarily, but sartorially. Popular prints traditionally issued from a world one step behind journalism and the fine arts, and several printmakers seemed reluctant to translate the stories of Grant's relatively rumpled appearance at Appomattox into print tributes. Philadelphia lithographer Joseph Hoover's print (fig. 88), for example, suggested that Lee surrendered his sword and, its caption stated, "his entire army" to Grant, and in such a mythologized landscape, the image distinction between these two great figures of the war was blurred. Hoover put Grant in a full-dress uniform with evidence of rank. He lacks the fancy gloves and high boots given to Lee, but otherwise their uniforms are much the same. Here the lithographer's notions of creating a picture for posterity do battle with widely reported truth. Other Appomattox prints, including Currier and Ives's depictions of the surrender, accoutred Grant in very much the same style as Lee. In such cases, patriotism and glorious tradition trumped fact, leaving to journalism and literature the details that many printmakers seemed unwilling to portray.

Whether they showed Grant in plain or fancy uniforms, all Appomattox prints helped give the man later famed for his costly strategy of "attrition," the "tough" warrior who oversaw "unlimited conquest," another image: that of a man of peace. But Grant himself helped create that image. It is easiest to recognize when one thinks of the prints that might have been created, but were not, of Grant the conqueror entering Richmond. As historian John Y. Simon has pointed out, Grant's aide Horace Porter revealed a significant aspect of the victor's character in recalling that, after Appomattox, "the general was asked whether he was going to run up to Richmond on the steamer, and take a look at the captured city, before starting for Washington. He replied: 'No; I think it would be as well not to go. I could do no good there, and my visit might lead to demonstrations which would only wound the

THE OLD BULL DOG ON THE RIGHT TRACK.

Figure 87. Currier and Ives, *The Old Bull Dog on the Right Track.* New York, 1864. Lithograph, 14 × 20 inches. Designed as a pro-Lincoln, anti-McClellan campaign cartoon (Lincoln refers tauntingly to McClellan's cowardly "gunboat" reputation), this lithograph also forcibly emphasized Grant's growing fame for bulldog tenacity. Here he is rendered literally as a bearded canine, vowing resolutely to capture the distant doghouse labeled "Richmond." Robert E. Lee, Jefferson Davis, P. G. T. Beauregard, and the other Confederate "curs" in the background gather around as the Confederate president proclaims, "You ain't got this kennel yet old fellow!" But they seem to cower as they wait for the inevitable onslaught. Grant had failed in June 1864 to seize the Weldon Railroad, which connected besieged Petersburg, Virginia, to North Carolina and served as a vital supply line for the Confederate army. But eight weeks later he launched another attack, and by August 23 the railroad was permanently under Union control. (*The Lincoln Museum*)

feelings of the residents, and we ought not to do anything at such a time which would add to their sorrow.'" His decision made it inevitable that "victory" prints would show the winning general graciously receiving his opponent rather than riding into the devastated Confederate capital in triumph.[19]

Print buyers could now find many means of pictorially celebrating Grant's triumphs. Lithographer Charles Lubrecht, who issued similar biographical prints honoring both Lincoln and Stonewall Jackson, produced *The Leader and His Battles / Ulysses S. Grant* (fig. 89), lavishly decorated with vignettes illustrating the highlights of Grant's Civil War career. These pictures ranged from the exaggerated

THE SURRENDER OF GENERAL LEE
AND HIS ENTIRE ARMY TO LIEUT GENERAL GRANT APRIL 9TH 1865.

Figure 88. A. L. Weise, *The Surrender of General Lee / And His Entire Army to Lieut. General Grant April 9th 1865*. Published by Joseph Hoover, Philadelphia, 1865. Hand-colored lithograph, 22 × 28 inches. Although the actual surrender ceremony inside a country house parlor inspired a number of prints that attempted to capture the scene realistically, quite a few others—like this one—depicted it outdoors. Inside or out, printmakers often gave Grant the dress uniform he had hoped to wear rather than the plain one he did. The myth of an outdoor surrender probably took hold when it was reported that Lee and Grant met on horseback the day *after* the surrender to discuss additional matters. It had also been reported that Lee was resting in an apple orchard nearby when he first decided he must surrender. Somehow, this combination of circumstances led some printmakers to show the surrender outdoors and, as in this case, beneath an apple tree. Here Grant is about to hand the "terms of surrender" to his vanquished foe in a wholly imaginary setting. Moreover, the artist placed both the Union and Confederate armies in the background, creating a grand vista in the manner of the surrender of Cornwallis the century before. (See John B. Jones, *A Rebel War Clerk's Diary at the Confederate States Capital*, 2 vols. [Philadelphia: Lippincott, 1866], 1:184; A. L. Long, *Memoirs of Robert E. Lee* [London: Low, Marston, Searle and Rivington, 1886], 422.) (*The Lincoln Museum*)

(Grant waving his hat to urge on his men at Shiloh) to the sublimely natural (a cigar-chomping Grant receiving the surrender of Vicksburg). But many printmakers were not content to limit their Grant portrayals to celebrations of his military triumphs—few of which, after all, translated into the kind of action-filled portraiture most viewers still associated with military heroics. They looked for something more.

Two years earlier, in 1863, a committee of artists, including Emmanuel Gottlieb Leutze and John Antrobus, whose own portrait of Grant later inspired a print (plate 11), had squabbled over the appropriate design for a medal that Congress had voted Grant as a tribute to his victory at Vicksburg. One idea had come from a New York lithographer named Alexander Kann. He proposed that the medal feature "busts of Lincoln, Grant & Washington," surmounted by the figure of Liberty to represent emancipation. The committee promptly rejected the suggestion. A simple profile of the general would appear on the medal's obverse; the figure of liberty, hovering over a battlefield scene, would grace the reverse. Such constraints would soon melt away, however.[20]

Grant achieved image parity when it was even more difficult to do so: after his commander in chief was transformed into a martyr. When Kimmel and Forster of New York issued *The Preservers of Our Union* in 1865, both the general and the president were portrayed as full equals, elevated above all other heroes of the war. The figure of Liberty occupied the center of the scene, holding victors' wreaths over the heads of both heroes. Alexander Kann's recommendation that Grant and Liberty be depicted together, rejected in 1863, now seemed entirely appropriate. So did an implied association with an earlier general, with whom General Sherman had dared to compare him only once in a private letter: George Washington. As Sherman told Grant in March 1864, the commanding general was so "brave, patriotic and honest" and had such a "simple faith in success" as to make him "Washington's legitimate successor." The *New York Times* helped explain why such comparisons now seemed less sacrilegious in a comment published some six weeks before Appomattox: "WASHINGTON is completing his second cycle. He was with JACKSON in 1832, when he suppressed treason. . . . He has been with ABRAHAM LINCOLN, and has gone with us through the war, teaching us to bear reverses patiently. He was with GRANT at the taking of Vicksburgh [*sic*], and will go with him to Richmond."[21]

The pantheon of heroes whose portraits the printmakers offered was shaped by the demands of Northern nationalism. In 1862 publisher George W. Childs of Philadelphia advertised T. B. Welch's engravings of Thomas Sully's portraits of George Washington and Andrew Jackson as "Household Pictures for the Entire Family," at five dollars each. Francis Preston Blair Sr., father of Lincoln's postmaster general and a onetime member of Jackson's "kitchen cabinet," urged their acquisition "to adorn the home of every American whose heart is touched with enthusiasm for the great Patriot Chiefs whose fame is the country's glory." "Suppressors of treason" like Jackson grew popular in the North during the war and outgrew their partisan im-

THE LEADER AND HIS BATTLES

CAPTURE OF FORT DONELSON.
FEBRUARY 16th, 1862.

BATTLE AT PITTSBURG LANDING,
APRIL 6th, 1862.

EN. PEMBERTON SURRENDERS VICKSBURG TO GEN. GRANT.
JULY 4th, 1863.

SURRENDER OF GENERAL LEE,
APRIL 9th, 1865.

ULYSSES S. GRANT,
LIEUTENANT-GENERAL. U. S. A.

US

BATTLE OF THE WILDERNESS, MAY, 1864,

BATTLE BEFORE RICHMOND, APRIL, 1865.

ages; afterward, others assumed this patriotic place in the household alongside Washington, especially Lincoln and Grant.[22]

In Civil War printmaking, Grant reigned longest, his popularity buoyed by his White House service, and his images were soon being published around the world. From Paris came *Le General Grant*, lithographed by L. Mercier, and from Madrid, *Ulysses S. Grant. / general en gefe*, lithographed for Garcia by N. Gonzalez.[23]

Yet where Grant's wartime image was concerned, one is left with the sense that printmakers might well have accomplished more. Nothing would have more effectively leavened his reputation for butchery and insobriety, for example, than early groupings portraying him in the warm embrace of his family. Printmakers were slow to realize this, and their potential subjects seemed unaware of the power such images exerted. Lincoln family prints were also delayed until their publication could help Lincoln no longer; not a single example was issued before his assassination. But the Lincoln example, once displayed, proved too powerful to ignore. When Grant changed his mind about the presidency and agreed to run for the White House in 1868, printmakers began an earnest effort to domesticate him. Now Grant family scenes would serve a subtle "political" purpose of demilitarizing the presidential candidate for a country in which the superiority of the civil to the military was sacred political doctrine.

One such effort by Philadelphia engraver Samuel Sartain (fig. 90) portrayed Grant—still in uniform—seated in a parlor with Julia and their children. Another example by Sartain moved the family outdoors, so Grant and his eldest son could be portrayed not only in uniform, but on horseback, as Julia, the children, and a family dog look on. Not one of these prints is contemporaneous with the war, though models had been available (Grant loved his family and brought them to headquarters as often as possible, offering opportunities for photography).[24]

Grant's 1868 presidential campaign inspired military images as well. A typical lithograph, published by Charles S. Crosby of Boston, portrayed Grant in uniform and identified him in its caption as a general, not a candidate. Grant's military record remained his greatest asset, and it rarely seemed threatening to Northerners (until talk of a third term arose). Nearly every Grant print issued in 1868 portrayed

opposite

Figure 89. Haasis and Lubrecht, *The Leader and His Battles / Ulysses S. Grant, / Lieutenant-General, U.S.A.* Published by Charles Lubrecht, New York, ca. 1865. Hand-colored wood engraving, 35⅜ × 27⅞ inches. What had now become the favored image of Grant—a three-quarters profile, based on photographs—rises over a flag-draped wreath of peace in this tribute to the general's battlefield triumphs. Pictured, clockwise from top left, were the capture of Fort Donelson, the Battle of Pittsburg Landing (Shiloh), the surrender at Appomattox, the battle before Richmond, the Battle of the Wilderness, and the surrender of Vicksburg. The last-named vignette was probably the best, showing a cigar-chomping Grant receiving the vanquished Confederate stronghold from General John C. Pemberton. However, Grant and the irritable Confederate general met outdoors on July 3; the July 4 surrender occurred indoors. Printmakers Haasis and Lubrecht specialized in such incident-rich tributes: they issued similar depictions of Abraham Lincoln and Stonewall Jackson in 1865 and 1867, respectively. (*The Lincoln Museum*)

him in uniform, testifying to the irresistible urge of image makers to continue merchandising him as a war hero, rather than a politician, during the presidential campaign. Anti-Grant political cartoons, too, recalled his military glory. Even S. Merinsky's scathing 1872 lampoon, *David and Goliath*, which quoted the Book of Samuel in castigating the giant (Grant) as an "uncircumcised Philistine," made Grant look bold and fierce and depicted him in uniform, clutching a spear and shield and wearing a plumed helmet to face his tiny opponent, Horace Greeley, who readies his Davidian sling.[25]

In subsequent prints, however, Grant did not always seem a giant. The explanation probably lies in his subsequent career. Unlike the generals who lived on principally in memory, making occasional appearances at parades and reunions, Grant became president of the United States, serving two full terms, and though few questioned his integrity, he left office surrounded by reports of corruption within his administration. He suddenly seemed less invincible than he had appeared on the battlefield. His death in 1885 inspired only a small, brief flurry of new printmaking.

Thure de Thulstrup did create a handsome biographical watercolor that year as the model for a print, dominated by a trompe l'oeil profile portrait surrounded by vignettes representing highlights of Grant's military career, but omitting his subsequent political career. The resulting chromo, entitled *Grant from West Point to Appomattox* (fig. 91), recalled most of Grant's crowning moments as a Civil War commander in small pictures that looked very much like the Grant scenes Thulstrup was then creating for Louis Prang's series of chromolithographs of the western campaigns.

In an anomalous development, Grant's death failed to provide printmakers the upsurge in demand they had counted on. Four years earlier, the assassination of President Garfield had created such bedlam at Currier and Ives's New York City retail shop that its manager, Edward West Currier, the founder's son, ordered barriers erected to control the crowd. "At times," he exulted, "they yelled so for pictures that the neighbors were scared and put their heads out of the windows to see what the matter was." Grant's passing inspired no similar demand, even though the firm marked his last heroic act—his race against cancer to complete his autobiography— by issuing a large-folio lithograph entitled *General Grant in His Library, Writing His Memoirs.*[26]

"The grand old 'General' has passed away," the younger Currier wrote to his father when he heard the news, "and New York will give him an imposing funeral. I do not know as yet whether we will have a 'boom' in prints or not. The date of the funeral is so far advanced that patriots do not enthuse much as yet."[27] Currier's worries proved well founded. "The Grant boom is exceedingly quiet," he noted ruefully the following week. "There has been an overproduction of everything in that line." A week later he summarized the experience by admitting, "The sale of Grant pictures was very small."[28]

That week, a photographer stopped in front of the firm's self-described "Grand

Figure 90. Samuel Sartain, *General Grant and His Family*. Designed by F[rederick A.] Schell. Published by Daughaday and Becker, Philadelphia, 1868. Mezzotint engraving, 24½ × 17½ inches. This is one of several Grant family prints issued during the presidential campaign of 1868 to domesticate the general's image. Almost all of them nevertheless depicted the war hero in uniform, and this one compounded its martial sensibility by portraying Grant's son, too, in military garb: the uniform of a West Point cadet. Note the picture of Lincoln in the background, perhaps included to remind viewers of the wartime bond between the general and the martyred commander in chief. Grant had allowed artist William Cogswell to paint his family from life, a group portrait subsequently engraved by Samuel Sartain's father, John, unleashing a flood of Grant family prints in time for election season. (Barber, *U. S. Grant*, 19, 54–55.) (*The Lincoln Museum*)

Central Depot for Cheap and Popular Pictures" and made a record of Currier and Ives's attempt to revive interest in the print portraits of Ulysses S. Grant (fig. 92). The photograph has been published before, usually accompanied by captions speculating only about the identity of the two men who pose in the emporium's doorway. No one has seemed to notice the black crape draped above the entrance or, more important, the pictures hanging in the window. There are perhaps a dozen in all, few easily distinguishable. But seven are unmistakable military portraits of the man whose wartime triumphs had been portrayed by this and nearly every other major printmaking firm in the North. Here, decorating Currier and Ives's shop window, was print after print of Ulysses S. Grant.

By the 1890s some who had overinvested in Grant images during the Civil War

Fort Donelson 1862.

The Battle of Shiloh 1862.

Drilling his Volunteers 1861.

The Siege of Vicksburg 1863.

In the Tower of Chapultepec 1847.

The Battle of Chattanooga 1863.

Graduated at West Point 1843.
Gen. Scott presenting diploma.

The Surrender of Gen. Lee 1865.

Commander in Chief 1864.

Copyright 1885 by L. Prang & Co. Boston.

Published by L. Prang & Co. Boston.

GRANT FROM WEST POINT TO APPOMATTOX.

had to unload their stock, including J. C. Buttre, who had issued one of the first prints of the general more than thirty years earlier. In his catalog of that year, which offered engravings by Buttre himself, as well as the work of others, his firm offered nineteen small prints of Grant, each 9½ by 12 inches in size, for twenty-five cents each. They included works by A. H. Ritchie, George E. Perine, H. B. Hall, John A. O'Neill, Frank Whitechurch, and others, most, if not all of them, designed originally as plates to illustrate books, now available in overstock as separate-sheet display pictures. Whereas only seven showed Grant as president, twelve depicted him as a general. Similarly, four of the six larger prints offered in the catalog showed the military Grant. Buttre offered his own 36-by-28-inch print for three dollars and Ritchie's and O'Neill's slightly smaller images at one dollar each.[29]

Unlike Lincoln, Grant would not be pictured going to heaven to meet George Washington. Fame in battle can carry an image only so far in a country devoutly dedicated to civil control of the military. But while the fashion endured for portrait prints of Civil War luminaries, Ulysses S. Grant reigned supreme.

The "Quintessence of Yankeedom"?

"Grant was short, Sherman tall," recalled one observer, "the former compact, the latter loosely built; the one broad and deep in the chest, the other narrow and almost effeminate." While Grant was "slow of speech," Sherman "talked incessantly and much more rapidly than any man I ever saw," as one Union officer remembered. "It would be easier to say what he did not talk about than what he did." To printmakers who portrayed them together in councils of war or military reviews—as did Ferdinand Mayer and Sons in an 1867 lithograph of an Ole Peter Hansen Balling painting (fig. 93)—they seemed, in the words of the Mayer caption, the greatest of all the "heroes of the republic."[30]

Sherman suffered from what modern media consultants would call "an image problem," one that was largely of his own making. His recent biographers concur that late in 1861, Sherman lapsed into deep mental depression. The general himself later referred to this period as "a perfect 'slough of despond.'" Historians dis-

---

opposite

Figure 91. L[ouis]. Prang and Company, after a watercolor by Thure de Thulstrup, *Grant from West Point to Appomattox*. Boston, 1885. Chromolithograph, 23⅞ × 17¾ inches. A faithful reproduction of the Thulstrup original, produced in the same large format, Prang's chromo replicated the clever trompe l'oeil effect Thulstrup created by overlaying the central portrait and imposing a thick black stripe to simulate a shadow at the bottom. Around this profile, clockwise from lower left, are depictions of Grant's graduation from West Point; the storming of Chapultepec during the Mexican War; the drilling of volunteers in 1861 (showing his beard as he would, in reality, trim it only later); supervising the capture of Fort Donelson; laying siege to Vicksburg; observing the action at Chattanooga; receiving his commission from Lincoln as lieutenant general (not as "commander-in-chief," as the picture suggested, which was Lincoln's title); and accepting Lee's surrender at Appomattox. The chromo appeared the year of Grant's death. (*Kenneth M. Newman, The Old Print Shop, New York*)

Figure 92. [Photographer unknown], [*Currier and Ives Employees Posing Outside the Nassau Street Shop*], late July or early August 1885. The shop window is filled with print portraits of the late President Grant—all of them showing him as a Civil War hero—as the firm seeks to attract new customers for its old lithographs. One can almost discern the outlines of the Ehrgott, Forbriger equestrian print of Grant (lower left), indicating that Currier and Ives sold works by other printmakers along with their own. The firm's new owner reported that disappointingly few of these pictures were sold while New Yorkers gathered en masse for Grant's funeral. (*Courtesy Harold Holzer*)

agree on how disabling the illness proved, but one thing is certain: Sherman was not spared the humiliation of seeing allegations of his insanity published in the press. "General Wm. T. Sherman Insane," is the way one headline bluntly trumpeted the news. Back at headquarters in St. Louis, even discounting for hyperbole, General Henry W. Halleck was sufficiently alarmed to declare Sherman "entirely unfit for duty" in 1861.[31]

Sherman's mental health revived, as did his reputation. But the episode aroused in the general a lifelong hatred for the press that not even satisfaction over his wartime triumphs and widespread popularity in the North could soften. Feuds with reporters seldom inspire tributes, so Sherman's unyielding loathing for war correspondents ("a set of sneaking, croaking scoundrels," he called them) cost him perhaps two years of positive attention in the public spotlight. Sherman's hatred for the press hardened even further when some reported that the general's unprepared men had been bayoneted while still in their tents at Shiloh. "General Grant and General Sherman have had more than their share of abuse," one supporter protested in a letter published in their defense in the *New York Tribune*.[32]

"HEROES OF THE REPUBLIC"

Figure 93. Ferdinand Mayer and Sons, after Ole Peter Hansen Balling, *"Heroes of the Republic."* New York, 1867. Lithograph with tintstone, 22¼ × 34¾ inches. Grant, Sherman, and the Union high command march in a grand, but wholly imaginary, review beneath a patriotic canopy of billowing American flags in this print adaptation of a painting made from life studies while the war still raged. Although Grant cooperated willingly in the production of his portrait for the original canvas, Sherman initially told the artist "to go to a hot place." Ultimately, he was lured to his brother's house, ostensibly for a family reunion, and "cornered" into posing. General Philip H. Sheridan is in the left foreground on his famous horse, Rienzi. (O. P. H. Balling, "An Artist's Close-up View of Lincoln, Grant, and Sherman," *Civil War Times* 3 [October 1964]: 17–18.) (*National Portrait Gallery*)

Eventually, Sherman moved to ban one especially irritating newspaperman from his army for filing a particularly critical report. Thomas W. Knox of the *New York Herald* replied: "I had no feeling against you personally, but you are regarded as the enemy of our set, and we must in self-defense write you down." Furious, Sherman had Knox court-martialed and expelled—and to Sherman went the dubious distinction of bringing the only such action against a journalist in American history. For as long as they could, Northern journalists wrote Sherman down. But they could not do so after he began winning battlefield glory, and in the end the general's patience was rewarded with "real" fame. He seemed to at least one observer to be "the concentrated quintessence of Yankeedom," all his features—a "tall, spare" build, long neck, and large head—combining convincingly to "express determination."[33]

Sherman's dislike and distrust of war correspondents extended to those who covered the campaigns pictorially. A *Frank Leslie's* editorial of December 7, 1861, attacking "pompous fools and martinets" who sought to prevent the weekly's special artists from covering the war, was by all accounts directed at Sherman. "You fellows make the best spies that can be bought," the general had reportedly raged at the "offending" special artist, banning him, too, from camp.[34]

As late as the end of 1863, Sherman was still doing his best to avoid correspondents and portrait-makers alike. "I have been importuned from many quarters for my likeness," he wrote to his brother, Senator John Sherman, on December 30. "I have managed to fend off all parties and hope to do so till the end of the war. I don't want to rise or be notorious." He treated painters, like O. P. H. Balling, the same way, attempting to avoid sittings until his fame was secure. As he told his brother, "If parties apply to you for materials in my behalf, give the most brief and general items, and leave the results to the close of my career."[35]

The pictorial results proved equally difficult to procure. One soldier who served under his command noted of Sherman, "He looks rather like an anxious man of business than an ideal soldier." An officer concurred: "There are no outward signs of greatness. He appears to be a very ordinary man." Encountering him for the first time, Major John C. Gray Jr., judge advocate for the Department of the South, observed: "General Sherman is the most American looking man I ever saw, tall and lank, not very erect, with hair like a thatch, which he rubs up with his hands, a rusty beard trimmed close, a wrinkled face, sharp, prominent red nose, small bright eyes, coarse red hands; black felt hat slouched over the eyes . . . dirty dickey with the points wilted down . . . and might sit to *Punch* for the portrait of an ideal Yankee."[36] Only when Sherman finally achieved fame would printmakers find themselves compelled to deal with all the factors that had inhibited the production of his parlor portraits: the hostility of the subject toward portrayals in *any* media, the dearth of available models, and, ultimately, the fact that, from Atlanta on, Sherman waged the kind of war that was not designed to inspire either picturesque battle scenes or heroic portraiture.

The problem of sources plagued even the western lithography firm of Ehrgott, Forbriger and Company, whose convenient location in Cincinnati should have increased its access to up-to-date Sherman photographs. The firm had issued a print portrait of General John A. Dix (fig. 94), whose original assignment to the command of the Department of Annapolis in July 1861 may explain the presence of a warship looming in the background of the print. The setting made less sense when Ehrgott, Forbriger replaced Dix's head with that of Sherman, the result (fig. 95) presenting the rising commander in a decidedly eastern, not to mention aquatic, setting. (Sherman had fought at Bull Run, but attracted his first real attention in the West.) To make matters worse, the portrait of Sherman was based on an early, outdated source. It showed the general looking perhaps ten years younger than he appeared during the rest of the Civil War, and wearing a close-shaved round beard, not his signature scruffy whiskers.[37]

What is more surprising than the inaccuracy of this early image is the paucity of portraits appearing thereafter to give audiences a correct impression of Sherman's wartime appearance. Notwithstanding his triumph at Atlanta (the most "gigantic" accomplishment of the war, according to Grant) and his subsequent March to the Sea, printmakers did not respond quickly to his sudden fame by issuing portraits. The inability of the print medium to capitalize on public interest in William T. Sherman can best be explained by the insurmountable problem of the lack of photographic models.[38]

A recent Sherman study featured a handsome cover illustration showing the general's determined features rising above an emblematic array of laurel leaves and military hardware, surrounded by an American flag. According to the book jacket, the portrait (fig. 96) is an "engraving by L. N. Rosenthal, 1864." There are some errors in the details here: the print is a lithograph, not an engraving, and it is the work not of Louis Rosenthal, but his brother, Max. More important, the original print portrait bears the date 1865, not 1864, and this fact is crucial to understanding the laggard evolution of the Sherman image. Only when he fell into the hands of the photographers who crowded the eastern theater of the war did William T. Sherman sit for the models that would then become the sources for the heroic portraiture that had been so long denied him—and that did not occur until he reached North Carolina from Savannah in 1865. William Sartain's faithful, undated mezzotint engraving, for example, was likely published that year, for 1865 is when the Brady Studio photograph on which it was based was made.[39]

A few months earlier, the New York print publishers Jones and Clark had issued one of the few authentic Sherman images published in 1864. Describing it in a *Harper's Weekly* advertisement on November 26 as "the largest and only correct portrait" of the general, the printmakers boasted that it was based on "a recent Photograph" and offered copies to prospective salesmen for fifty cents apiece. "Agents wanted," Jones and Clark declared, "in the Army and elsewhere." Most likely, the publishers expected Sherman's soldiers to clamor for the print, and it seems probable, recalling the anecdote of the bogus Grant photographs, that they did.[40]

Several weeks later, General Sherman achieved his final goal on the march from Atlanta, and on December 22 he sent President Lincoln one of the best-remembered military reports of the entire war: "I beg to present you as a Christmas-gift the city of Savannah, with one hundred and fifty heavy guns and plenty of ammunition, also about twenty-five thousand bales of cotton." An appreciative Lincoln replied on December 26: "Many, many thanks for your Christmas-gift—the capture of Savannah. When you were about leaving Atlanta for the Atlantic coast, I was *anxious*, if not fearful; but feeling that you were the better judge, and remembering that 'nothing risked, nothing gained' I did not interfere. Now, the undertaking being a success, the honor is all yours."[41]

Sherman's letter was reproduced in facsimile—suggesting the general's cooperation in the enterprise—beneath the caption when J. C. Buttre of New York issued

JOHN. A. DIX.
MAJ.GEN^{L.} U.S.A.

Figure 94. Ehrgott, Forbriger and Company, *John A. Dix. / Maj. Genl. U.S.A.* Cincinnati, ca. 1863. Lithograph, 9½ × 9⁷⁄₁₆ inches. Born in 1798, Dix was a former United States senator and, briefly, secretary of the treasury. He was already well known to many Americans when the Civil War began. His first wartime command was the Department of Annapolis, which explains the background of this print: a force of armed soldiers marching on land and a warship steaming offshore. Like other images from Ehrgott, Forbriger's midwar series of military portraits, the design would be used again (see fig. 95). (*Library of Congress*)

W. T. SHERMAN.
MAJ. GEN.ᴸ U.S.A.

Figure 95. Ehrgott, Forbriger and Company, *W. T. Sherman. / Maj. Genl. U.S.A.* Cincinnati, ca. 1863. Lithograph, 9½ × 9⁷⁄₁₆ inches. If the combination of equestrian, military, and naval accoutrements suited a portrait of General Dix (see fig. 94), the design here seemed less welcoming of General Sherman, whose head was affixed to the generic body in the Dix print to form this second state of the image. To compound its incongruity, the Sherman portrait itself was based on a beardless, side-whiskered photograph that showed the general as he looked before he grew the red beard that became something of a trademark. (*Library of Congress*)

the imposing engraving, *Sherman at Savannah, Ga.* (fig. 97) in 1865. The print was based on an "original picture" by Colonel Otto Boetticher, a Prussian-born Union soldier-artist who had served in the Sixty-eighth New York Volunteers before being captured and confined to military prison (an experience that inspired his most famous work, a depiction of Union prisoners at Salisbury, North Carolina, playing baseball [see fig. 29]). For group equestrian scenes like *Sherman at Savannah*, Boetticher had a rather more conventional approach. Horses rear up or kick up dust, and discrete knots of officers exchange meaningful glances as the great event unfolds. Boetticher's scene of Sherman's arrival in Savannah bore close resemblance to his own *Grant and Lee / (Meeting near Appomattox Courthouse, Va., the Day after the Surrender of Lee's Army)*, published by Hatch and Company in 1866. Although one scene purports to show the South in spring and the other in winter, the ground and sky are the same in both, as are the overall designs. But compared to such improbable group equestrian scenes as O. P. H. Balling's more famous contribution (see fig. 93), the Boetticher print was masterful.[42]

Furthermore, Sherman would remark of Savannah that its streets were "perfectly regular, crossing each other at right angles." Many of its intersections, he noted, were nothing more than "small enclosures in the nature of parks." Sherman thought the trees lining the streets particularly beautiful, and he admired a statue of Count Pulaski in a large park above the city. But he rather dismissed Savannah's reputation for grandeur, pointing out that its houses "would hardly make a display on Fifth Avenue or the Boulevard Haussmann of Paris." Not only was Boetticher's vision of the city surprising for its absence of any trees, it made the central part of Savannah look grander than the Place de Concorde, much less the Boulevard Haussmann.[43]

Fame came late for Sherman, almost too late for him to be depicted as a hero before the fighting ceased, and at the conclusion of the conflict he stumbled and nearly experienced the fall from fame he had earlier feared. Unlike Grant, when Sherman accepted the surrender of Confederate General Joseph Johnston in North Carolina on April 26, 1865, he did not enhance his reputation, he endangered it.

Sherman and Johnston first met to discuss surrender terms on April 17, barely a week after Lee had capitulated to Grant at Appomattox. Sherman carried with him to this initial meeting something of a trump card: the as yet unknown news that Lincoln had been assassinated. Sherman handed Johnston the dispatch and "watched him closely. The perspiration came out in large drops on his forehead, and he did not attempt to conceal his distress. . . . We talked about the effect of this act on the country at large and on the armies, and he realized that it made my situation extremely delicate."[44]

But rather than use the disquieting news to exact concessions from his adversary, the conqueror, whom historian Michael Fellman called "the harshest Union scourger of the South," instead became, in Fellman's words, "the maker of the softest and kindest peace." Sherman went beyond the generous terms Grant had offered Lee and included a "general amnesty" that did not specifically exclude civilians, with the

MAJ. GEN. W^{M.} T. SHERMAN.

Figure 96. Max Rosenthal, *Maj. Gen. Wm. T. Sherman*. Signed in stone, left, "Max Rosenthal / Del." "Engraved" (printed) by L[ouis]. N. Rosenthal, published by William Smith, Philadelphia, 1865. Lithograph with tintstone, 25⅞ × 19⅛ inches. American flags and victory laurels cradle a portrait of Sherman published to celebrate his wartime triumphs. The tools of war gathered in the foreground—a musket, saber, telescope, pistol, fieldpiece, cannonball, and trumpet—are presented as relics of the conquest of Atlanta, the skyline of which is visible in the background. (*National Portrait Gallery*)

Figure 97. Major and Knapp, *Sherman at Savannah, Ga. / From the Original Picture by Brt. Col. Otto Boetticher*, with a facsimile of Sherman's letter to Lincoln. Published by J[ohn] C. Buttre, New York, 1865. Lithograph, 26 × 34 inches. The grand vista of Savannah hovers in bright winter sunshine in the background as William T. Sherman and his staff of twenty individually identified officers march into the captured city. Artist Boetticher, who was breveted a lieutenant colonel in 1865 "for gallant and meritorious conduct," had been a captive at Salisbury prison in North Carolina, where he made perhaps the best known of his wartime pictures: a scene of Union prisoners playing baseball (see fig. 29). Here he created one of the best of the equestrian group print portraits of the Civil War, a well-drawn picture whose horses assume imaginatively varied positions and, for once, kick up considerable dust. (*The Old Print Gallery, Washington, D.C.*)

understanding that Confederate troops outside Johnston's jurisdiction would surrender as well. Johnston wanted a return to the *status quo ante bellum*, and Sherman was not himself unwilling to see the South return to its prewar situation: they agreed that the Confederacy's prewar legislatures would be reconstituted and civilian property rights recognized (without specifically excluding slaves). Southerners would be guaranteed "their political rights and franchises, as well as their rights of person and property, as defined by the Constitution of the United States and of the States respectively." No mention was made of emancipation, the Thirteenth Amendment then approaching ratification, or the rights of ex-slaves.[45]

A horrified Secretary of War Edwin M. Stanton promptly ordered Grant to disapprove the surrender and direct Sherman "to resume hostilities at the earliest moment." All political issues, Stanton reminded Grant, were to be held by the president "in his own hands." Grant relayed the message, and Sherman was compelled to meet with Johnston for a second time and require him to accept terms similar to those Lee had accepted from Grant. Sherman's humiliation was complete, tempered only by the fact that the war was finally over. In full fury, the hero of Atlanta adopted both malevolent tone and imperial voice to vow revenge: "Sherman, who was not scared by the crags of Lookout Mountain, the barriers of Kenesaw, and long and trackless forests of the South, is not to be intimidated by the howlings of a set of sneaks who were hid away to brag as danger was rampant, but now shriek with very courage."[46]

The damage to Sherman's popular reputation proved slight and temporary. His explanation—that he had only been following the wishes Lincoln had expressed when the late president conferred with his commanders at City Point, Virginia, on March 27 and 28—eventually satisfied many Northerners, who, after all, had for months digested reports detailing the opposite side of Sherman's military ethos: his harshness. Lincoln had "said that he contemplated no revenge," Sherman insisted in 1872, although he admitted that he could not recall Lincoln's precise "language at the time."[47]

The surrender inspired only two known prints, a fraction of the number of engravings and lithographs produced to commemorate the meeting of Grant and Lee at Appomattox. Philadelphia lithographer Pierre S. Duval, who produced *Interview between Sherman & Johnson [sic]* (fig. 98), realistically portrayed "the small frame-house," as Sherman later described it. The lithographer thus resisted the impulse to which several Appomattox printmakers had succumbed by exaggerating the size of the historic parlor where Lee and Grant had met earlier that month. Moreover, the printmaker came close to achieving a sense of mood in his portrayals of the rigid and defiant-looking Johnston gazing fixedly as Sherman dispassionately reads a piece of paper he holds in his hands.

Currier and Ives entitled its version *The Surrender of Genl. Joe Johnston Near Greensboro, N.C. April 26th 1865*, taking no notice of the controversy over peace terms. Johnston has removed his hat and holds his sword as if he is about to offer it to Sherman. The Union general, hat firmly planted on head, scowls menacingly at his vanquished foe, his arms folded on his chest. The iconography of Sherman's final scene in the Civil War drama had thus metamorphosed quickly. Currier and Ives's principal error was to place the scene outdoors, with both Union and Confederate armies lined up in the background, when in fact the generals' second meeting, like the first, had occurred inside the modest Bennett House.

The effort either predated or ignored Sherman's presumptuous attempt to impose his own conservative political beliefs on peace. The printmakers ignored his hysterical reaction to the criticism that followed, including his request that his superior, General Henry Halleck, "keep slightly *perdu*" after criticizing the first Bennett House peace, lest Sherman's own men take revenge for "public insult to a brother officer."[48]

By the time retrospective prints were coming off the press, Sherman's reputation was fully restored. He was among the first to tell his side of the story of the war, in a skillful memoir in 1875. He became a prolific public speaker, a ubiquitous presence at Civil War reunions, a lionized hero, and yet a man who refused to capitalize on his fame by standing for public office or engaging in party affairs. It was inevitable that his likeness would grace some of the postwar prints that looked nostalgically at the war from the safe distance of twenty years. Basing one such print at least in part on a well-known stereopticon photograph of Sherman on horseback by Alexander Gardner, Thure de Thulstrup produced a handsome equestrian watercolor of Sherman at the Siege of Atlanta (plate 12), published for Louis Prang's portfolio of Civil War chromolithographs.[49]

According to the pamphlet issued by Prang to accompany the print, it was in-

INTERVIEW BETWEEN SHERMAN & JOHNSON

Figure 98. P[ierre]. S. Duval, *Interview between Sherman & Johnson* [sic]. New York, ca. 1865. Lithograph, 5⅝ × 8¾ inches. Sherman studies the surrender terms as his vanquished opponent, Confederate General Joseph E. Johnston, waits with evident unease in this rare depiction of the meeting at the Bennett House in Durham, North Carolina. The print erred in showing the principals with their staffs; Sherman remembered that "we were alone together" (William Tecumseh Sherman, *Memoirs* [1875; reprint, New York: Library of America, 1990], 837). Unlike Appomattox, the Bennett House surrender quickly had a shadow cast over it when the War Department disallowed Sherman's terms, and this scene never rivaled the meeting of Lee and Grant in iconographic memory. (*The Lincoln Museum*)

tended to celebrate Sherman's dogged artillery attack on Atlanta, "maintained . . . [an] entire month" even as the infantry slowly closed in on the city, "capturing the various defences and fortified positions." Sherman is portrayed with his aides, including Colonel O. M. Poe, his chief of engineers, surveying the scene with typical grim detachment.[50]

But G. P. A. Healy's 1868 painting, *The Peacemakers*, issued in 1871 as a chromolithograph (fig. 99), best pleased Sherman as an iconographical record of his wartime service. The original canvas has most often been described, particularly in captions for illustrated histories and magazines, as a Lincoln portrait—or more precisely, a portrait of Lincoln and his commanders in council of war. But a careful examination of the work will remind viewers that Sherman is shown emphatically talking and gesturing, and the others merely listening.

Only in part for this reason, the chromo stands as one of the most important print portraits of the controversial general. It was also perhaps the first work in whose creation Sherman cooperated himself; what was more, he elicited the participation of Grant. By then each hero had adopted the other's old attitude toward sitting for portraits: Sherman was now eager to pose, but Grant was so tired of posing he "had determined not to sit again." It is surely no coincidence that the finished work, and the print it inspired, gave prominence to Healy's friend Sherman. With one eye surely still focused on the North Carolina surrender controversy, Sherman insisted that the scene at City Point portrayed not a council of war, but a conference on peace, in which four warriors explored the idea of leniency toward the South. Healy agreed, painting a symbolic rainbow visible through a porthole in the background. The image not only justified Sherman's scorned generosity at the Bennett House, it delineated his image precisely as he thought it should be remembered: that of the fiercest of all warriors who nonetheless knew how and when to end the fight by shaking hands.[51]

Sherman also proved that he knew when it was time to make peace with image makers, although it surely would have accrued to his benefit had he softened his attitude toward them during the war. He began corresponding regularly with Healy and Daniel Huntington. He sat for sculptor Augustus Saint-Gaudens, and he collected art himself, including a set of Edwin Forbes's war etchings. He gave suggestions to painters like James E. Taylor and once, observing a sculptor at work on a bust of Grant, took the tools himself to make corrections. "Pictures like these," he told Taylor of his Civil War works in 1883, "in one glance give a better idea than a hundred pages of the best descriptive writing." The man who disdained sittings during the war proved true to his word: once his career was over, and left to history and art to interpret, he was the very model of enthusiastic cooperation.[52]

Still, Sherman's transformation from relentless warrior to generous peacemaker never really manifested itself in popular prints. The ugly side of the kind of war Sherman waged was rarely dealt with, nor was his own dark side ever fully confronted. Instead, once given access to photographic models, image makers focused

Figure 99. [Printmaker unknown], after George Peter Alexander Healy, *The Peacemakers*. New York, ca. 1871. Chromolithograph, 21⅝ × 29⅝ inches. Perhaps the best-known "council of war" image of the entire Civil War, Healy's painting of Abraham Lincoln's final meeting with, from left, General Sherman, General Grant, and Admiral David Dixon Porter combined the muscularity of military portraiture with the promise of lasting peace, as symbolized by the rainbow visible outside the window of the steamship cabin in which the historic session took place. The artist was Sherman's friend, which may help explain the fact that the general was shown in the foreground of the painting, speaking and gesturing as the others listen. Taking a keen interest in the production of the canvas, Sherman secured from Porter diagrams and descriptions of the cabin and wrote to Healy to provide a detailed description of the meeting. (*Chicago Historical Society*)

relentlessly on Sherman's stern visage, transforming it into a virtual icon of modern war.

Buttre's catalog of 1894, published thirty years after the March to the Sea, still offered eight small print portraits of Sherman at twenty-five cents each, together with three larger portraits, two by Ritchie and one by Buttre, for one dollar, and the dramatic image of Sherman at Savannah. But Sherman's was not the only portrait promoted. The same catalog offered eleven engravings of McClellan, six of Philip Sheridan, six of Burnside, five of Meade, six of Farragut, and three of Porter. The vogue for Civil War battle prints would come and go and come again, but America's taste for the Civil War military portrait remained constant and endured as long as the appetite existed for parlor prints themselves.[53]

Ultimately, however, the frustrating silence of the written record from the nineteenth century leaves us with more questions than answers about the military portraits of the Civil War. It is difficult to say whether the era's changes or its traditional elements were more significant. No longer were the heroes of war portrayed with their black servants in the background holding their horses, for example, as the first images of Washington and Lafayette had appeared in the early republic. Such blatantly aristocratic elements vanished in Civil War art (though not in fact: Grant had a black servant who fetched his horses and cigars). But the images were not otherwise notably democratized. Grant's image in prints, in fact, was consistently made more formal than he actually appeared. Nor were the images shorn in any obvious way of their hidden origins in monarchy and militarism. Though Civil War politics reverberated with hysterical allegations of Caesarism and conspiracy for military dictatorship, no witness from the century has left a syllable of comment on the potential these images held for creating the aura that might surround a man on horseback. No one commented on the distance these images stood from the antimilitarist republican origins of the United States.[54]

Of course, George Washington complicated the matter from the start, the Founding Father and first president being himself a great military hero. But popular prints existed at a level well below systematic analysis. If they were dangerous to republics when they celebrated military heroes, no one seems to have noticed. If potential dictators might have used them to advantage, none in fact recognized the opportunity. Essentially, the Union military portraits of the Civil War remain innocent expressions of curiosity about and reasonable gratitude for the North's military protectors. They suggested no sense that these saviors of the country or their images in any way actually threatened the republic, and in that faith the republic proved correct.

The Entire Field Could Be Observed

Civil War Battle Prints

After viewing a 1996 exhibition of Currier and Ives prints, a *New York Times* art critic observed that the Civil War "was never one of Currier & Ives's great subjects. In part this was because war photography had usurped the journalistic role of print illustration. But also because, one suspects, the middle-class audience on whom the firm depended for sales was badly unnerved by an event that had taken the country by the neck, shaken it violently, and put it down again, forever changed."[1]

That observation contains the sorts of errors inevitable in making any brief assessment of the state of the graphic arts during the Civil War. The fact of the matter is that the war did become a "great subject" for Currier and Ives. The intensity of coverage, measured by number of titles published, put the Civil War on a par with any other subject for which the firm has become famous. For example, Currier and Ives produced only some thirty steamboating prints during the company's long history. By contrast, the firm issued at least fifty-three different lithographs of Civil War battle scenes in "small folio size" (roughly 8¼ by 12¾ inches), most of them in one four-year period. That adds up to more than one per month for the forty-eight months of the Civil War. If large-folio prints (over 14 by 20 inches) are included the number reaches sixty, about double the number of steamboating scenes published over thirty-odd years. Military genre scenes and wartime portraits of military heroes would add still more titles to the impressive amount of war coverage.[2]

Moreover, photography by no means usurped the role of "illustration" previously held by engraving and lithography. Photographs could not be reproduced in newspapers or books during the Civil War, and illustration, understood as adding images to printed matter, remained almost entirely the realm of the engraver and lithographer. As for "illustrating" the events of the war in images for the Victorian home, it is not clear that printmakers felt competition from photography at all. In fact, photographs proved an aid in the lithographers' work, providing accurate portrait models of heroes, together with images of the scenes of campaigns and weapons of war.

Besides, photographs could not compete with prints in depicting action, heroism, color, and patriotism. Photographers longed to lend their works the same appeal, especially of patriotism, but it proved difficult to contrive. Moreover, camera operators had to stay away from battlefields until the fighting had ceased. They could not stand up behind their bulky box cameras, which were mounted on tall tripods, while bullets and cannon balls flew around them. They might take photographs of carnage or hallowed sites after the bullets quit flying, but they could not photograph the action itself. The buyers of popular prints found their morale raised by the vigorous action and flag-waving patriotism of action prints. Photographs could not inspire that response.

Finally, it would be best to dismiss the assumption that the audience of popular prints was "middle class." Perhaps it was, but class was not the most distinguishing characteristic of the print buyer. The middle classes read the urban daily newspapers, with their coverage of art exhibitions, but they could find no similar analysis or celebration of the humble popular lithograph—and only rarely an advertisement for their sale. Popular prints apparently appealed most to a less sophisticated audience, perhaps especially to country people to whom urban-based printmakers like Currier and Ives sold pictures by catalog, through advertisements in newspapers at holiday season, or via itinerant peddlers. The makeup of the audience helps explain the lack of visual sophistication in such pictures. Of course, city dwellers purchased prints as well—in New York at Currier and Ives's headquarters on Nassau Street, for example—but they were likely not the city's elite.

The quantity of Currier and Ives's small-folio battle prints (figs. 100–104) did not guarantee their quality, as they tended to be produced quickly, capitalizing on headlines. The surviving copyright records confirm the speed with which the firm worked. *The Battle of Pittsburg, Tenn., April 7th, 1862* (Shiloh), for example, was registered for copyright protection on June 3. *The Battle of Williamsburg, Va., May 6th, 1862* was registered on June 27, and *The Battle of Fair Oaks, Va., May 31st, 1862* (part of the Richmond campaign) was deposited only two weeks after the battle, on June 14, remarkably speedy coverage in an era when only words, and not pictures, could travel by telegraph, and when the mass production of images remained a tedious process still accomplished mostly by hand.[3] By 1863 Currier and Ives could count on even prompter performance from its artists and lithographers. *Maj. Genl. George G. Meade at the Battle of Gettysburg* was registered on July 13, only ten days after the guns fell silent in Pennsylvania.[4]

The small battle lithographs, the most journalistic of Civil War prints, thus document the importance of the war to Currier and Ives as a producer of popular prints and to its customers as seekers of patriotic and newsworthy images of the war. The sturdy presence of these rough images as part of the visual record of the Civil War deserves more extensive comment than the images usually receive as mere illustrations. It nevertheless requires an effort of historical imagination to understand them. As was the case with other artifacts found in the homes of the nonelite, the later reputation of the small battle pictures was never high. Neither was that of the

THE BATTLE OF SHARPSBURG, M.D. SEPT. 16TH 1862.

In this Battle the Federal troops under Gen! M.C Clellan, contended with the great Rebel army commanded by Generals Lee, "Stonewall" Jackson, Hill and Longstreet, for three days. The Rebels fought with desperate determination and courage, but the indomitable valour and heroism of the gallant Union Soldiers finally prevailed and defeated the enemy with great slaughter.

Figure 100. Currier and Ives, *The Battle of Sharpsburg, Md. Sept. 16th 1862.* New York, ca. 1862. Lithograph, 8¾ × 12¾ inches. Confederates face an attack led personally by General George B. McClellan (left, riding an undersized white horse and aiming an antique flintlock pistol) in this simplistic view of the Union victory at Antietam. The charging phalanx of Union soldiers at left is drawn in uninspired fashion, but the soldiers using bayonets in the left foreground show genuine energy. The print was captioned with this patriotic message: "In this Battle the Federal troops under Genl McClellan, contended with the great Rebel army commanded by Generals Lee, 'Stonewall' Jackson, Hill and Longstreet, for three days. The Rebels fought with desperate determination and courage, but the indomitable valour and heroism of the gallant Union Soldiers finally prevailed and defeated the enemy with great slaughter." (*Library of Congress*)

similar images published by the company's competitors, such as Hartford's E. B. and E. C. Kellogg. Hastily composed according to formula, some perhaps drawn and hand-tinted in assembly-line fashion by a series of specialists in portraits, figures, horses, landscape, and the like, they do not often appeal to modern-day museum curators selecting images for exhibition. They have never been much to collectors' tastes, either. Not a single Civil War print appeared among the eighty-four illustrations selected for Frederic A. Conningham's famous *Currier and Ives Prints: An Illustrated Check List.*

To revise the reputation of these prints for artistic merit or journalistic accuracy would be a mistake. Accuracy may have been nearer their reach than usually thought possible, because James Merritt Ives, one of the firm's principals and himself an artist, served briefly during the war as a captain in the Twenty-third Regiment of the New York State Militia.[5] But the prints were inspired less by direct witness of action than by other prints, by imagination, and by the woodcuts in the illustrated newspapers that were, in turn, based on the observations of the "special artists" at the front.

Their limitations as works of art were many. To the lamentably crude results of slapdash and unprofessional craftsmanship—unacceptable foreshortening, horses

THE BATTLE OF MALVERN HILL, Va JULY 1ST 1862.

Charge of the 36th New York Volunteers, at the Battle of Malvern Hill, July 1st 1862, and Capture of the Colors of the 14th Regt. N.C. Infantry.

Figure 101. Currier and Ives, *The Battle of Malvern Hill, Va. July 1st 1862. / Charge of the 36th New York Volunteers, at the Battle of Malvern Hill, July 1st 1862, and Capture of the Colors of the 14th Regt. N.C. Infantry.* New York, 1862. Lithograph, 8¾ × 12¾ inches. The line in the center of this print, formed by the rifles of the charging Union soldiers, appears to mark a section of the image drawn in less well-defined fashion by one artist. Another artist may have drawn the fleeing and terrified and wounded Confederate soldiers in the lower half of the print. Note the central dominance of the American flag. The battle was not a Union victory in any clear sense; the failure of the attempt to capture Richmond in 1862 in fact dealt a blow to Northern morale. (*Library of Congress*)

drawn too small, mismatched figure proportions, and distorted perspective—must be added a failure to embrace the dramatic diagonal in composition of action scenes. Instead, the prints were mostly designed on the horizontal. Some of them look as though they were divided into sections to be finished rapidly by different wielders of the lithographic crayon or sketching pencil.

The Battle of Malvern Hill, Va. July 1st 1862 (fig. 101), for example, seems to be constructed in two sections divided by a horizontal line drawn across the middle of the print. The more interesting lower half depicts terrified, wounded, and fleeing members of the Fourteenth North Carolina Infantry. The upper half, dominated by an American flag in the center of the composition, depicts the charge of the Thirty-

BOMBARDMENT AND CAPTURE OF FREDERICKSBURG, VA.— DEC. 11TH 1862.
BY THE ARMY OF THE POTOMAC, UNDER GEN!. BURNSIDE.

At sunrise ... opened on the City with 143 pieces of Artillery and set it on fire in several places. The attempt was then made to complete the pontoon bridge across the Rappahannock, but the rebel sharpshooters drove us back; Volunteers were then called for, to cross the river in small boats and dislodge the enemy; thousands sprung out of the ranks but only a hundred were ..... who crossed the river in the most dashing style, drove back the sharpshooters at the point of the bayonet, and captured over a hundred of them. The bridges were then completed and the army crossed in safety.

Figure 102. Currier and Ives, *Bombardment and Capture of Fredericksburg, Va.—Dec. 11th 1862. / By the Army of the Potomac, Under Genl. Burnside.* New York, ca. 1863. Lithograph, 7½ × 12½ inches. Union artillery opens fire over the Rappahannock River at the town of Fredericksburg, Virginia, as Ambrose E. Burnside looks on astride a white charger. This print surely emphasized the positive news from Fredericksburg, noting in its caption that the Federals were able to "dislodge the enemy," place pontoon bridges, cross the river "in safety," and capture 100 Confederate sharpshooters. The print did not suggest visually, nor did the caption mention, that two days later Burnside and his army suffered a resounding defeat at the ensuing Battle of Fredericksburg. In this instance, government propaganda could hardly have produced a more falsifying version of events than did this simple patriotic print. (*Library of Congress*)

BATTLE OF CHANCELLORSVILLE, Vᴬ MAY, 3ᴿᴰ 1863.

This terrific Battle was fought between the "Army of the Potomac" under Genᶦ Hooker; and the Rebel Army, under command of Generals Lee, "Stonewall" Jackson, Longstreet and Hill.— The Rebels advanced in overwhelming numbers, but the brave Union Soldiers fought with desperate gallantry, holding the Rebels in check, and inflicting dreadful slaughter among them.

Figure 103. Currier and Ives, *Battle of Chancellorsville, Va. May, 3rd 1863.* New York, ca. 1863. Lithograph, 8¼ × 12¾ inches. A viewer examining this print without knowledge of the Union loss at Chancellorsville would be unsure which side won the battle. Union troops sweep across the lithograph from right to left, waving the American flag as they attack, and Confederates seem to flee in the left foreground. The trees are too wintry for May in Virginia; foliage in fact aided the spectacular strategic maneuver of General Stonewall Jackson, who surprised the Union left flank by a rapid march on a hidden road. The battle could not have had the same result in winter. Neither image nor text referred to General Lee's triumph or General Joseph E. Hooker's stunning defeat. (*Library of Congress*)

sixth New York Infantry. The New Yorkers form a phalanx in two ranks as rigidly and tightly aligned as toy soldiers. (Little wonder a cartoonist for the picture weekly *Vanity Fair* made sport of the pretensions of Civil War artists to eyewitness acquaintance with battle by showing an artist behind his closed office door making his sketch on a table top with toy soldiers lined up on it [fig. 105].) In *The Battle of Malvern Hill* the stylistic differences between the facial likenesses in the two halves of the print seem great enough to suggest the work of two different artists.

A few of these prints are redeemed by a riveting portrait likeness of a general on horseback, and others capitalize on a pyramidal composition, featuring flag and of-

THE BATTLE OF GETTYSBURG, Pᴬ JULY 3ᴰ 1863.

This terrific and bloody conflict between the gallant "Army of the Potomac," commanded by their great General George G. Meade, and the host of the rebel "Army of Virginia" under General Lee, was commenced on Wednesday July 1ˢᵗ and ended on Friday the 3ᵈ at 5 O'Clock P.M. — The decisive Battle was fought on Friday, ending in the complete rout & dispersion of the rebel Army. — Undying fame and a Nations thanks, are ever due the heroic soldiers, who fought with such unflinching bravery in this long and desperate fight.

Figure 104. Currier and Ives, *The Battle of Gettysburg, Pa. July 3d 1863*. New York, 1863. Lithograph, 8 × 12¾ inches. In the Union triumph at Gettysburg, Currier and Ives finally had a subject to celebrate for Northern print buyers who focused on developments in the East, and the firm responded with three separate depictions of different highlights of the victory. This print, apparently intended to show the climactic Confederate charge of July 3, emphasized the solidity of the Union line. The print made no secret of its sympathies. Its caption offered "undying fame and a Nations [*sic*] thanks" to "the heroic soldiers, who fought with such unflinching bravery" during the "long and desperate fight." Note the resemblance of the Confederate with a head injury, the infantryman crouching away in retreat, and the soldier with upraised arms in the foreground to similar figures in *The Battle of Malvern Hill* (see fig. 101), symptomatic of the firm's occasional reliance on stock figure-painting. (*Library of Congress*)

ficer at the top and infantrymen at the base, that echoed the hierarchical military sociology of successful battle paintings of the era. For the most part, however, these battle pictures constitute evidence of the humble lack of sophistication of their patriotic purchasers.

The small lithograph from Currier and Ives that could lay claim to most distinction is *The Fall of Richmond, Va. on the Night of April 2nd 1865* (plate 13). This justifiably renowned print combined a memorable image of the city skyline with the dramatic diagonal of a long bridge spanning the James River, thronged with fleeing residents of Richmond. To these interesting features Currier and Ives added its

OUR OWN ARTIST SKETCHING "A VIEW OF GEN. BANKS' ARMY ON THE SPOT, FROM A DRAWING BY OUR SPECIAL ARTIST."

Figure 105. Benjamin H. Day Jr., *Our Own Artist Sketching "A View of Gen. Banks' Army on the Spot, from a Drawing by Our Special Artist."* Woodcut cartoon from *Vanity Fair*, September 14, 1861. After the war, *Harper's Weekly* suggested quite the opposite of what this cartoon seemed to admit. The newspaper boasted that its battlefield artists had worked "in the field, upon their knees, upon a knapsack, upon a bulwark, upon a drum-head, upon a block, upon a canteen, upon a wet-deck, in the gray dawn, in the dark twilight, with freezing or fevered fingers" to create war pictures "quivering with life, faithful, terrible, romantic, the value of which will grow every year" (*Harper's Weekly*, June 3, 1865). (*Library of Congress*)

tried-and-true accent of sensationalism, fire: the city is engulfed in flames. The print also invited close inspection of its details, such as the individual buildings depicted in the cityscape. Looking closely at the image of the bridge, a viewer was rewarded with an interesting array of infantry, cavalry, carriages, and quartermaster wagons laden with goods escaping in a long narrow line of terror from the conflagration behind them. Actually, the preferred escape route, taken by Jefferson Davis and other government officials at about eleven that night, was the railroad. But the print was reasonably accurate and has offered generations of Americans, mostly unfamiliar with such scenes on their own soil, a harrowing view of defeat, glowing red in fiery destruction.[6]

From the first emblematic prints focused on the American flag to the images of Richmond in flames and Lee's surrender at Appomattox, the Currier and Ives era of Civil War battle images, featuring prints that were produced near the time of the actions portrayed, exploited their news value but never lost sight of the flag. Their ultimate purpose was patriotic and their use in the home inspirational. Such images, with only a handful of exceptions, were published with undisguised pro-Union feeling and were too one-sided to dominate national memory after the war, when many people began striving for sectional reconciliation.

The popular prints of the American Civil War that have persisted for more than a century as illustrations in books and popular magazines were mostly post-Reconstruction products. Printed in the 1880s and 1890s, their dominance is in substantial degree a function of color, and color was the forte of chromolithography, a technique available during the war but not dominant in American print production until later. Modern collectors and museum-goers should keep in mind that they are likely to see more colored Currier and Ives prints today than Americans did in the 1860s. Color is widely regarded as desirable, and it has occasionally been added by obliging dealers and collectors over the years to lithographs originally published in black and white.

Besides color, the chromolithographs of the 1880s and 1890s also offered images affected by the first great era of reconsideration of the war. Inaugurated in the 1880s by the United States government's publication of the war's official records, the period witnessed a spate of articles serialized in middlebrow magazines and later collected in multivolume works—especially the heavily illustrated *Battles and Leaders of the Civil War*. Scribner's Campaigns of the War series of books also appeared then. The battle chromolithographs that were produced around the same time in Chicago and Boston should be thought of as part of that broader movement of recollection. They shared its two driving but ultimately irreconcilable principles: celebration, as in battlefield reunions and heroizing memoirs, and a quest for accuracy, which was the thrust of the voluminous *Official Records* and other monuments of serious scholarship. Impartiality was as yet unachievable, though the chromolithographs made some strides in that direction, critical to their broader acceptability. Confederate soldiers were no longer depicted, as they had been in Currier and Ives's *Battle of Malvern Hill*, as the hapless and terrified victims of an invincible Northern phalanx.

It was crucial, of course, that Reconstruction had ended. Lithographs and engravings existed in a creative world parallel to but not identical with the realm of the printed word, and these postwar prints took inspiration from more than written sources. The most important influence, and probably the most neglected in writing on prints, may have been the cyclorama—a visual (and commercial) inspiration rather than a reflective, political, or intellectual one. Prints were part of the urge to commemorate and recollect and get the story right, but they were particularly influenced by the advent of the visually sensational cycloramas in Northern cities. These huge circular paintings, first made popular in Europe, offered Americans spectacle and illusion on a cinematic scale. The chromolithographs of battles that followed in the wake of the cycloramas might be thought of as the nineteenth century's equivalent of "movie tie-ins" or "spin-offs." In other words, the spectacular cycloramas popularized depictions of Civil War battles, and chromolithographers attempted to imitate their success and offer the print-buying public a little piece of a cyclorama for display at home.

Evidence of direct influence can be found in *Battle of Shiloh. April 6th 1862* (fig. 106), a chromolithograph of a panoramic Shiloh painting then on exhibit in Chicago, published by Cosack and Company in 1885 (one of several Civil War prints produced as promotional items by the McCormick Harvesting Machine Company). The colorful print offered a panoramic view of the battle (with a McCormick machine, not a part of the original panorama, drawn into the scene in the left foreground) adapted from the larger painting. Theophile Poilpot's original canvases laid out the customary sweep of action on both sides, along with the usual homely details and heroic anecdotes. These were legendary in their day but are lost to most viewers now.

For example, the curious figure of an old man with a white beard at the base of a tree in the left center of the print represented a sixty-year-old private of the Ninth Illinois Volunteer Infantry. James Getty refused to fall back with his unit when it ran short of ammunition (hence his exposed position in front of the Union lines of battle in the print) and kept on firing and loading with other units. A canny old soldier, he carefully obtained signed statements from officers of the other units attesting to the fact that he had spent the day fighting and not skulking. The anecdote appeared in print in 1864 in a regimental history and, after twenty years of retelling, was ripe for pictorial depiction in the 1880s.[7]

General Ulysses S. Grant's close presence on the battlefield (at right) betrayed the obligation of the painter Poilpot to the pro-Grant interpretation of the battle. Actually, the Battle of Shiloh was one reason Grant's path to fame was less than direct. Hailed in the earliest press reports as a great victory, the battle quickly underwent a significant change in reputation when journalist Whitelaw Reid, an eyewitness, reported that the Union soldiers were taken by surprise and that defeat was narrowly averted by the arrival of another army under Don Carlos Buell.[8] What redeemed the reputation of the Battle of Shiloh was Grant's later fame, beginning with the fall of Vicksburg. Gradually Grant's explanation of his preparation for battle—and William T. Sherman's as well, for he commanded a division at Shiloh and was involved in the later controversy—prevailed. When the time came for a retrospective look at the Civil War's military history, the Battle of Shiloh would gain inclusion in the print portfolio pantheon.

No image of Grant at Shiloh, including Poilpot's, accurately renders the general's appearance during the battle. As Grant recalled in his memoirs twenty-three years later, he was suffering from a recent injury at the time and could not walk without a crutch! Two nights before the Confederates attacked, Grant's horse had stumbled during a reconnaissance in the rain and darkness. The horse fell on Grant and would surely have mangled his leg had the ground not been soft from the downpours. Even so, the general's boot had to be cut off, and for two or three days he was unable to walk without crutches (three days would mark the end of the two-day battle at Pittsburg Landing). His ankle hurt so badly on the night after the first day that he could not sleep.[9] The general could and did ride horseback during the battle, but Poilpot's image offers not a hint of suffering on Grant's part or of the crutches he needed when he dismounted.

Civil War generals were depicted in prints only in heroic good health or, in a different genre, as martyrs to the cause, mortally wounded in combat. Conditions between robust health and martyrdom—hints of human frailty—seldom crept into the heroic universe of popular military portraiture: no crutches, bandages,

Figure 106. Cosack and Company, *Battle of Shiloh. April 6th 1862. / The McCormick Machines Come Victoriously Out of Every Contest and Without a Scratch.* Buffalo, New York, 1885. Chromolithograph, 23 × 34⅞ inches. Both sides can be observed in this print, based on a panorama painting, with General Grant at right and General Albert Sidney Johnston at left, behind the reaper, receiving a mortal wound. The print emphasized not only the battle but the durability of McCormick's machines; the farm machinery company copyrighted the chromo along with the printmaker. (*Chicago Historical Society*)

splints, slings, medicines, prostheses, or beds. Common soldiers appeared bloody, battered, and bandaged, but artists exempted generals from such signs of human vulnerability.[10]

The Cosack and Company Shiloh print and others like it offer the key to the origins of the largest and most popular set of Civil War prints ever issued, thirty-six chromolithographs published by Kurz and Allison of Chicago between 1884 and 1894, for cycloramas also inspired this series of Civil War battle pictures. The images are to this day hardy perennials of Civil War illustration, yet their origin and inspiration have remained obscure; despite their persistent presence on book dust jackets and in other popular pictorial media, they still beg for systematic explanation and analysis. Nitpickers murmur complaints at their historical inaccuracies, but given the survival of the brightly colored chromos over the years and their continuing reproduction despite their obvious mistakes, they deserve more and closer attention.

The printmakers responsible for introducing these popular chromos remain obscure. Little is known about Louis Kurz, and even less about his partner, Alexander Allison. Kurz was the company's principal artist. Born in Austria in 1834 or 1835, he emigrated to the United States with his family in the wake of the European political upheavals of 1848. By the 1850s he had moved to Chicago and established himself as a scene- and mural-painter for opera houses and theaters. That early specialty helps explain the distinctive look of his later Civil War chromos, with their sweepingly panoramic horizons.[11]

Kurz launched his career as a lithographer in Milwaukee in partnership with Henry Seifert. He then served in the Union army, returning after the war to help found the Chicago Lithographing Company. Early on, he demonstrated his affinity for print portfolios, rather than random images unrelated one to another, by producing a series entitled *Chicago Illustrated*, views of the city in twenty-five parts (though only thirteen were ultimately issued), with four tinted prints in each part, at $1.50 per issue.[12]

Kurz's postwar career with the Chicago Lithographing Company ended abruptly with the Great Fire of 1871. He then went back to Milwaukee, where he opened a firm that he named, using the German term for chromolithography, the American Oleograph Company. Not until 1878 did he return to Chicago to stay. Two years later he established his partnership with Allison, who was probably a financial backer and manager. This time Kurz named the company, in Currier and Ives style, for himself and his new associate. But Currier and Ives did not provide the only model, for Kurz and Allison advertised the production of "chromos a la Prang"—a reference to Boston's Louis Prang. The new partners would describe themselves as "Art Publishers."[13]

Aside from this background information, we have only the prints themselves, their titles, and their dates of publication as evidence of their origins and purpose. Yet even this meager evidence has not been fully exploited, for in the subject of the first print and the timing of the remainder lies the explanation of the origins of the series. The firm's first Civil War battle chromo was an image of the Battle of Gettysburg published in 1884. Given the battle's modern reputation, this may well seem the most likely subject for an initial offering in a series of Civil War prints, but Kurz and Allison hailed from Chicago and were to some degree immune to the reputation of the great eastern battles.[14]

Others had already attempted to capture the famous battle visually, of course. Serious students of Gettysburg and ambitious visual chroniclers were always daunted by the battle's vast scale. Lithographic artist John B. Bachelder, for example, dedicated his life from 1863 until his death in 1894 to memorializing the battle, but he could never quite find a piece of paper large enough to capture his vision. Neither a long and narrow print published about the time of the country's centennial nor various maps based on his meticulous research gave him room to point out to the viewer all the details he wished to convey; he finally became director of the Gettysburg Battlefield Association and worked to memorialize the battlefield on a different scale by marking and preserving the field itself.

In another Gettysburg project, artist Peter F. Rothermel in 1875 offered engraver John Sartain $3,000 to reproduce his 16-by-9-foot painting of the defense against Pickett's Charge "in his best style of line and stipple with a thin veil of mezzotint."[15] But despite the skill of artist and engraver, the result (fig. 107) telescoped the fighting and seemed, as did similar black-and-white efforts by H. B. Hall and others, more an echo of the old battle prints than a recognition of the yearning for grander

THE BATTLE OF GETTYSBURG.

From the Original Picture Painted for the State of Pennsylvania under Award of Commission Appointed by the Legislature.

Figure 107. John Sartain, after Peter Frederick Rothermel, *The Battle of Gettysburg. / From the Original Picture Painted for the State of Pennsylvania under Award of Commission Appointed by the Legislature.* Philadelphia, copyrighted 1872, [published 1879]. Steel engraving with mezzotint, 24⅞ × 38¼ inches. Artist Rothermel had his canvas photographed in four sections, then pieced them together, doing "requisite touching along the lines," for the engraver to use as a model for the plate. Still, it took Sartain four years to complete it. The central figures, highlighted by their white shirts, were painted hatless, allowing Rothermel to emphasize their humanity and individuality—something not easily done with faces shadowed by the visors of kepis or the brims of soft hats. A chromolithographed, full-color version of this print was issued in 1889 by Donaldson Brothers of New York. (John Sartain to Emily Sartain, March 13, 1875, Sartain Papers, Historical Society of Pennsylvania, Philadelphia; Mark Thistlethwaite, *Painting in the Grand Manner: The Art of Peter Frederick Rothermel* [Chadds Ford, Pa.: Brandywine River Museum, 1995], 108.) (*Library of Congress*)

and more colorful depictions. The Battle of Gettysburg was well on its way to senti-mentalization, as in Thomas Hovenden's *In the Hands of the Enemy after Gettysburg* (fig. 108), which suggested that Union and Confederate soldiers were brothers in suffering. But Kurz and Allison supplied the color lacking in these black-and-white prints and harked back, too, to the clash of arms as Currier and Ives had depicted the battle during the war.

The inspiration for the Kurz and Allison Gettysburg chromo (fig. 109), produced in 1884, was more visual than historical: not the reputation of the battle itself, but the mighty impact of a cyclorama painting representing the battle. Understanding that crucial relationship has been impeded by the modern association of Paul Philippoteaux's great cyclorama painting with the town in Pennsylvania where the battle occurred. While we can see the cyclorama in Gettysburg today, Philip-poteaux's work was first shown in Chicago, where Kurz lived, in 1883 (the painting now on view in Gettysburg is a copy of the Chicago original created for the city of Boston, which did not arrive in Gettysburg until many years after 1883).

The influence of the Gettysburg cyclorama on the Kurz and Allison print is read-ily recognizable as soon as the viewer makes the connection between the two works. The print openly copied vignettes from the painting and in at least one instance perpetuated a historical error made by artist Philippoteaux: Confederate General Lewis Armistead, leading a contingent of Pickett's famous charge about to break through Union lines, falls backward off his horse, mortally wounded, in both paint-ing and print (fig. 110). In truth, when he led the long lines of Confederate infantry to the famous cluster of trees at Gettysburg, Armistead marched on foot all the way across the wheat field, and he was on foot when he received his mortal wound. The print was obviously inspired by the dramatic section of the great painting depicting the so-called high-water mark of the Confederacy. The chromo also copied the dis-tinctive stone and rail fence angling to the vanishing point of the painting (fig. 111), as well as the wounded prisoner being aided to the rear by two of his comrades in a basket-carry.

Understanding the inspiration by the Gettysburg cyclorama helps us to make sense of the record of production of the Kurz and Allison prints by year:

1884	1	1890	4
1885	0	1891	6
1886	3	1892	1
1887	3	1893	4
1888	7	1894	1
1889	6		

These publication dates reveal that it is a mistake to think of the Kurz and Allison prints as a series that began publication in 1884. The chromolithographers made a print of Gettysburg in 1884 specifically to capitalize on the popularity of the cy-clorama on view in Chicago beginning in 1883. The firm then went on with its other print business and did not begin publication of the Civil War print series until 1886.

What had happened in between? Most likely, the printmakers glimpsed the work of their rival and inspiration, Louis Prang, in a series called *Prang's War Pictures: Aquarelle Facsimile Prints*. Prang first displayed the works in his portfolio to Philadelphia critics in late June 1886 and had likely had the earliest examples ready for purchase earlier in the year, or perhaps at the end of 1885.[16] One look must have convinced Louis Kurz and Alexander Allison that they had missed an opportunity the year before. They resurrected their old Battle of Gettysburg chromo and designed more prints in the same 28-by-22-inch format.

Figure 108. James Hamilton, after Thomas Hovenden, *In the Hands of the Enemy after Gettysburg.* Signed, lower left, "Hovenden, N.A. / 1889"; lower right, "Hamilton." New York, 1889. Etching, 17 × 25 inches. A Union family ministers tenderly to a wounded Confederate soldier, who we are meant to believe receives care at least equal to that being offered injured Union soldiers in the South, in this scene of sectional reconciliation composed a quarter-century after the battle. Propped up comfortably on a pillow, the soldier wears a slipper on his healthy foot, surely loaned to him by his benefactors, and is about to receive a cup of coffee from the matron of the house as a wounded youngster in the foreground applies bandages to his injured foot. This scene of mercy and forgiveness unfolds in the warm glow of a Victorian Yankee gathering, in a room whose wall hangings include an American flag and a portrait of Abraham Lincoln. (*Library of Congress*)

THE BATTLE OF GETTYSBURG.

Figure 109. Kurz and Allison, *The Battle of Gettysburg*. Chicago, 1884. Chromolithograph, 18 × 22 inches. Much of the entire field can be observed in this panoramic depiction of the climax of Pickett's Charge on the third day of the Gettysburg battle. The wounded Confederates being led to the rear as prisoners of war provide a curious focus in the foreground and constitute the best set piece in the picture, actually detracting from the drama of General Armistead's death at the so-called high-water mark of the Confederacy. The chromo owed an obvious debt to the Gettysburg cyclorama (see figs. 110, 111). (*Chicago Historical Society*)

Prang's portfolio was likely the model for both subject matter (Civil War battles) and the idea of a series of prints in the same format. But Kurz and Allison showed no interest in Louis Prang's ambitions for bringing art to the masses. The firm did not contract with military artists of recognized reputation to make models for its chromos, and it did not advertise its battle prints as substitutes for art. Kurz and Allison remained true to the popular tradition in lithography embodied in the work of Currier and Ives; Prang was aiming higher.

Prang no doubt employed the French word for watercolor in the title of his portfolio of Civil War prints as a sign of his high artistic aspirations. It would be difficult to imagine Kurz and Allison peddling its somewhat rustic prints with fancy French words, and therein lies the best clue to the hauntingly distinctive appearance of the firm's chromolithographs. What inspired Louis Prang—the great possibilities of

Figure 110.
Paul Philippoteaux,
detail from the
Battle of Gettysburg
cyclorama, 1884,
showing the death of
General Armistead
(right center). The
spectacular pose was
copied by Kurz and
Allison for its 1884
chromo. (*Gettysburg
National Military
Park, National Park
Service*)

chromolithography—did not move Kurz and Allison. Prang capitalized on the essential quality of chromolithography, the fact that "the colors . . . make up the picture itself," as art historian Peter Marzio tells us.[17] That quality distinguished chromolithographs from the mass of lithographic images produced during the Civil War, like those of Currier and Ives discussed earlier in this chapter. In the early prints, heavy dark crayon lines outlined the images, and color, if provided at all, was applied by hand over the image later.[18]

Suddenly the obvious distinguishing quality of the Kurz and Allison images stands before the viewer in, one is tempted to say, bold outline: the figures of Civil War soldiers that crowd the foreground of the chromos are outlined in heavy dark lines, chromolithography notwithstanding. Kurz and Allison did not let the color form the image, except in the background landscapes. The firm produced color

Figure 111. Paul Philippoteaux, detail from the Battle of Gettysburg cyclorama, 1884, showing stone and rail fence, duplicated by Kurz and Allison after the cyclorama was unveiled in the printmakers' home city of Chicago. (*Gettysburg National Military Park, National Park Service*)

prints that were reminiscent of the lithographic images in which the war was first presented to Americans (fig. 112). From the start, the prints had a deliberately quaint appearance: they were self-conscious pieces of Americana.

Kurz and Allison prints were also distinguished by the panoramic point of view (inspired by cycloramas and by Kurz's previous career as a scene painter for the stage): the prints usually depict both armies at once, with the generals behind the lines, as though the battle had been fought in a glass bowl. The firm's chromos were distinguished as well by what did *not* inspire them: photography. Unlike most artists and illustrators in the 1880s, Kurz and Allison seemed immune to the charms of Civil War photography. Ill-fitting uniforms, slouching posture, imperfect and unmatched equipment, ordinary-looking men with jug ears and big Adam's apples and crossed eyes—all the realities of military life revealed in photography—never

BATTLE OF KENESAW MOUNTIAN.

Figure 112. Kurz and Allison, *Battle of Kenesaw Mountain*. Chicago, 1891. Chromolithograph, 22 × 28 inches. As in the news-conscious prints of the 1860s, this chromo featured two armies fighting at extremely close range, divided by billowing smoke, battle flags waving. What sets the image apart is the landscape, in this case the looming natural wonder, Kennesaw Mountain, here depicted with near–Rocky Mountain grandeur—and vivid color. (*The Lincoln Museum*)

enter Kurz and Allison prints. Neither do the sharp contrasts of light and shade created by the camera.

Such visual independence was the more remarkable because photographic influence was rising fast in Civil War military art and illustration. No one put stronger wind into the sails of Civil War illustration than the Century Company with the numerous pieces of artwork it commissioned for the articles and recollections that were later gathered into *Battles and Leaders of the Civil War*. The company obviously strove for a photographic atmosphere. Many of the illustrations were simply artistic renderings in line of Civil War photographs, and those based entirely on the imaginations of illustrators often had a postphotographic look to them, with high contrast between light and shadow.

By the standards of Civil War art and illustration of their day, the Kurz and Allison prints were resolutely *anti*photographic. The printmakers spurned a photographic look for a nostalgic one—nostalgic not for the war but for the lithographic medium in which it was first brought home to common people. By 1888, when Louis Prang's competing series of battle prints was complete, Kurz and Allison had reached an elevated plateau of skill in rendering Civil War battles. The previous year, the firm had produced images of three battles that were easily conjured up in the viewer's imagination by remarkable physical features that played famous parts in the battles: Burnside's Bridge at Antietam (fig. 113), the pontoon bridges over the Rappahannock at Fredericksburg, and Vicksburg, the Mississippi city on the cliffs, under siege. These picturesque prints may well have been the best of the series.

Kurz and Allison proved unusually willing to depict battles in which black soldiers took a prominent part, featuring four such actions and offering among them the greatest heroic representation in the print medium of the famous "gallant rush" of the Fifty-fourth Massachusetts at Fort Wagner. The firm also portrayed the most brutal racial atrocity of the war, the murder of black prisoners of war at Fort Pillow by Confederate troops under General Nathan Bedford Forrest (plate 14).

This unusual subject matter is perhaps more remarkable than any other quality of Kurz and Allison's work and goes a long way toward making up for the firm's many historical inaccuracies. In terms of the respect shown for the contribution of black troops to Union victory in the war, the Kurz and Allison prints do not seem at all like post-Reconstruction images. No one else in the late nineteenth century produced such heroic depictions of black soldiers, for that was a period of intensifying white racism when many white Americans were fast forgetting the contribution of African Americans to the war effort. In the same period, in fact, Currier and Ives was turning its back on its Civil War heritage to produce a gross series of racist caricatures called "Darktown" prints, more than seventy of which were issued between 1884 and 1897.[19]

Kurz and Allison did make many historical mistakes in its pictures. Its *Battle of Pea Ridge* (fig. 114), for example, published in 1889, featured Indians in buckskin and warpaint. As the modern experts on the battle, Earl Hess and William Shea, report—in a rare effort in a battle history to comment on the visual as well as verbal treatments of the battle—the "1889 Kurz and Allison print shows Confederate cavalry, including a large contingent of Plains-type Indians, charging Federal guns. Like all such prints it is highly stylized and wildly inaccurate. In truth, no Indians took part in the mounted charge on Foster's farm."[20]

The Kurz and Allison prints also initiated the visual diminution of the role of the navy in the Civil War. The firm's only naval image, of the battle between the *Monitor* and the *Merrimac*—also inspired by a cyclorama—viewed the encounter from a landlubber's perspective, depicting the shoreline in the foreground, with longboats rescuing floundering sailors, while the great naval ships were barely visible in the background.

The crucial difference between the two great and influential series of Civil War chromos issued by Kurz and Allison and by Prang lay in their relative debts to popular lithography on the one hand and to painting and photography on the other: Kurz and Allison's prints were antiphotographic; Prang's were postphotographic. Kurz and Allison consciously sought a quaintly antique, lithographic-crayon image appealing to the lithograph's traditional, simple audience. Prang went to great lengths to provide the illusion of original art colors and eyewitness composition. Prang was self-consciously "modern"; Kurz and Allison was self-consciously nostalgic for the Civil War days of black-outline lithography. Prang was uplifting; Kurz and Allison worked in the popular world of the cyclorama and spectacle.

BATTLE OF ANTIETAM.

Figure 113. Kurz and Allison, *Battle of Antietam.* Chicago, 1887. Chromolithograph, 18 × 22 inches. Called Rohrbach Bridge before the battle, Burnside Bridge was one of four stone bridges spanning Antietam Creek. On September 17, 1862, General Ambrose E. Burnside (not depicted in Kurz and Allison's print) received General George B. McClellan's orders to attack across the bridge early in the day (how early later became a matter of bitter controversy). Delay and the high ridge on the Confederate side of the bridge (inadequately represented here) caused Union forces to meet stiff resistance. Louis Kurz, employing his eye for panoramic inclusion to good effect, focused on the picturesque bridge but surveyed the ranks of both armies and the verdant, late-summer Maryland countryside as well. (Stephen W. Sears, *Landscape Turned Red: The Battle of Antietam* [New York: Ticknor and Fields, 1983], 260–61, 353–57.) (*The Lincoln Museum*)

BATTLE OF PEA RIDGE, ARK.

Figure 114. Kurz and Allison, *Battle of Pea Ridge, Ark.* Chicago, 1889. Chromolithograph, 18 × 22 inches. Both sides can be observed in this depiction of a decisive battle in Arkansas, which reveals the charm and curious inaccuracies of the famous Chicago print series. Note, for example, the odd flag carried by the Confederate troops. The artist here sought to impart a sense of violent action and thus frequently showed horses running with all four feet off the ground or rearing spectacularly. (*Chicago Historical Society*)

Prang's artists seem to have aimed higher than primitive parlor-wall patriotism. American flags did not dominate the infantry battles depicted. Carefully researched regimental and headquarters flags appeared instead, and flags were often seen hanging in folds instead of furling outward in emblematic, patriotic inspiration. The copywriters who provided descriptions of the images to help sell them sounded patriotic notes, and reactions to the pictures from contemporary viewers often waxed patriotic, but the images themselves clearly separated their message from the simpler flag-waving Currier and Ives patriotism.

Sophistication imbued the Prang enterprise. An "elegant portfolio of special design to hold the whole collection" was "furnished to subscribers free of charge." The title was stamped in gold on the cover along with a military device. The large folio opened—like a book—to reveal a box holding the prints with a window opening the size of the images and titles. Around the borders ran a plush maroon velvet mat.[21]

The early Prang prospectus offered the prints at five dollars for shipments of two at a time; the whole set was worth forty-five dollars. A pamphlet describing "the special incident" represented in the print accompanied each chromo. The pamphlets themselves came to 188 pages and together constituted, in Prang's estimation, "a valuable work of reference." Subscribers also received a bonus chromolithograph of Ulysses S. Grant (a sure sign that these images were created for a Northern audience). By 1890 the price was two dollars per print, and by 1900 "this splendid gallery of Art" could be "placed in your home," an advertisement noted, "for only $2.00 and then 6 cents a day in payments," a total of twenty dollars, including a bonus chromo of *The Naval Battle of Manilla Bay* from the more recent Spanish-American War. But even thirty-five years after Lee's surrender, the Civil War set was still being touted as "a pictorial history . . . as well as a gallery of magnificent art work worthy of a place in the best collection of American Art." As General Logan was quoted as judging: "The Prang War Pictures are marvellously well-executed, the color and drawings being true to nature."[22]

The full set of prints included the following titles (listed with copyright date):

Battle of Chattanooga, 1886
"Sheridan's Final Charge at Winchester," 1886
Sheridan's Ride, 1886
Battle of Mobile Bay, 1886
Siege of Vicksburg, 1886
Monitor and Merrimac (*Monitor and Merrimac: The First Fight between Ironclads*), 1886
Capture of New Orleans, 1886
Battle of Fredericksburg (*Laying the Pontons [sic] at Fredericksburg*), 1887
Battle of Gettysburg, 1887
Battle of Spotsylvania, 1887
Battle of Kenesaw Mountain, 1887
Capture of Fort Fisher, 1887
Battle of Port Hudson (*Passing the River Batteries*), 1887
Kearsarge and Alabama, 1887
Battle of Antietam, 1887
Battle of Allatoona Pass (*Allatoona Pass, or "Hold the Fort"*), 1887
Battle of Atlanta (*Siege of Atlanta: The Artillery Review*), 1888
Battle of Shiloh (*The Hornet's Nest*), 1888

Louis Prang had begun publishing chromolithographs as early as 1857 and naturally included war-inspired images in his offerings after 1861. He struck publishing gold after the war by devising the Christmas card, and from 1875 on, as Prang recalled, "the Xmas card became the leading article of manufacture in my establishment."[23] Despite that commercial claim to fame, Prang actually prided himself on bringing art to the masses. In addition to painstaking technique in printing, Prang hired respected artist-illustrators to create the models for many of his prints. A journalist visiting his studios in 1885 saw "chromos and the oil paintings from which they were made" hanging "side by side in identical frames. So close are the reproductions that often even the artist could not tell which was brush and which was printing-press."[24]

For his Civil War series, Prang contracted with Thure de Thulstrup, a Swedish-born military illustrator, and Julian O. Davidson, an American naval painter, to create the models in watercolor. (They were paid from $250 to $460 for each picture.) Prang clothed his artistic aspirations in the bloated boasts of the most commercial advertising language, describing the series as "exquisite Fac-simile Prints, rendered in the highest style of modern art, after masterly original paintings by the most famous living American artists."

Both of the Civil War artists were veterans of the Century Company's great "Battles and Leaders" project and were imbued with its postphotographic ideals of illustration. The literature accompanying the *Battle of Gettysburg* print included a sketch after a photograph of the battleground of Pickett's Charge by Tipton, apparently the basis of the image of the landscape in the print.[25] The artists, assisted by photographs and interviews with participants in the battles, would create models for popular prints "worthy, from the rare quality of their artistic execution, of a place in the best collections of American Art, as well as in the homes, whether rich or humble, of the surviving heroes of the War, or their descendants."[26]

The series offered depictions of six land battles from the eastern theater of the war (figs. 115, 116) and six from the western, as well as six naval battles. Color was their true appeal, as the prospectus for the series made emphatically clear: "Their superiority over black and white prints, in illustrating military scenes, is at once apparent; for the flags and the uniforms of officers and troops are vividly reproduced, the fire and smoke of battle graphically portrayed, and all the surroundings represented in colors of nature and of actual war."[27] This piece of advertising serves to remind modern students of prints yet again that the bulk of engravings and lithographs before chromolithography were black and white; many that are colored today were not colored by their publishers and have been altered by print dealers and collectors over the last hundred years. Seeing a series of colored prints of the Civil War was unusual enough in the 1880s to cause one reviewer to state (erroneously) that Prang's were "the first illustrations in colors ever issued of the Civil War."[28]

As for their "modern" look, artist Thulstrup was obviously influenced by photography. Inspiration for his watercolor on which Prang modeled the chromolithograph of the Battle of Atlanta (detail, fig. 117; see also plate 12) was likely a photograph of General William T. Sherman taken in the breastworks at Atlanta (fig. 118). Thulstrup used the photograph more than once for a model, and for Prang's

Figure 115. L[ouis]. Prang and Company, after Thure de Thulstrup. *Laying the Pontons* [sic] *at Fredericksburg.* Boston, 1887. Chromolithograph, 15 × 22 inches. The city of Fredericksburg, Virginia, looms in the distance as volunteers cross the Rappahannock River by boat, assigned to dislodge Confederate sharpshooters on the other side. "As a grand illustration of American valor," Prang declared in his brochure for the chromo, "the battle of Fredericksburg will rank with the great historic combats of mankind" (*Text to Number Two of Prang's War Pictures*, advertising brochures in the Thomas J. Watson Library, The Metropolitan Museum of Art, 18). (*The Lincoln Museum*)

project he made considerable variation from the original photographic pose, turning it into a right profile rather than a left and facing Sherman more toward the horizon than toward the viewer of the picture. But the overall image of Sherman on horseback retained the profile portrait and the static quality of a photographic pose.

Thulstrup's Sherman provides a sharp contrast to F. O. C. Darley's Sherman-inspired image (fig. 119), called *A Cavalry Raid*, which provided the basis for an engraving later associated with Sherman's March to the Sea (fig. 120). Some of the Prang prints depict generals, horses, and aides in still, almost placid poses—not the rearing horses and boldly gesticulating leaders traditional in heroic military portraiture. The point of view of the Prang images is that of the eyewitness, not the panoramic vision opted for by Kurz and Allison, and the soldiers are individuals, not the mustachioed and bearded cookie-cutter soldiery that crowded the Kurz and

Figure 116. L. Prang and Company, after Thure de Thulstrup. *Battle of Gettysburg*. Boston, 1887. Chromolithograph, 15 × 22 inches. "The closing act" of the "bloody drama" of Gettysburg, the promotional material for this chromo declared, was "here portrayed to us in vivid colors." The print shows General Winfield Scott Hancock (on horseback, left) arriving on the field during Pickett's Charge on July 3, 1863. The picture, the firm declared, "is of historic value, and of great interest to all who were with, and who glory in the achievements of the Army of the Potomac" (*Text to Number Four of Prang's War Pictures*, 25, 35). (*The Lincoln Museum*)

Allison chromos. The staff members in the Atlanta image, for example, are mostly portrait likenesses.

The literature offered with Prang's depiction of the Battle of Atlanta provided a useful key to the portrait likenesses in the chromolithograph. The Atlanta brochure also revealed the patriotic purpose and pro-Republican outlook of the firm and the artwork produced. News of Sherman's victory, explained the little brochure on the print, played an important role at home:

The Northern States, then in the midst of a Presidential campaign, were fighting "the enemy in the rear." A political party had in its platform declared the war a failure; advocated that the South be allowed to secede and establish a separate government, with slavery as her corner-stone. The success of the national forces

Figure 117. L. Prang and Company, after Thure de Thulstrup. Detail of *Battle of Atlanta* (see plate 12). Boston, 1888. Chromolithograph, 15 × 22 inches. Sherman is the mounted figure farthest to the viewer's right. To his left is his chief of engineers, Colonel O. M. Poe. In the left foreground, with his back turned to the viewer, is Lieutenant Colonel C. Ewing, Sherman's inspector-general. The three officers at the rear, behind the black servant holding a horse's reins, are, from left to right, Brigadier General W. F. Barry, chief of artillery; Brigadier General John M. Corse, inspector-general; and Colonel L. M. Dayton, an aide-de-camp. Prang's pamphlet promoting the print gave it a more apt title: *Siege of Atlanta: An Artillery Review.* (*The Lincoln Museum*)

was, therefore, at that time, a political necessity, and the brilliant success of Sherman's army, "way down in Dixie," carried forward the impending campaign to the triumphant re-election of President Lincoln.[29]

The anonymity of the brochure's phrase "a political party" was an absurd gesture to nonpartisanship in the heyday of the two-party system, and virtually any American reader would have known that the passage referred to the Democrats. Only Republicans saw the history of Civil War politics the way they were depicted here. The Democratic platform in the 1864 election did proclaim the war a failure, but it did not advocate letting the South secede and establish a separate government, and it

Figure 118.
[Photographer unknown],
[*William T. Sherman in the Field*].
The photograph was evidently
consulted by artist Thure de
Thulstrup for his watercolor of
Sherman at the Siege of Atlanta
(see fig. 117 and plate 12).
(*Library of Congress*)

did not advocate the creation of a government based on the cornerstone of slavery. That was the stuff of extreme Republican mythmaking, and Louis Prang and Company apparently swallowed it whole.

The merging of the Republican point of view on the war with American patriotism is thus readily discernible in Prang Civil War chromos. The Boston printmaker tried especially to reach Civil War veterans with the prints, engaging a man named John V. Redpath as its general agent to sell the war pictures. Redpath, in turn, apparently recruited Civil War veterans to sell the prints, and these subagents referred to themselves as "comrades."[30] Thus Prang tried the same marketing technique used by New York's Endicott and Company for its naval series.

In any image aimed at veterans, accuracy of depiction was a goal. The reviewer for the *Boston Daily Globe*, likely well bolstered with information provided by Prang's agents in the firm's hometown, asserted that Prang's war pictures were not "made in the haphazard manner of many so-called military pictures, but as the result of careful painstaking, and the liberal expenditure of time and money. Battle-fields have been visited by the artists, access to official reports has been obtained, and war-time photographs in possession of the government and military societies have been se-

Felix O.C.Darley's Study drawing - A Cavalry Raid-1865.

Figure 119. Felix Octavius Carr Darley, *A Cavalry Raid*, ca. 1865. Pencil and charcoal on paper, 25 × 42 inches. The study drawing shows Union soldiers tearing up a Confederate railroad line and setting buildings ablaze in the background. A slave family (right foreground) flees the scene. (*West Point Museum, United States Military Academy*)

cured." The Boston newspaper reporter also referred to "correspondence with soldiers," the submission of "sketches to those best qualified to judge of the scenes represented," and the resulting "high degree of realism." Of Thulstrup the newspaper noted that "his studios . . . [were] filled with weapons, flags, and uniforms of every description used in both armies."[31] In depicting the *Battle of Winchester*, Thulstrup apparently copied the Union brigade colors from the original in the West Point museum and conferred with Theodore F. Rodenbough, who served on Sheridan's staff at the battle. Prang maintained that General John A. Logan, of Kennesaw Mountain fame, "made the final corrections in the artist's sketch" of the scene of that battle represented in the series.[32]

Thulstrup referred to Grant's famed *Memoirs* for the inspiration of the *Battle of Chattanooga* (plate 15). Grant and his staff stood on Orchard Knob, "from which the entire field could be observed," and with General George H. Thomas and his staff watched the Union assault of the corps commanded by General Gordon Granger. Prang's literature described the moment this way: "Grant lifting his field glass to his eye; on his left stands General Granger; while the heroic proportions of General Thomas, then newly christened the 'Rock of Chicamauga [*sic*],' stand out boldly

Figure 120. A[lexander]. H[ay]. Ritchie, after F. O. C. Darley, *On the March to the Sea*. Published by [Lucius] Stebbins, New York, 1868. Engraving, 28 × 42 inches. One of the best-known Civil War prints, this engraving is widely reproduced in books and magazines, usually to illustrate the harshness of Sherman's march through Georgia. It also inspired a number of copies and reissues, notably H. H. Willes's engraving, published in 1888, a full twenty years after the appearance of the Ritchie version. For this engraved adaptation, Ritchie added detail to F. O. C. Darley's impressionistic drawing (see fig. 119), making it clear that Union troops were blowing up the structure in the center of the print, as well as wrecking rails and pulling down telegraph poles (right). Ritchie also added an extra dose of poignancy by making the displaced slaves flee on foot, rather than with a mule, and adding a father for the children so that the slaves form an inseparable family. Finally, Ritchie added the inevitable emblem of Union strength, blessing even this controversial enterprise: the American flag. (*Library of Congress*)

against the horizon. Near this historic trio may be seen a signal officer vainly endeavoring to communicate with General Sherman, for whose relief the attack immediately in front has been made. . . . To the right is the corps headquarters flag and color-guard with their horses."[33]

Thulstrup's *Sheridan's Ride* (plate 16), perhaps the most successful of all the images of that famous event, laid claim to depicting an unusual moment in a celebrated act of heroism: "The most dramatic episode of the famous 'Ride,' which lights up the sombre pages of the history of the Great Rebellion, even as the 'Charge of the Six Hundred' sparkles among the shadows of European warfare, has hitherto escaped the notice of artist and author. It has been reserved for M. de Thulstrup to mark this incident by the accompanying picture which might well be entitled 'The Home Stretch.'"[34]

In a way, *Prang's War Pictures* signaled the end of American military innocence. It was now easy to compare an American conflict—with its horrific scale and blood-drenched sacrifice—to major Old World conflicts. The *Battle of Allatoona* (plate 17), for example, could be characterized as depicting "a charge of the last reserves, like that of the Imperial Guard at Waterloo."[35] Describing the prints for the *Public Service Review* in 1887, a military reporter observed:

> There is no walk of art in America in which the artist has made longer strides during the past decade than the painting of military scenes. At the end of the Civil War the military art of America consisted entirely in the superficial and rarely even approximately accurate designs of the newpaper draughtsmen. To-day we have a class of artists who, at their best, can challenge comparison with the greatest battle-painters of contemporary Europe.[36]

In America, military prints, too, had come of age.

Epilogue. Toward a New Union Image?

In 1864 Hartford printmaker Lucius Stebbins published a Henry W. Herrick litho-graph entitled *Reading the Emancipation Proclamation* (fig. 121). Unlike the pre-ponderant number of emancipation prints that began appearing that year to coin-cide with the presidential election campaign, or those widely distributed after Abraham Lincoln's assassination in 1865, this image did not show the president as a fatherly Moses figure reading or signing the document from the rarefied isolation of his White House office. In fact, except for a small portrait in the bottom margin of the print, it did not show Lincoln at all. Rather, it depicted an armed Union sol-dier reading the text of this liberating document aloud, by torchlight, to a slave fam-ily gathered around the fireplace in their tiny cabin. There is no franker depiction of Lincoln's most important act in all of American iconography, for the proclama-tion itself freed no slave until, under the terms of the decree, Federal troops ad-vanced into slaveholding rebel states and liberated the slave population in their wake, or slaves themselves broke out from the plantations to achieve freedom. Slaves were freed by the sword as well as the pen, but Stebbins's was the first print to suggest it.[1]

One can detect something else visible in the background of the scene: a family hearth, above which sits a bare, undecorated wall, inviting future decoration in the homes of freed people. Popular prints could fill that void, and picture publishers doubtless hoped that emancipation would create a new audience for the graphic arts. If we judge by the works that soon came off Northern presses depicting freed-men, that is precisely what happened. The war changed not only American society but American popular prints as well.

That change could be seen immediately after emancipation in prints issued as re-cruiting posters. One such pictorial handbill, *Freedom to the Slaves* (plate 18), prob-ably published in 1863, showed a white officer holding his saber aloft beneath a huge American flag, urging shackled, kneeling slaves toward a future that promised both education and the opportunity to own land. "All slaves were made freemen by

Figure 121. H[enry]. W. Herrick, after J. W. Watts, *Reading the Emancipation Proclamation*. Published by Lucius Stebbins, Hartford, Connecticut, 1864. Lithograph, 14 × 25 inches. Several generations of a slave family listen as a Union soldier reads to them the liberating words of Lincoln's Emancipation Proclamation. Note the symbolic discarded whip in the foreground. An alternate edition of this image was issued under the title *The Midnight Hour*, a reference to the precise moment, on January 1, 1863, when the proclamation took effect. (*Library of Congress*)

opposite
Figure 122. [Printmaker unknown], *Major Martin R. Delany. U.S.A. / Promoted on the Battle Field for Bravery*. Published by John Smith, Philadelphia, ca. 1865. Hand-colored lithograph, 21¾ × 17¼ inches. As a sentinel stands guard beneath the American flag, the first black staff officer of the Union army is shown in full dress uniform, complete with sash and saber. Delany saw little action before war's end, but the onetime newspaperman and physician became a symbol for African Americans hungry for heroes of their own, and, for print publisher Smith, an avenue to this hitherto largely unexplored audience for popular prints. (*National Portrait Gallery*)

MAJOR MARTIN R. DELANY. U. S. A.

PROMOTED ON THE BATTLE FIELD FOR BRAVERY

THE END OF THE REBELLION IN THE UNITED STATES, 1865.

Figure 123. Kimmel and Forster, *The End of the Rebellion in the United States, 1865*. New York, 1866. Lithograph, 18½ × 24¼ inches. The losers of the Civil War—among them Robert E. Lee (surrendering his sword) and Jefferson Davis (carrying bags of stolen Confederate gold)—gather beneath a storm cloud in this symbol-laden tableau representing the return of national authority. The figure of Justice (left foreground), holding her balanced scales and brandishing a sword, stares appreciatively at the wounded African American soldier in the foreground. Liberty (top right) waves the American flag as she ponders the formerly enslaved black, rising from his knees, his chains shattered. Among the other characters portrayed are William T. Sherman (leading troops, left), Ulysses S. Grant (gesturing, on horseback), and (below Grant) Secretary of State William H. Seward and the new president, Andrew Johnson. On the Confederate side, surmounted by a symbolic palmetto tree that is weighed down by the dead serpent of rebellion, one can find Lincoln's assassin, John Wilkes Booth. But attention is clearly drawn to the African Americans, who are pictured closest to the central sarcophagus decorated with likenesses of Washington and Lincoln. This print was a companion piece to an earlier allegorical print by Kimmel and Forster, *The Outbreak of the Rebellion*, in which no people of color were depicted at all. (*Library of Congress*)

Abraham Lincoln," the message on the back of the handbill declared (plate 19), stretching the truth. "Come, then, able-bodied COLORED MEN, to the nearest United States Camp, and fight for the STARS AND STRIPES." Thus the American flag, once the exclusive emblem of white Unionists, now seemed finally, at least in the graphic arts, to belong to people of color as well. By 1864, after all, an African

American sergeant major named Christian Fleetwood would report that at the Battle of New Market, he had "seized . . . the American Flag" amidst a "deadly hail storm of bullets," as comrades cried "Boys, save the colors."[2]

In a period chromolithographed recruiting poster, *Come and Join Us Brothers* (plate 20), the transfiguration was made complete: now an African American was portrayed clutching the flag himself, perhaps for the first time in American iconography. The flag mania that had once gripped the white North was at last extended to the black population as well. Beneath one version of the chromo was further proof of this transformation: the stirring lines to the chorus of a famous war song, its call to arms appearing for the first time in the caption to a print designed specifically for African Americans: "Rally Round the Flag, boys! Rally once again, / Shouting the Battle Cry of FREEDOM."[3]

Some two years later, Philadelphia publisher John Smith could issue a lithographic portrait of Major Martin R. Delany (fig. 122), who that year became the first African American to serve as a staff officer in the Union army. The man whom Lincoln had praised as "extraordinary" was respectfully portrayed dominating a Union campsite. Significantly, the Stars and Stripes appeared, too, floating above a cluster of nearby tents, as if consecrating Delany's precedent-setting commission.[4]

This image revolution reached its zenith with Kurz and Allison's depiction of the Fifty-fourth Massachusetts Regiment, *Storming Fort Wagner* (plate 21). The print commemorated the moment that the regiment's white colonel, Robert Gould Shaw, suffered a fatal wound while leading his troops against the Confederate position near Charleston, South Carolina. But the flag billowing at the apex of the design is held aloft by an African American, and the dead and dying soldiers falling beneath it are shown sacrificing their lives for it.

By the time New York printmakers Kimmel and Forster issued their allegorical lithograph, *The End of the Rebellion in the United States* (fig. 123), it was clear that in war and iconography alike, African Americans had, under that flag, raised themselves from shackled slaves to armed freedom fighters. Not only did these representative before-and-after figures appear in the prominent foreground of the print, but, in a composition crowded with heroes (Grant and Sherman among them), the symbols of the newly reunited nation, Columbia, Liberty, and Justice, all cast their gaze squarely on the two African Americans in the scene. The figure of Liberty, contemplating the liberating effects of the long and bloody Civil War, holds aloft the American flag while an eagle soars majestically overhead.

At last, "the entire field could be observed."

NOTES

INTRODUCTION

1. John G. Nicolay and John Hay, *Abraham Lincoln: A History*, 10 vols. (1890; reprint, New York: Century Company, 1914), 5:59.

2. Roy P. Basler, ed., *The Collected Works of Abraham Lincoln*, 9 vols. (New Brunswick, N.J.: Rutgers University Press, 1953–55), 5:10.

3. One of the best narrative descriptions of the attack on Fort Sumter is found in Richard N. Current, "The Confederates and the First Shot," *Civil War History* 7 (1961): 357–58; the notion that popular pictures "testified to convictions" was first advanced in Robert Philippe, *Political Graphics: Art as a Weapon* (New York: Abbeville Press, 1980), 172. We owe much to his succinct interpretation of the significance of popular prints.

4. *New York Times*, April 15, 1861.

5. The official report to the president appears in Nicolay and Hay, *Abraham Lincoln*, 4:60; see also Stephen D. Lee, "The First Step in the War," in *Battles and Leaders of the Civil War*, ed. Robert Underwood Johnson and Clarence Clough Buel, 4 vols. (1887; reprint, Secaucus, N.J.: Castle Publishing, 1991), 1:79, 81; Patricia L. Faust, ed., *Historical Times Illustrated Encyclopedia of the Civil War* (New York: Harper and Row, 1986), 15.

6. *Harper's Weekly*, May 11, 1861. "The entire profits of the sale of the PORTRAIT OF MAJOR ANDERSON," promised publisher E. Anthony in the advertisement, would "hereafter be deposited in [the] Bank" and "paid over to the committee authorized to take charge of such contributions by the great Union Meeting of April 20th." There is no record of whether the pledge was fulfilled.

7. For the most influential guidance given women of the day on the use of prints, see Catharine E. Beecher and Harriet Beecher Stowe, *The American Woman's Home or, Principles of Domestic Science . . .* (1869; reprint, Hartford, Conn.: Stowe-Day Foundation, 1994), 91–92.

8. J. Cutler Andrews, *The North Reports the Civil War* (Pittsburgh: University of Pittsburgh Press, 1983), 5.

9. For election results in New York City, see *The Tribune Almanac for the Years 1838 to 1864, Inclusive . . .* (New York: New York Tribune, 1868), 41. Lincoln's arrival in New York is described in Victor Searcher, *Lincoln's Journey to Greatness* (Philadelphia: John C. Winston Company, 1960), 186; Richard N. Current, *Lincoln and the First Shot* (New York: J. B. Lippincott, 1963), 160; "wildly excited crowds" described in Jacob D. Cox, "War Preparations in the North," in Johnson and Buel, *Battles and Leaders*, 1:84–86; flag fever noted in James M. McPherson, *Battle*

Cry of Freedom: The Civil War Era (New York: Oxford University Press, 1988), 274.

10. Advertisement for flags is in *Harper's Weekly*, May 25, 1861.

11. Nast's original painting, *The Departure of the 7th Rgt. to the War, April 19th 1861*, is in the Seventh Regiment Armory in New York City.

12. A small copy of the lithograph by Sarony is in the Macculloch Hall Museum in Morristown, New Jersey. For copies of the print published in books, see William Swinton, *History of the Seventh Regiment, National Guard, State of New York, During the War of the Rebellion . . .* (New York: Fields, Osgood, and Company, 1870), frontis., and D. T. Valentine, *Manual of the Corporation of the City of New-York, 1862* (n.p., 1862).

13. A photograph of the New York City rally is reproduced in William C. Davis, *First Blood: Fort Sumter to Bull Run* (Alexandria, Va.: Time-Life Books, 1983), 32–33; the oration is quoted in Richard M. Ketchum, ed., *The American Heritage Picture History of the Civil War* (New York: Doubleday, 1960), 73. See also *New York Evening Express*, April 22, 1861; Gerald L. Carr, *Frederic Edwin Church: Catalogue Raisonné of Works of Art at Olana Historic Site*, 2 vols. (Cambridge: Cambridge University Press, 1994), 1:275; *Harper's Weekly*, May 4, 1861; Francis Lieber, *No Party Now, but All for Our Country* (Philadelphia: Crissey and Markley, 1863), 1; and memorandum from Francis Lieber to B. J. Lossing, inserted in copy of *No Party Now* in the Huntington Library, San Marino, California. Lieber, a prosaic college professor, even wrote a poem about the flag-raising over Columbia College that day.

14. Carr, *Frederic Edwin Church*, 1:275 (quoting the *New York World* for April 20, 1861); the advertisement for the flag envelope is in the *New York Daily Tribune*, May 6, 1861.

15. All three prints are in the Library of Congress. They are discussed, and their copyright dates given, in Bernard F. Reilly Jr.,

American Political Prints, 1766–1876: Catalog of the Collections in the Library of Congress (Boston: G. K. Hall, 1991), 466–67. The Library of Congress's copy of *The Spirit of 61*, however, does not include the verses quoted. They may be found in the copy reproduced in Ketchum, *American Heritage Picture History of the Civil War*, 71.

16. Reilly, *American Political Prints*, 468–69.

17. Carr, *Frederic Edwin Church*, 1:275; Henry Ward Beecher, *Freedom and War. Discourses on Topics Suggested by the Times* (Boston: Ticknor and Fields, 1863), 93.

18. Beecher, *Freedom and War*, 116, 121–22.

19. Ibid., 120, 123–24.

20. Carr, *Frederic Edwin Church*, 1:276; David C. Huntington, *The Landscapes of Frederic Edwin Church* (New York: George Braziller, 1966), 61.

21. Carr, *Frederic Edwin Church*, 1:276–77; "Our Banner in the Sky" (New York: Goupil and Company, [1861]), original at Olana, Hudson, New York.

22. "Our Banner in the Sky."

23. Carr, *Frederic Edwin Church*, 1:499.

24. Ibid., 1:276.

25. Reilly, *American Political Prints*, 469–70. Artist Bauly, who lived at 737 Eighth Avenue in Manhattan, exhibited a work entitled *The Last of the Crew* at the National Academy of Design exhibition of 1859; little else is known about him. See *National Academy of Design Exhibition Record, 1826–1860*, 2 vols. (New York: New-York Historical Society, 1943), 2:25.

26. Carr, *Frederic Edwin Church*, 1:277–78.

27. John R. Howard, ed., *Henry Ward Beecher: Patriotic Addresses in America and England from 1850 to 1885, on Slavery, the Civil War, and the Development of Civil Liberty* (New York: Fords, Howard, and Hulbert, 1887), 676–77, 696, 851.

28. Ibid., 851. The occasion for Beecher's comment was a eulogy to Ulysses S. Grant.

29. Mark de Wolfe Howe, ed., *Touched*

with Fire: *Civil War Letters and Diary of Oliver Wendell Holmes, Jr.* (Cambridge: Harvard University Press, 1946), vii.

30. We have deemphasized print portraits of Abraham Lincoln, as these were the subject of a previous book we wrote with Gabor S. Boritt: *The Lincoln Image: Abraham Lincoln and the Popular Print* (New York: Scribner's, 1984).

31. Advertisements by G. S. Heskes and Company, *Harper's Weekly*, October 29, 1864, and November 19, 1864; H. H. Lloyd, *Harper's Weekly*, October 19, 1864.

32. "Our Artists During the War," *Harper's Weekly*, June 3, 1865. For pictures within pictures, see, for example, the painting *The Hero's Return* by Trevor McClurg, ca. 1860s, showing a wounded veteran coming home to his simple cottage—above whose hearth are displayed prints of Washington and Lincoln. The original is in the Civil War Library and Museum, Philadelphia, and it is illustrated in Harold Holzer and Mark E. Neely Jr., *Mine Eyes Have Seen the Glory: The Civil War in Art* (New York: Orion Books, 1993), 235.

33. Again, we are indebted for the comparison to "the analogous sacred print" to Robert Philippe, *Political Graphics*, 172.

34. For Holmes, see David E. Shi, *Facing Facts: Realism in American Thought and Culture, 1850–1920* (New York: Oxford University Press, 1995), 56.

35. "Editor's Easy Chair," *Harper's New Monthly Magazine* 23 (1861): 844.

CHAPTER ONE

1. *New York Tribune*, April 12, 1864.

2. John T. Morse, ed., *The Diary of Gideon Welles, Secretary of the Navy under Lincoln and Johnson*, 3 vols. (Boston: Houghton Mifflin, 1911), 1:107; Francis Walker quoted in *Lee's Terrible Swift Sword: From Antietam to Chancellorsville—An Eyewitness History*, ed. Richard Wheeler (New York: HarperCollins, 1992), 204.

3. *Harper's Weekly*, October 19, 1861, November 30, 1861, March 1, 1862, September 5, 1863.

4. T. Harry Williams, *Lincoln and His Generals* (New York: Alfred A. Knopf, 1952), 16–18; for another view of Scott by the same printmaker, see *The Hercules of the Union Slaying the Great Dragon of Secession*, showing Scott striking a blow against the Confederacy, when in fact he favored a more passive policy of constriction. For the apparent differences in audiences and use for cartoons as opposed to other display prints, see Harold Holzer, Gabor S. Boritt, and Mark E. Neely Jr., *The Lincoln Image: Abraham Lincoln and the Popular Print* (New York: Scribner's, 1984), esp. 3–4, 34–40.

5. Original in the Abraham Lincoln Museum, Lincoln Memorial University, Harrogate, Tennessee.

6. Teresa R. Knox, "The Origins and Antecedents of the Military Portrait in Britain," and Carter E. Foster, "History and Heroes: The Military Narrative in the Wake of Benjamin West," both in *The Martial Face: The Military Portrait in Britain, 1760–1900*, ed. Peter Harrington (Providence, R.I.: Brown University Press, 1991), 15, 47.

7. Noble E. Cunningham Jr., *Popular Images of the Presidency: From Washington to Lincoln* (Columbia: University of Missouri Press, 1991), 19; Barry Schwartz, *George Washington: The Making of an American Symbol* (New York: Free Press, 1987), 194–95; Mark Twain, *Adventures of Huckleberry Finn*, Riverside Edition (Boston: Houghton Mifflin, 1958), 144.

8. See Bernard Reilly, *American Political Prints, 1766–1876: A Catalogue of the Collections in the Library of Congress* (Boston: G. K. Hall, 1991), 40, 43, 156, 280–81, 290–91, 295–96.

9. Horace Porter, *Campaigning with Grant* (1897; reprint, New York: Da Capo Press, 1986), 441.

10. Roy P. Basler, ed., *The Collected Works of Abraham Lincoln*, 9 vols. (New Brunswick,

N.J.: Rutgers University Press, 1953–55), 4:385–86.

11. J. Cutler Andrews, *The North Reports the Civil War* (Pittsburgh: University of Pittsburgh Press, 1955), 80, 668. The first woodcuts in the illustrated press appeared in *Harper's Weekly*, June 15, 1861.

12. Copyright Records of the Eastern District of Pennsylvania, May 17, 1861–March 22, 1862, and the Southern District of New York, June 1861–October 1861, in the Library of Congress. Ellsworth's letter reproduced on illustrated card, *Col. Ellsworth's Last Letter to His Parents*, published in 1861 by Mumford and Company, Ohio, reproduced in William C. Davis, *First Blood: Fort Sumter to Bull Run* (Alexandria, Va.: Time-Life Books, 1983), 68.

13. Copyright Records, Eastern District of Pennsylvania, May 17, 1861–March 22, 1862, Library of Congress; Winfred Porter Truesdell, *Catalog Raisonné of the Portraits of Col. Elmer E. Ellsworth* (Champlain, N.Y.: The Print Connoisseur, 1927), list follows 26; Davis, *First Blood*, 68.

14. Harold Holzer examined the Ellsworth uniform at the New York State Capitol on several occasions in 1984 and 1985; see also Charles A. Ingraham, "Colonel Ellsworth; First Hero of the Civil War," in Truesdell, *Catalog Raisonné of the Portraits of Col. Elmer E. Ellsworth*, 24.

15. Original print in the Lincoln Museum, Fort Wayne, Indiana.

16. George Templeton Strong, *Diary*, 4 vols. (New York: Macmillan, 1952), 3:146; see "Colonel Ellsworth Requiem March," lithographed cover by Edward Mendel (Chicago: Root and Cady, ca. 1861), in the collection of the Lilly Library, Indiana University, Bloomington.

17. Original prints in the Prints and Photographs Division, Library of Congress; Copyright Records of the Southern District of New York, June–October 1861, Library of Congress.

18. Copyright Records, Southern District

of New York, June–October 1861, Library of Congress; James M. McPherson, *Battle Cry of Freedom: The Civil War Era* (New York: Oxford University Press, 1988), 405; Franz Sigel, "The Flanking Column at Wilson's Creek," in Johnson and Buel, *Battles and Leaders*, 1:305; William L. Shea and Earl J. Hess, *Pea Ridge: Civil War Campaign in the West* (Chapel Hill: University of North Carolina Press, 1992), 30. We rely on Shea and Hess's excellent monograph for our understanding of Sigel.

19. Shea and Hess, *Pea Ridge*, 278–82.

20. Ibid., 7, 231–36; E. B. Long and Barbara Long, *The Civil War Day by Day: An Almanac, 1861–1865* (New York: Doubleday, 1971), 91; sheet music, "General Sigel's Grand March," by Henry Werner, copyright October 1, 1861, in the Library of Congress.

21. E. B. Long and Barbara Long, *The Civil War Day by Day: An Almanac, 1861–1865* (New York: Doubleday, 1971), 91. Sigel also inspired prints from the firm headed by Peter Ehrgott and Adolphus Forbriger, German-born lithographers working in Cincinnati.

22. See Peter Paret, *Imagined Battles: Reflections of War in European Art* (Chapel Hill: University of North Carolina Press, 1997), 62–64.

23. The pro-Confederate etchings of Baltimore's gifted engraver, Adalbert J. Volck, embodied anti–German American animus. See George McCullough Anderson, *The Work of Adalbert Johann Volck, 1828–1912* (Baltimore: privately printed, 1970), esp. 38–39 and the etching *Valiant Men Dat Fite Mit Sigel*, which pictured the general's troops as murderers of women and children. On atrocities, see Michael Fellman, *Inside War: The Guerilla Conflict in Missouri during the American Civil War* (New York: Oxford University Press, 1989), 202.

24. *Harper's Weekly*, August 27, 1861, June 29, 1861.

25. Stephen W. Sears, ed., *The Civil War Papers of George B. McClellan: Selected Corre-*

spondence, 1860–1865 (New York: Ticknor and Fields, 1989), 473.

26. One early print, in the Library of Congress collection, placed McClellan's face on the body of an earlier war hero, Franklin Pierce. McClellan's reputation was also spreading through Europe, as suggested by the appearance of another French-made lithograph, *Bataille de Gaines Mill*, in the Anne S. K. Brown Military Collection, John Hay Library, Brown University.

27. Stephen W. Sears, *George B. McClellan: The Young Napoleon* (New York: Ticknor and Fields, 1988), 196; essential for understanding the new style of leadership is John Keegan, *The Mask of Command* (New York: Viking, 1987), esp. 197, 208.

28. Basler, *Collected Works of Lincoln*, 5:107.

29. The pioneering study is Milton Kaplan, "Heads of State," *Winterthur Portfolio* 6 (1970): 144–49. Kaplan counted twenty-eight different lithographs by Ehrgott, Forbriger but omitted nineteen variants discovered by the authors of this book at a Gettysburg, Pennsylvania, Civil War book fair in July 1996. For a generic study of the phenomenon of interchangeable military portrait prints, see George Somes Layard, *Catalogue Raisonné of Engraved British Portraits from Altered Plates* (London: Philip Allan and Company, 1927), vii.

30. E. A. Duyckinck, *History of the War for the Union, Civil Military and Naval* (New York: Johnson and Fry, 1862). See frontispieces to volumes 1–14, 15–16, 17–18, 19–20, 21–22, 23–24, 25–26, 27–28, 29–30, 31–32.

31. Advertisement on the back page of ibid.

32. Lucas's advertisement is in *Harper's Weekly*, September 5, 1863, 574.

33. David Dixon Porter, *The Naval History of the Civil War* (1886; reprint, New York: Benchmark Publishing, 1970), iv.

34. *A List of Songs, Waltzes, Polkas, Marches &c . . . Published and for sale by Lee and Walker* (Philadelphia: Lee and Walker, n.d.), original in the Library of Congress.

35. Printmaker Sachse, operating in the border state of Maryland, returned to pro-Confederate subjects as soon as the war was over. One of his typical peacetime efforts was *Grave of Stonewall Jackson at Lexington, Virginia*, original in the Anne S. K. Brown Military Collection at the John Hay Library, Brown University.

36. Copyright Records, Southern District of New York, April 1863–August 1863, Library of Congress; Richard Wheeler, *Witness to Gettysburg* (New York: New American Library, 1987), 168.

37. *National Portrait Gallery Permanent Collection: Illustrated Checklist* (Washington, D.C.: Smithsonian Institution, 1982), 89–90.

38. Basler, *Collected Works of Lincoln*, 4:519.

39. Ezra J. Warner, *Generals in Blue: Lives of the Union Commanders* (Baton Rouge: Louisiana State University Press, 1964): 160–61.

CHAPTER TWO

1. Harry T. Peters, *America on Stone: The Other Printmakers to the American People . . .* (New York: Doubleday, Doran and Company, 1931), 269; Rosenthal series in the Print Collection of the Chicago Historical Society.

2. Rare indeed was such a depiction as Endicott and Company's *Military Execution of James Griffin, alias John Thomas Barnett, a Private of the 11th Pa. Cavalry, for Desertion and Highway Robbery, at Portsmouth, Va., Sept. 17th, 1862*, original in the Library of Congress, as are both Bufford lithographs.

3. Original prints of *Soldiers Rest, Washington D.C.* by Charles Magnus (1864) and *Graves of the Highlanders* are in the Print Collection, Chicago Historical Society.

4. Richard Orr Curry, *A House Divided: A*

Study of Statehood Politics and the Copperhead Movement in West Virginia (Pittsburgh, Pa.: University of Pittsburgh Press, 1964), esp. chap. 6.

5. Joseph A. Saunier, *A History of the Forty-seventh Ohio Veteran Volunteer Infantry . . .* (Hillsboro, Ohio: Lyle Printing, 1903), 17.

6. See Harold Holzer and Mark E. Neely Jr., *Mine Eyes Have Seen the Glory: The Civil War in Art* (New York: Orion Books, 1993), chap. 1.

7. Alan Trachtenberg, *Reading American Photographs: Images as History, Mathew Brady to Walker Evans* (New York: Hill and Wang, 1989), 107–11. Though we disagree with Trachtenberg's interpretation, we learned much about photographs from this pioneering and properly influential book.

8. Saunier, *History of the Forty-seventh Ohio*, 19.

9. Ibid., 31.

10. See Sibley tent in Jack Coggins, *Arms and Equipment of the Civil War* (Garden City, N.Y.: Doubleday, 1962), 18–19.

11. C. E. Dornbusch, *Regimental Publications and Personal Narratives of the Civil War: A Checklist*, vol. 1 (New York: New York Public Library, 1962), pt. 5, Indiana and Ohio, locates four of these portfolios, three in Ohio. We found substantial parts of another set in Chicago. The Library of Congress, of course, received a copyright set. Otherwise, they do not seem to have traveled far from the Midwest.

12. See Matthew Paul Lalumia, *Realism and Politics in Victorian Art of the Crimean War* (Ann Arbor, Mich.: UMI Research, 1984.)

13. Nicolai Cikovsky Jr. and Franklin Kelly, *Winslow Homer* (New Haven, Conn.: Yale University Press, 1995), 19–20; Gordon Hendricks, *The Life and Work of Winslow Homer* (New York: Harry N. Abrams, 1979), 46–47.

14. Cikovsky and Kelly, *Winslow Homer*, 21; Marc Simpson, *Winslow Homer: Paintings of the Civil War* (San Francisco: Fine Arts

Museums of San Francisco/Bedford Arts, 1988), 18–19.

15. Cikovsky and Kelly, *Winslow Homer*, 393; Katherine Morrison McClinton, *The Chromolithographs of Louis Prang* (New York: Clarkson N. Potter, 1973), 67–70, 144; Lloyd Goodrich, *The Graphic Art of Winslow Homer* (New York: Museum of Graphic Art, 1968), 10; see also Julian Grossman, *The Civil War: Battlefields and Campgrounds in the Art of Winslow Homer* (New York: Harry N. Abrams, 1991), 140–46.

16. *New York Tribune*, December 17, 1864.

17. See Simpson, *Winslow Homer*, esp. 217, 220, 235.

18. *New York Tribune*, December 17, 1864.

19. Ron Tyler, *Prints of the West* (Golden, Colo.: Fulcrum, 1994), 106, 120–22.

20. Earl J. Hess, *The Union Soldier in Battle: Enduring the Ordeal of Combat* (Lawrence: University Press of Kansas, 1997), 64.

21. *The War of the Rebellion: A Compilation of the Official Records of the Union and Conferate Armies*, 128 vols. (Washington, D.C.: Government Printing Office, 1880–1902), ser. 1, vol. 25, pt. 1, p. 193.

22. Ibid., ser. 1, vol. 20, pt. 1, p. 444.

23. Paddy Griffith, *Battle Tactics of the Civil War* (1987; reprint, New Haven, Conn.: Yale University Press, 1989), esp. chap. 6.

24. *Catalogue of Forbes Historical Art Collection of Battles, Incidents, Characters and Marches of the Union Armies* (n.p., n.d.), unpaginated introduction.

25. Ibid., 17–20.

26. See Francis Trevelyan Miller, ed., *The Photographic History of the Civil War*, 10 vols. (New York: Review of Reviews, 1911), 8:187.

27. William Forrest Dawson, ed., *A Civil War Artist at the Front: Edwin Forbes' Life Studies of the Great Army* (New York: Oxford University Press, 1957), no pagination.

28. *Uniform and Dress of the Army and Navy of the Confederate States of America*, modern edition with introduction by Richard Harwell (New York: St. Martin's Press, 1960).

CHAPTER THREE

1. P. G. T. Beauregard, *Soldiers of Shiloh and Elkhorn* (n.p., 1862), broadside; copy kindly supplied by T. Michael Parrish.

2. W. W. Blackford quoted in Herman Warner Williams, *The Civil War: The Artists' Record* (Boston: Beacon Press, 1961), 46.

3. George M. Fredrickson, *The Inner Civil War: Northern Intellectuals and the Crisis of the Union* (New York: Harper and Row, 1965), 77, 247 n. 25. See Chapter 4, "Penalties of Defeat: Northern Reaction to the Battle of Bull Run," in Michael C. C. Adams, *Fighting for Defeat: Union Military Failure in the East, 1861–1865* (1978 [as *Our Masters the Rebels*]; reprint, Lincoln: University of Nebraska Press, 1992), 71–86.

4. See, for example, *The Battle of Bull's Run*, ca. 1861, by an unknown printmaker, showing the flight of civilian spectators in the wake of the Confederate victory, original lithograph in the Library of Congress.

5. Harriet Beecher Stowe, "House and Home Papers, VII," *The Atlantic*, 14 (1864): 95.

6. Reid Mitchell, *The Vacant Chair* (New York: Oxford University Press, 1993), 31, opposite 82.

7. Ibid., 31, 84. See also Harold Holzer and Mark E. Neely Jr., *Mine Eyes Have Seen the Glory: The Civil War in Art* (New York: Orion Books, 1993), 220–22; David W. Blight, "No Desperate Hero: Manhood and Freedom in a Union Soldier's Experience," in *Divided Houses: Gender and the Civil War*, ed. Catherine Clinton and Nina Silber (New York: Oxford University Press, 1992), 59.

8. Frederic A. Conningham and Colin Simkin, *Currier and Ives Prints: An Illustrated Check List*, rev. ed. (New York: Crown Publishers, 1970), 197.

9. Catharine E. Beecher and Harriet Beecher Stowe, *The American Woman's Home or, Principles of Domestic Science . . .* (1869; reprint, Hartford, Conn.: Stowe-Day Foundation, 1994), 91; Franklin Walker and G. Ezra Dane, eds., *Mark Twain's Travels with Mr. Brown, Being Heretofore Uncollected Sketches Written by Mark Twain for the San Francisco* Alta California *in 1866 and 1867* (New York: Alfred A. Knopf, 1940), 240.

10. Copyright Records of the Southern District of New York, October 1862–March 1863 and April 1863–August 1863, Library of Congress; *Currier and Ives Catalogue Raisonné*, 2 vols. (Detroit, Mich.: Gale Research, 1964), 2:945–46, 1001–3. For a view that diminishes the alleged impact of war on Americans' private lives, see Anne C. Rose, *Victorian America and the Civil War* (Cambridge: Harvard University Press, 1992), esp. 12.

11. Conningham and Simkin, *Currier and Ives Prints*, 162–66.

12. John W. Hanson, *Historical Sketch of the Old Sixth Regiment of Massachusetts Volunteers* (Boston: n.p., 1866), 198; Louis P. Masur, ed., *"The Real War Will Never Get in the Books": Selections from Writers during the Civil War* (New York: Oxford University Press, 1993), 21.

13. James Marten, "For the Good, the True, and the Beautiful: Northern Children's Magazines and the Civil War," *Civil War History* 41 (March 1995): 58–59, 61.

14. James M. McPherson, *Ordeal by Fire* (New York: Alfred A. Knopf, 1982), 357.

15. Marten, "For the Good," 64.

16. William F. Thompson, *The Image of War: The Pictorial Reporting of the American Civil War* (1949; reprint, Baton Rouge: Louisiana State University Press, 1994), 100.

17. See *The Brave Wife*, lithographed by Currier and Ives, 1861, discussed in Chapter 1. Currier and Ives, which dominated the period market for genre prints, not surprisingly extended that dominance to the subject of "war spirit at home," hence the large number of Currier and Ives prints in this chapter.

18. Clinton and Silber, *Divided Houses*, 243; Fredrickson, *Inner Civil War*, esp. chap. 7.

19. *Frank Leslie's Illustrated Newspaper,*

April 23, 1864; C. Vann Woodward and Elizabeth Muhlenfield, eds., *The Private Mary Chesnut: The Unpublished Civil War Diaries* (New York: Oxford University Press, 1984), 145.

20. Mary M. Roberts, *American Nursing: History and Interpretation* (New York: Macmillan, 1954), 9–11; Donald Fleming, "Social Darwinism," in *Paths of American Thought*, ed. Arthur M. Schlesinger Jr. and Morton White (Boston: Houghton Mifflin, 1963), 137; Stephen B. Oates, *A Woman of Valor: Clara Barton and the Civil War* (New York: Free Press, 1994), 374; Kristie Ross, "Arranging a Doll's House: Refined Women as Union Nurses," in Clinton and Silber, *Divided Houses*, 99, 110.

21. William Quentin Maxwell, *Lincoln's Fifth Wheel: The Political History of the United States Sanitary Commission* (New York: Longmans, Green and Company, 1956), 37; Jeannie Attie, "Warwork and the Crisis of Domesticity in the North," in Clinton and Silber, *Divided Houses*, 250, 252.

22. *Sanitary Commission Bulletin*, March 15, 1864, 289, and February 15, 1864, 244–45, 301–2.

23. Caption on an original print in the Lincoln Museum, Fort Wayne, Indiana.

24. *Sanitary Fair Bulletin*, January 1, 1864, 202, 205; Alvin Robert Kantor and Marjorie Sered Kantor, *Sanitary Fairs: A Philatelic and Historical Study of Civil War Benevolence* (Glencoe, Ill.: SF Publishing, 1992), 172–74.

25. "The Brooklyn Sanitary Fair," *Lincoln Lore*, no. 1749 (November 1983): 2–4.

26. Kantor and Kantor, *Sanitary Fairs*, 91.

27. Ibid.; Charles Eberstadt, *Lincoln's Emancipation Proclamation* (New York: Duschnes Crawford, 1950), 41; "The Brooklyn Sanitary Fair," 4; William Y. Thompson, "Sanitary Fairs of the Civil War," *Civil War History* 4 (March 1958): 57–58.

28. *History of the Brooklyn and Long Island Fair, February 22, 1864* (Brooklyn, N.Y.: n.p., 1864); Harry T. Peters, *America on Stone: The Other Printmakers to the American People . . .*

(New York: Doubleday, Doran and Company, 1931), 113; a copy of the rare print *Sanitary Fair Logan Square Philad. June 1 1864* is in the Abraham Lincoln Museum, Lincoln Memorial University, Harrogate, Tennessee.

29. Original print, after a painting by Christian Schussele and published by John Dainty of Philadelphia in 1865, in the Print Collection of the Chicago Historical Society.

30. Mark E. Neely Jr., Harold Holzer, and Gabor S. Boritt, *The Confederate Image: Prints of the Lost Cause* (Chapel Hill: University of North Carolina Press, 1987), 79–96.

31. See Holzer and Neely, *Mine Eyes Have Seen the Glory*, 227.

32. Linda M. Kruger, "Home Libraries: Special Spaces, Reading Places," in *American Home Life, 1880–1930: A Social History of Spaces and Services*, ed. Jessica H. Foy and Thomas J. Schlereth (Knoxville: University of Tennessee Press, 1992), 101.

33. J. Matthew Gallman, *The North Fights the Civil War: The Home Front* (Chicago: Ivan R. Dee, 1994), 16–17, 109–15.

34. Conningham and Simkin, *Currier and Ives Prints*, 219–20; John H. Rhodes, *History of Battery "B", 1st Rhode Island Light Artillery*, quoted in Williams, *The Civil War: The Artist's Record*, 222; George Edgar Turner, *Victory Rode the Rails: The Strategic Place of the Railroads in the Civil War* (Indianapolis: Bobbs-Merrill, 1953).

35. Adams, *Fighting for Defeat*, vii–viii, 28; Alan Trachtenberg, *Reading American Photographs: Images as History, Mathew Brady to Walker Evans* (New York: Hill and Wang, 1989), 103–10.

36. Gallman, *The North Fights the Civil War*, 109–15.

CHAPTER FOUR

1. Nathaniel Hawthorne, "Chiefly About War Matters by a Peaceable Man," *Atlantic Monthly* 10 (1862): 57–59. On technology

and the image of the *Monitor*, we are indebted especially to Earl J. Hess, "Northern Response to the Ironclad: A Prospect for the Study of Military Technology," *Civil War History* 31 (June 1985): 126–43.

2. The most important student in rescuing the reputation of Palmer apparently did not recognize these prints as paired, but naval print specialists did in *Currier and Ives Navy: Lithographs from the Beverley R. Robinson Collection* (Annapolis, Md.: U. S. Naval Academy Museum, 1983), 86–87. Mary Bartlett Cowdrey, "Fanny Palmer, An American Lithographer," in *Prints: Thirteen Illustrated Essays on the Art of the Print Selected for the Print Council of America*, ed. Carl Zigrosser (New York: Holt, Rinehart, and Winston, 1962), 225. Walton Rawls, *The Great Book of Currier and Ives' America* (New York: Abbeville, 1979), 202, 210, 222; Copyright Records, Southern District of New York, March 1, 1865–May 12, 1865, Library of Congress. Bingham's flatboatmen had been popularized and made accessible in an 1847 American Art Union engraving of 10,000 copies.

3. Cowdrey, "Fanny Palmer," 222. See also Stephen Daniels, *Fields of Vision: Landscape Imagery and National Destiny in England and the United States* (Princeton: Princeton University Press, 1993), 174–99. Flatboats were already on their way out when Bingham painted them, but the role of nostalgia in Palmer's image was secondary. Michael Edward Shapiro, "The River Paintings," in Shapiro et al., *George Caleb Bingham* (St. Louis, Mo.: Saint Louis Art Museum, 1990), 153.

4. Palmer may have owed a visual debt to *Bound Down the River*, an 1860 lithograph printed by Endicott and Company of New York and published by M. Knoedler, which depicted a steamboat being loaded from the riverbank by moonlight. Particularly reminiscent of the Endicott lithograph are the arrangement of the cotton bales on the steamboat on the Mississippi in the "peace"

print and the moonlit sky in the "war" print. *Bound Down the River* is reproduced on the back cover of *The Old Print Gallery Showcase* (Washington, D.C.) for December 1993.

5. Cowdrey, "Fanny Palmer," 219–25. Her important contribution to Currier and Ives is suitably noted in Albert K. Baragwanath, *Currier and Ives* (New York: Abbeville Press, 1980), esp. 50, and in Daniels, *Fields of Vision*, 174–99.

6. Currier and Ives capitalized on *The Mississippi in Time of Peace* again in a smaller print published in 1870 as *Bound Down the River* (borrowing a title from Endicott and Company). See *Old Print Shop Portfolio* (New York) 54, no. 5 (1995): 101.

7. Palmer is not mentioned in Herman Warner Williams's *The Civil War: The Artists' Record* (Boston: Beacon Press, 1961); the only woman artist who is mentioned by Williams confined her vision to women's accustomed sphere in the nineteenth century, the home front.

8. Copyright Records, Southern District of New York, 1863, Library of Congress.

9. The changes went undetected in *Currier and Ives Navy*, 72–74, where the prints happen to be reproduced side by side in order to show the variety in coloring by Currier and Ives's assembly-line artists. For the third version, see Rawls, *Great Book of Currier and Ives' America*, 307 (*Bombardment and Capture of Island Number Ten*). See Tony Gibbons, *Warships and Naval Battles of the Civil War* (New York: Gallery Books, 1989), esp. 16–21, and the excellent cutaway drawings in Jack Coggins, *Arms and Equipment of the Civil War* (Garden City, N.Y.: Doubleday, 1962), esp. 140, for the details of naval architecture.

10. John D. Milligan, *Gunboats Down the Mississippi* (Annapolis, Md.: United States Naval Institute, 1965), 53–60.

11. Henry Walke, *Naval Scenes and Reminiscences of the Civil War . . .* (New York: F. R. Reed, 1877), 113–14.

12. David Dixon Porter, *The Naval History*

of the Civil War (1886; reprint, New York: Benchmark Publishing, 1970), 182.

13. William C. Davis, *Duel between the First Ironclads* (Baton Rouge: Louisiana State University Press, 1975), 117.

14. *Old Print Shop Portfolio* 58 (1998): 33.

15. Henry Bill's depiction of the *Monitor* and *Virginia*, in the Print Collection of the Chicago Historical Society.

16. James Phinney Baxter, *The Introduction of the Ironclad Warship* (Cambridge: Harvard University Press, 1933); William N. Still, "The Historical Importance of the U.S.S. *Monitor*," in William B. Cogar, *Naval History: The Seventh Symposium of the United States Naval Academy* (Wilmington, Del.: Scholarly Resources, 1988), 76–77.

17. John Taylor Wood, "First Fight of Iron-clads," in *Battles and Leaders of the Civil War*, ed. Robert Underwood Johnson and Clarence Clough Buel, 4 vols. (1887; reprint, Secaucus, N.J.: Castle Publishing, 1991), 1:692; see also Gibbons, *Warships and Naval Battles*, 2. Another Currier and Ives print of the battle, based on F. Newman's allegedly eyewitness sketch, showed the stern but not the bow of the Confederate ironclad rounded. *Currier and Ives Navy*, 68. See Harold Holzer and Mark E. Neely Jr., *Mine Eyes Have Seen the Glory: The Civil War in Art* (New York: Orion Books, 1993), 97, for the original painted sketch. The Newman print also correctly depicted the pilot house ahead of the smokestack; Palmer's unlikely vessel had no pilot house.

18. *Currier and Ives Navy*, 70.

19. James M. McPherson, *Battle Cry of Freedom: The Civil War Era* (New York: Oxford University Press, 1988), 373–78.

20. *Descriptive Text to Prang's War Pictures* (Boston: L. Prang and Company, 1888), 10.

21. Ibid., 11, 16.

22. Ibid., 57.

23. Porter, *Naval History of the Civil War*, 130.

24. Harry T. Peters, *America on Stone: The Other Printmakers to the American People . . .* (New York: Doubleday, Doran and Company, 1931), 378–79, 172–75.

25. Copy in the Peters Collection, Museum of the City of New York.

26. Davis, *Duel between the First Ironclads*, 42.

27. Porter, *Naval History of the Civil War*, 127.

28. Jack Coggins, *Arms and Equipment of the Civil War* (Garden City, N.Y.: Doubleday, 1962), 135–37; Gibbons, *Warships and Naval Battles*, 300.

29. Letter dated April 11, 1865, in Museum of the City of New York.

30. On the democratization of war art, see Matthew Paul Lalumia, *Realism and Politics in Victorian Art of the Crimean War* (Ann Arbor, Mich.: UMI Research, 1984).

31. Charles Lee Lewis, *Farragut, Our First Admiral* (Annapolis, Md.: United States Naval Institute, 1943), 334 (for example).

32. *Official Records of the Union and Confederate Navies in the War of the Rebellion*, 30 vols. (Washington, D.C.: Government Printing Office, 1894–1922), ser. 1, 21:445 ("devilish" quote), 415. Hereafter cited as *ORN*.

33. Ibid., 420, 665; "teakettles" quotation in Francis Trevelyan Miller, ed., *The Photographic History of the Civil War*, 10 vols. (New York: Review of Reviews, 1911), 6:72.

34. *ORN*, ser. 1, 21:722, 417; John Keegan, *The Mask of Command* (New York: Viking, 1987), 208–9. On courage, see Gerald E. Linderman, *Embattled Courage: The Experience of Combat in the American Civil War* (New York: Free Press, 1987).

35. Charles Lee Lewis, *David Glasgow Farragut*, 2 vols. (Annapolis, Md.: United States Naval Institute, 1941–43), 2:293; James Russell Soley, *The Blockade and the Cruisers* (New York: Scribner's, 1883), 60–61.

36. *Currier and Ives Catalogue Raisonné*, 2 vols. (Detroit, Mich.: Gale Research, 1964), 2:400.

CHAPTER FIVE

1. Francis Bicknell Carpenter, *Six Months at the White House with President Lincoln: The Story of a Picture* (New York: Hurd and Hougthon, 1866), 46.

2. William C. Darrah, *Cartes de Visite in Nineteenth Century Photography* (Gettysburg, Pa.: William C. Darrah, 1981), 4; Robert Philippe, *Political Graphics: Art as a Weapon* (New York: Abbeville Press, 1980), 172.

3. *New York Tribune*, October 27, 1862.

4. Roy P. Basler, ed., *The Collected Works of Abraham Lincoln*, 9 vols. (New Brunswick, N.J.: Rutgers University Press, 1953–55), 4:261.

5. Basler, *Collected Works of Lincoln*, 8:52, 101.

6. The 1864 vote was so large that both Abraham Lincoln and Horace Greeley, close students of election statistics, assumed the country's population must have increased since 1860. See ibid., 8:150; *New York Tribune*, December 2, 1864. For an expert analysis of campaign ephemera from this and previous elections, see Roger A. Fischer, *Tippecanoe and Trinkets, Too: The Material Culture of American Presidential Campaigns, 1828–1984* (Urbana: University of Illinois Press, 1988).

7. Darrah, *Cartes de Visite*, 4. Currier and Ives, for example, issued at least five portrait lithographs of McClellan by 1864. See Frederic A. Conningham and Colin Simkin, *Currier and Ives Prints: An Illustrated Check List*, rev. ed. (New York: Crown Publishers, 1970), 172.

8. John T. Morse, ed., *The Diary of Gideon Welles, Secretary of the Navy under Lincoln and Johnson*, 3 vols. (Boston: Houghton Mifflin, 1911), 2:66–67, 153. The California Union ticket was illustrated in the Robert A. Siegel Auction Galleries catalog for Sale No. 786, New York, April 8–9, 1997, 56.

9. See Charles Eberstadt, *Lincoln's Emancipation Proclamation* (New York: Duschnes Crawford, 1950).

10. Original in the Library of Congress.

11. Stanley Kaplan, "The Miscegenation Issue in the Campaign of 1864," *Journal of Negro History* 34 (July 1949): 317; Conningham and Simkin, *Currier and Ives Prints*, 172.

12. Arthur M. Schlesinger Jr. and Fred L. Israel, *History of American Presidential Elections, 1789–1968*, 4 vols. (New York: Chelsea House, 1971), 4:1179; Stephen W. Sears, ed., *The Civil War Papers of George B. McClellan: Selected Correspondence, 1860–1865* (New York: Ticknor and Fields, 1989), 596.

13. For examples of the use of blacks to symbolize the slavery issue in 1860 prints, see Rufus Rockwell Wilson, *Lincoln in Caricature* (New York: Horizon Press, 1953), 19, 31, 33, 39, 51.

14. Iver Bernstein, *The New York City Draft Riots: Their Significance for American Society and Politics in the Age of the Civil War* (New York: Oxford University Press, 1990), 5, 33, 38–39. The image of the Irish American laborer would become, if anything, even more brutish and grotesque. See "The Usual Irish Way of Doing Things" in *Harper's Weekly*, September 2, 1871, a reaction to the so-called Orange Riot of July 1871.

15. Bruce Tap, *Over Lincoln's Shoulder: The Committee on the Conduct of the War* (Lawrence: University Press of Kansas, 1998), 124; George Wilkes, *McClellan: From Ball's Bluff to Antietam* (New York: Sinclair Tousey, 1863), 13, 14, 16.

16. Schlesinger and Israel, *History of American Presidential Elections*, 2:1200.

17. Stephen W. Sears, *George B. McClellan: The Young Napoleon* (New York: Ticknor and Fields, 1988), 352.

18. Sears, *Civil War Papers of George B. McClellan*, 568.

19. Schlesinger and Israel, *History of American Presidential Elections*, 2:1202.

20. We owe an important debt, for the view of politicians as underestimating technical military knowledge, to Tap, *Over Lincoln's Shoulder*, esp. 240.

21. Copyright Records, Southern District of New York, September–December 1864, Library of Congress.

22. Ward Hill Lamon, *Recollections of Abraham Lincoln, 1847–1865*, ed. Dorothy Lamon Teillard (1895; reprint, Washington, D.C., 1911), chap. 9.

23. Only one print from the 1860 campaign is known to have linked the Democrats with this stock Irish laborer character: *The Political Quadrille* showed Lincoln dancing with an African American, and his Democratic opponent, Stephen A. Douglas, doing likewise with an Irishman.

24. See David E. Long, *The Jewel of Liberty: Abraham Lincoln's Re-election and the End of Slavery* (Mechanicsburg, Pa.: Stackpole Books, 1994), 153–69, 172–77.

25. See *Miscegenation: The Theory of the Blending of the Races, Applied to the American White Man and Negro* (New York: Croly and Wakeman, 1864), 61. The copy that the publishers sent to Lincoln, together with an introductory letter, in an effort to lure him into the trap, is in the Library of Congress. Lincoln never responded to the tract.

26. Lincoln believed that he would lose New York in 1864. On October 13 he made a list of the voting states and predicted which way they would vote in November. Although he calculated that he would win 120 electoral votes to McClellan's 114, thus holding on to the presidency, he placed New York State's 33 votes in McClellan's column. For a reproduction of the chart in Lincoln's hand, see Stefan Lorant, *Lincoln: A Picture Story of His Life* (New York: W. W. Norton, 1969), 234.

27. Bromley and Company advertising sheet (see fig. 76); Kaplan, "The Miscegenation Issue," 317.

28. *New York Weekly Day-Book*, July 9, 1864; Long, *The Jewel of Liberty*, 169–70; Mary Elizabeth Massey, *Women in the Civil War* (1966 [as *Bonnet Brigades*]; reprint, Lincoln: University of Nebraska Press, 1994), 154–55.

29. That readers of the generally pro-war *Harper's Weekly* would be offered remaindered prints of McClellan strongly suggests that printmakers still believed their offerings had some universal appeal.

CHAPTER SIX

1. Rachel Sherman Thorndike, ed., *The Sherman Letters* (New York: Charles Scribner's Sons, 1894), 220.

2. *Harper's Weekly* for November 5, 1864, featured a cover illustration of "Phil Sheridan's ride to the front, October 19, 1864." See also *Academy of Fine Arts. Sheridan's Ride. Now on Exhibition* (Philadelphia, n.d.), original pamphlet in the Macculloch Hall Library and Museum, Morristown, New Jersey.

3. *Harper's Weekly*, December 31, 1864, February 4, 1865. The ad offered prints of "any one of the Corps Commanders of our army" but highlighted the engravings of Lincoln, Grant, Sherman, and Sheridan. See also engraver George E. Perine's advertisement for "Two Splendid Steel Engravings of Lieut.-Gen. Grant and President Lincoln, Printed on 19 x 24-plate paper. Price $1 each," the former purportedly bearing an endorsement from Grant's father as "the best engraved likeness I have ever seen," in *Harper's Weekly*, July 23, 1864.

4. For the Ritchie adaptation, see Ulysses S. Grant, *Personal Memoirs*, 2 vols. (New York: Charles L. Webster and Company, 1892), 1:i.

5. Geoffrey Perret, *Ulysses S. Grant, Soldier and President* (New York: Random House, 1997), 73–74; John Y. Simon, ed., *The Papers of Ulysses S. Grant*, 22 vols. to date (Carbondale: Southern Illinois University Press, 1967–1998), 1:frontis., i–ii, 106, 231, 264, 312, 3:63, 76–77; John Y. Simon, introduction to *U. S. Grant: The Man and the Image*, by James G. Barber (Washington, D.C.: National Portrait Gallery, 1985), 19.

6. Simon, introduction to Barber, *U. S. Grant*, 19.

7. Horace Porter, "Reminiscences of General Grant," *Harper's New Monthly Magazine* 71 (September 1885): 589; William F. Thompson, *The Image of War: The Pictorial Reporting of the American Civil War* (1949; reprint, Baton Rouge: Louisiana State University Press, 1994), 119.

8. Horace Porter, *Campaigning with Grant* (1897; reprint, New York: Da Capo, 1986), vii.

9. Copyright Records for the Eastern District of Pennsylvania, May 17, 1861–March 22, 1862, Library of Congress.

10. Sylvanus Cadwallader, *Three Years with Grant as Recalled by War Correspondent Sylvanus Cadwallader*, ed. Benjamin P. Thomas (New York: Alfred A. Knopf, 1955), 138–39.

11. John Y. Simon and David L. Wilson, eds., "Samuel H. Beckwith: 'Grant's Shadow,'" in *Ulysses S. Grant: Essays and Documents*, ed. John Y. Simon and David L. Wilson (Carbondale: Southern Illinois University Press, 1981), 94–95. *New York Herald*, April 9, 1862, and *Cincinnati Gazette*, April 19, 1862, in *The North Reports the Civil War*, ed. J. Cutler Andrews (Pittsburgh: University of Pittsburgh Press, 1955), 178.

12. Porter, *Campaigning with Grant*, 13–14.

13. John Keegan, *The Mask of Command* (New York: Viking Press, 1987), 220–21.

14. Shelby Foote, *The Civil War: A Narrative*, 3 vols. (New York: Random House, 1974), 3:3–5; Porter, *Campaigning with Grant*, 22.

15. For the impact of Appomattox prints on the Lee image, see Mark E. Neely Jr., Harold Holzer, and Gabor S. Boritt, *The Confederate Image: Prints of the Lost Cause* (Chapel Hill: University of North Carolina Press, 1987), 68–78.

16. Cadwallader, *Three Years with Grant*, 350–51.

17. Ibid., 351.

18. Grant, *Personal Memoirs*, 2:490; Porter, *Campaigning with Grant*, 473.

19. See, for example, Russell F. Weigley, *History of the United States Army* (New York: Macmillan, 1967), 251, 264; Porter, *Campaigning with Grant*, 493; Ulysses S. Grant, *Memoirs and Selected Letters* (New York: Library of America, 1990), 750.

20. Simon, *Papers of Ulysses S. Grant*, 9:504; the original of the Grant medal is in the Division of Military History of the National Museum of American History at the Smithsonian Institution in Washington, D.C.; a photograph of the obverse and reverse is in the Prints Division, Chicago Historical Society.

21. Michael Fellman, *Citizen Sherman: A Life of William Tecumseh Sherman* (New York: Random House, 1995), 174; *New York Times*, February 23, 1865.

22. W. G. Brownlow, *Sketches of the Rise, Progress, and Decline of Secession; with a Narrative of Personal Adventures among the Rebels* (Philadelphia: George W. Childs, 1862), unpaginated advertisements at rear.

23. Both prints are in the Anne S. K. Brown Military Collection at the John Hay Library, Brown University.

24. See Neely, Holzer, and Boritt, *The Confederate Image*, 137–68.

25. The Crosby and Merinsky lithographs are in the Library of Congress collection.

26. Edward West Currier to Nathaniel Currier, September 25, 1881, Currier and Ives Papers, Archives of American Art, Washington, D.C., microfilm; Frederick A. Conningham and Colin Simkin, *Currier and Ives Prints: An Illustrated Check List*, rev. ed. (New York: Crown Publishers, 1970), 105.

27. Edward West Currier to Nathaniel Currier, July 27, 1885. Currier and Ives Papers, microfilm.

28. Edward West Currier to Nathaniel Currier, August 3, 1885, and August 10, 1885, ibid.

29. *Engravings for Sale by J. C. Buttre* (New York: J. C. Buttre, 1894), 40, 103.

30. Barber, *U. S. Grant*, 39; John Chipman Gray and John Codman Ropes, *War Let-*

ters, 1862–1865 (Boston: Houghton Mifflin, 1927), 425, 427.

31. Fellman, *Citizen Sherman*, 100–101, 248; John F. Marszalek, *Sherman: A Soldier's Passion for Order* (New York: Free Press, 1993), 169; John F. Marszalek, *Sherman's Other War* (Memphis: Memphis State University Press, 1981), 67–68.

32. Fellman, *Citizen Sherman*, 126; Andrews, *The North Reports the Civil War*, 179–81.

33. Philip Shaw Paludan, *"A People's Contest": The Union and Civil War, 1861–1865* (New York: Harper and Row, 1988), 109; Fellman, *Citizen Sherman*, 129; Marszalek, *Sherman*, 211–13.

34. Thompson, *The Image of War*, 79.

35. Thorndike, *The Sherman Letters*, 220, 223; Burke Davis, *Sherman's March* (New York: Random House, 1980), 9.

36. Davis, *Sherman's March*, 9; Stephen W. Sears, ed., *The Civil War: A Treasury of Art and Literature* (New York: Hugh Lauter Levin Associates, 1992), 67–68.

37. Original prints in the Library of Congress.

38. Simon, *Papers of Ulysses S. Grant*, 12:155.

39. Charles Royster, *The Destructive War: William Tecumseh Sherman, Stonewall Jackson, and the Americans* (New York: Alfred A. Knopf, 1991). The book jacket design is credited to Semadar Megged.

40. *Harper's Weekly*, November 26, 1864.

41. Abraham Lincoln Papers, Library of Congress; Roy Basler, ed., *The Collected Works of Abraham Lincoln*, 9 vols. (New Brunswick, N.J.: Rutgers University Press, 1953–55), 8:181.

42. Neely, Holzer, and Boritt, *The Confederate Image*, 78.

43. William Tecumseh Sherman, *Memoirs* (1875; reprint, New York: Library of America, 1990), 708; Davis, *Sherman's March*, 166.

44. Sherman, *Memoirs*, 837.

45. Fellman, *Citizen Sherman*, 237; Roys-ter, *The Destructive War*, 347–48; Sherman, *Memoirs*, 845.

46. Sherman, *Memoirs*, 847–48; Fellman, *Citizen Sherman*, 250; Grant, *Personal Memoirs*, 2:515–18.

47. Fellman, *Citizen Sherman*, 240–41.

48. Ibid., 253.

49. Michael Kammen, *Mystic Chords of Memory: The Transformation of Tradition in American Culture* (New York: Alfred A. Knopf, 1991), 108, 125.

50. *Text to Number Ten of Prang's War Pictures: "Siege of Atlanta: An Artillery Review"* (Boston: L. Prang and Company, n.d.), 35–36.

51. Sherman, *Memoirs*, 812–17; Barber, *U. S. Grant*, 48; George P. A. Healy, *Reminiscences of a Portrait Painter* (Chicago: A. C. McClurg and Company, 1894), 70; Marie de Mare, *G. P. A. Healy: American Artist* (New York: David McKay, 1954), 238–41 (Marie de Mare was G. P. A. Healy's granddaughter); Fellman, *Citizen Sherman*, 237.

52. Marszalek, *Sherman*, 482–83.

53. *Engravings for Sale by J. C. Buttre*, 18, 34, 58, 62, 73, 82, 103–4.

54. See Michael C. C. Adams, *Fighting for Defeat: Union Military Failure in the East, 1861–1865* (1978 [as *Our Masters the Rebels*]; reprint, Lincoln: University of Nebraska Press, 1992), esp. 119.

CHAPTER SEVEN

1. Holland Cotter, "Currier and Ives, as Telling as Ozzie and Harriet," *New York Times*, July 14, 1996, Arts and Leisure, 33.

2. Frederic A. Conningham, *Currier and Ives Prints: An Illustrated Check List* (New York: Crown, 1949), provides the basis for this enumeration of titles. Numbers of surviving prints encountered in print shops and antique stores provide a rough measure of the representativeness of the title count for number of prints purchased.

3. Copyright Records, Southern District

of New York, June 1861–October 1862, Library of Congress.

4. Ibid., April 1863–August 1863.

5. Harry T. Peters, *Currier and Ives: Printmakers to the American People* (New York: Doubleday and Doran, 1942), 8; Ives obituary in the *Port Chester (New York) Journal*, January 10, 1895; Frederick Phisterer, *New York in the War of the Rebellion*, 3d ed., 6 vols. (Albany, N.Y.: J. B. Lyon Company, 1912), 1:621–22.

6. Michael Ballard, *A Long Shadow: Jefferson Davis and the Final Days of the Confederacy* (Jackson: University Press of Mississippi, 1986), 44–48.

7. Bruce Catton, *Grant Moves South* (Boston: Houghton Mifflin, 1960), 323; Marion Morrison, *A History of the Ninth Regiment Illinois Volunteer Infantry* (Monmouth, Ill.: John S. Clark, 1864), 26–27.

8. Catton, *Grant Moves South*, 252–54. Marion Morrison remembered "the feeling which prevailed in the North with reference to it. There was rejoicing over it as a victory. Still it was regarded as a dearly bought victory. There was a very decided feeling that somebody was at fault. That the rebels had completely surprised our army. That our pickets were out but a very short distance. Hence, the surprise. Gen. Grant, as chief in command, was faulted. It was charged that he was drunk at the time. That he had disobeyed orders, and landed his men on the wrong side of the river, etc. I heard a citizen of Chicago, not a month ago, say that if Gen. Grant had made his appearance in Chicago immediately after the battle of Shiloh, he would have been mobbed, such was the feeling of indignation." *History of the Ninth Regiment*, 34.

9. Ulysses S. Grant, *Memoirs and Selected Letters* (New York: Library of America, 1990), 224–25, 234.

10. Ibid., 234.

11. George C. Groce and David H. Wallace, *The New-York Historical Society's Dictionary of Artists in America, 1564–1860* (New

Haven, Conn.: Yale University Press, 1957), 378–79; Peter C. Marzio, *The Democratic Art: Pictures for a Nineteenth-Century America* (Boston: David R. Godine, 1979), 178.

12. Groce and Wallace, *Dictionary of Artists in America*, 379; Alan E. Kent, "Early Commercial Lithography in Wisconsin," *Wisconsin Magazine of History*, 36 (1953): 249–53; Harry T. Peters, *America on Stone: The Other Printmakers to the American People* . . . (New York: Doubleday, Doran and Company, 1931), 259; Marzio, *Democratic Art*, 179.

13. In 1921 Kurz and Allison went out of business and sold their stock; the new owners, Daleiden and Company, promoted the inventory as "Famous Kurz & Allison Pictures . . . Pictures for the School and Hall." Peters, *America on Stone*, 259; Groce and Wallace, *Dictionary of Artists in America*, 259; Marzio, *Democratic Art*, 178–79, 259.

14. Marzio, *Democratic Art*, 78.

15. Mark Thistlethwaite, *Painting in the Grand Manner: The Art of Peter Frederick Rothermel* (Chadds Ford, Pa.: Brandywine River Museum, 1995), 21.

16. See *Prospectus. Prang's War Pictures*, published in Boston in 1890, copy bound in *Descriptive Text to Prang's War Pictures* (Boston: L. Prang and Company, 1888). The bound volume examined here was the copy belonging to the Huntington Library in San Marino, California, and was once the property of early Civil War bibliographer John Page Nicholson. The *Prospectus* quotes a letter dated January 1886 concerning the Battle of New Orleans print, issued second in the series, and quotes a Philadelphia newspaper account, from June 28, 1886, of the unveiling there (13–14).

17. Peter C. Marzio, *The Democratic Art: An Exhibition on the History of Chromolithography in America, 1840–1900* (Fort Worth, Tex.: Amon Carter Museum of Western Art, 1979), 11.

18. In most instances, that is. A few chromolithographs were produced during the

Civil War, but most battles were commemorated at first in black-and-white lithographs, some of them hand colored afterward.

19. Conningham, *Currier and Ives Prints*, 68–70; Joseph Glatthaar, *Forged in Battle: The Civil War Alliance of Black Soldiers and White Officers* (New York: Free Press, 1990), esp. chap. 11.

20. William L. Shea and Earl J. Hess, *Pea Ridge: Civil War Campaign in the West* (Chapel Hill: University of North Carolina Press, 1992), 323.

21. Portfolio examined at the Huntington Library, San Marino, California. It had light blue endpapers decorated with sketches of Civil War soldiers in a repeated pattern and was dubbed "Prang's Easel Portfolio."

22. "Prang War Pictures. Set of Twenty Were $80.00. A Few Sets Now at $20.00." Advertisement of Historical Art Company, Boston, in *Current History* 10 (April 1900): 20.

23. Louis Prang, "Autobiographical Notes," typescript in the Archives of American Art, Washington, D.C.

24. Katherine Morrison McClinton, *The Chromolithographs of Louis Prang* (New York: Clarkson N. Potter, 1973), 21, 140–41.

25. *Text to Number Four of Prang's War Pictures* (Boston: L. Prang and Company, n.d. for the entire series), 24. The set of descriptive texts examined at the Thomas J. Watson Library, The Metropolitan Museum of Art.

26. *Prang's War Pictures*, undated prospectus, collection of Harold Holzer.

27. *Prospectus. Prang's War Pictures. Aquarelle Facsimile Prints* (Boston: L. Prang and Company, 1888).

28. *Prospectus* bound in Huntington Library copy of *Descriptive Text to Prang's War Pictures*, 12.

29. *Text to Number Ten of Prang's War Pictures*, 37.

30. *Catalogue. Prang's War Pictures. Aqua-*

relle Facsimile Prints. John V. Redpath, General Agent for the United States, Globe Building, Boston (Boston: L. Prang and Company, 1888). Description in catalog entry of Thomas T. Moebs, Americana and Fine Books, List Number 114 (1996).

31. Ibid.

32. *Prospectus*, 5, 10.

33. *Text to Number Seven of Prang's War Pictures*, 8–9.

34. *Text to Number Three of Prang's War Pictures*, 19.

35. *Text to Number Nine of Prang's War Pictures*, 29.

36. *Prospectus*, 13.

EPILOGUE

1. On self-emancipation, see James M. McPherson, *Drawn with the Sword: Reflections on the American Civil War* (New York: Oxford University Press, 1996), 192–207 and "Works Cited."

2. Noah Andre Trudeau, *Like Men of War: Black Troops in the Civil War, 1862–1865* (Boston: Little, Brown, 1998), 290.

3. William A. Gladstone, *United States Colored Troops, 1863–1867* (Gettysburg: Thomas Publications, 1990), 18. The author, also a major collector, owns the second state of the print containing the words to "Battle Cry of Freedom."

4. Lincoln proposed a commission for Delany in February 1865. See Roy P. Basler, ed., *The Collected Works of Abraham Lincoln*, 9 vols. (New Brunswick, N.J.: Rutgers University Press, 1953–55), 8:272–73. Delany is the subject of Dorothy Sterling's *The Making of an Afro-American Hero: Martin Robison Delany, 1812–1885* (Garden City, N.Y.: Doubleday, 1971; reprint, New York: Da Capo Press, 1996), 230–51.

ACKNOWLEDGMENTS

We have been filing away research notes for this book—and in the process, relying on a number of helpful friends and colleagues—for more than eleven years. We are indebted to those who provided their time and assistance.

Crucial help and guidance was provided along the way by curators of public collections throughout the country, who made their holdings available for study and provided photographic reproductions for use in this volume. Bernard Reilly and his staff at the Prints and Photographs Division of the Library of Congress helped us during our visits and afterward with requests to examine original prints. Daniel Lorello opened the resources of the New York State Archives and the New York State Library, and Deborah Evans in the Photoduplication Division of the Library of Congress handled countless requests for pictures, as did the rights and reproductions specialists at the National Portrait Gallery, the Lilly Library of Indiana University, and other repositories.

Peter Harrington led us through the Anne S. K. Brown Military Collection at the John Hay Library at Brown University. Larry Viskochill opened the files of the print collection at the Chicago Historical Society, and Gerald Prokopowicz, Carolyn Texley, and Cindy Van-Horn supplied photographs from the holdings of the Lincoln Museum in Fort Wayne, Indiana. David Meschutt, formerly of the West Point Museum at the United States Military Academy, was most helpful in granting permission to use pieces from his archives. Alice Caulkins of the Macculloch Hall Museum in Morristown, New Jersey, onetime home of artist Thomas Nast, helped us to locate several rare images, and Charles Dittrich, senior at Gettysburg College, instructed us in the use of the HarpWeek CD-ROM program at the school's Musselman Library.

At the Metropolitan Museum of Art, Elliot Davis of the American Art Department took the time to advise Harold Holzer on Winslow Homer and Louis Prang, encouraged our use of the museum's Thomas J. Watson Library, and helped make us aware of the rarely consulted, seldom exploited *Text to Prang's War Pictures*. The Huntington Library made Mark Neely the R. Stanton Avery Research Fellow for 1997–98, which permitted research in its extensive Civil War holdings.

This book is the richer for the help of dealers and collectors. Judith Blakely of the Old Print Gallery in Washington, D.C., Kenneth M. Newman of the Old Print Shop in New York, and Donald Cresswell of the Philadelphia Print Shop all generously provided us with photographs of items from their catalogs, for which we are extremely grateful. William Gladstone of West Palm Beach, Florida, allowed us entrée to, and the right to reproduce items from, his superb collection of graphic arts representing the African American experience in the Civil War, and our good friend Frank J. Williams of Hope Valley, Rhode Island, made available his great library and collection for research and reproduction.

Professor John Y. Simon, editor of *The Papers of Ulysses S. Grant*, provided a valuable reading of Chapter 6. Professor John F. Marszalek of Mississippi State University read and contributed as well to that chapter, and Professor Craig L. Symonds of the United States Naval Academy at Annapolis commented most usefully on the section dealing with marine prints. Sylvia Neely provided a critical reading of the entire manuscript.

We owe a thank you as well to George Craig of the Civil War Round Table of New York, who urged publication of a Union sequel to our 1987 book, *The Confederate Image*.

We are grateful as well to our assistants, who eased the considerable burden of collaborating long distance—between New York and St. Louis—on what proved an unexpectedly demanding and complicated project. Our thanks go to Larisa Elzon of the Metropolitan Museum of Art, to Re Becca Ames, formerly of the Metropolitan, and to Susie Foxworth Green of St. Louis University. Thanks, too, to the Pennsylvania State University for providing Mark Neely time and encouragement in the later stages of this work, and to Philippe de Montebello, director of the Metropolitan Museum of Art, for his constant enthusiasm for scholarship, even when it is pursued by his administrative staff.

Finally, we acknowledge the encouragement and patience of Lewis Bateman, our editor at the University of North Carolina Press, who never stopped believing in this project.

INDEX OF ILLUSTRATIONS

Italic numbers give the location of the illustration; other references are to discussion in the text.

GENERAL INDEX

The names of printing and publishing firms appear in small capital letters. The titles of prints that are discussed but not illustrated are given here; all references to the illustrated prints are to be found in the preceding Index of Illustrations.